# THE
# PREPPER'S
# CANNING &
# PRESERVING
# BIBLE

The Guide to Preserving, Water Bath & Pressure Canning, Pickling, Fermenting, Dehydrating & Freeze Drying. Prepare Your Pantry Now for any situation!

by

## Gordon Flay

# Contents

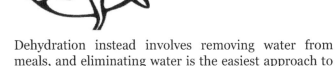

# Introduction

Food preservation is a strategy for preventing food from developing harmful bacteria. Often after preparing a meal, we cover the pots with lids to preserve and protect the food, also keeping flies and insects out. By doing this, we are defending against any illness brought on by harmful bacteria; this however is a solution for short-term storing. Food preservation instead aims at keeping food fresher for a longer time.

Drying, cooling, fermenting are some of the earliest preservation techniques. Canning, pasteurization, irradiation, and the addition of chemicals are instead examples of more contemporary techniques. Modern food preservation has benefited greatly also from advancements in packing materials.

The two most common causes of food spoiling are pathogens (disease-causing microbes) like molds & bacteria attacking the food, or oxidation, which results in the breakdown of vital biochemical substances in plant & animal cells. The many techniques for food preservation that have been developed are all intended to lessen or eliminate one or all of these harmful consequences of food spoilage.

Modern food preservation techniques were created as a result of the development of technology. Immediately after slaughter or harvest, foods made from plants or animals start to deteriorate. Any mechanical harm sustained during postharvest processing may cause the stored enzymes in the cells of animal & plant tissues to be released. These enzymes start dissolving the biological components. As a result food quality degrades due to the chemical processes that the enzymes catalyze, including the emergence of bad flavors, degradation of texture, and depletion. For preservation, chemicals and other organic materials are also used. Among the most common preservatives that have been utilized to prevent microbial development for centuries, there are edible oils, salts, and sugars.

The heating and freezing processes for preserving food are also quite widespread. As a result of the use of these procedures, microbial growth is halted. Microbes that cannot withstand high temperatures are destroyed by boiling. And, thanks to the low temperatures the Microbes' ability to develop is hindered.

Among the most common preserving techniques, we have Canning and Dehydrating. In Canning, the food is sealed at high temperatures in canning jars. Canning is used to preserving meat, fruits & other produce. Dehydration instead involves removing water from meals, and eliminating water is the easiest approach to preventing food spoiling.

The process of canning includes heating the jars and their contents to a boiling point by placing them in a water bath canner. The heat generated during this operation is sufficient to eradicate the bacteria that may lead to mold growth. This process also removes the oxygen and air generating a vacuum seal.

# |Part 1| Water Bath & Pressure Canning Intro

## Section 1: What is Canning

Canning is a very effective and secure technique for food preservation if done correctly. During the canning process foods are put in jars and heated to a temperature that kills bacteria that might ruin the food or provide a health risk. The high temperature inactivates enzymes and eliminates germs by maintaining the food's safety and quality. Enzymes that may ruin the food are likewise rendered inactive. During heating, the air in the jar is expelled, and when it cools, a vacuum seal is created. This seal prevents air from returning to the product and recontamination of the food with bacteria. Many different foods can be preserved by canning.

Foods that have a high acidic level (PH less than 4.6) can be safely preserved using the water bath canning method. Pressure canning instead must be used to process low-acid items like meats for example. Attention Low-acid products MUST be necessarily pressure canned in order to be protected against the Clostridium botulinum.

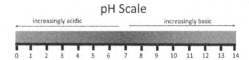

pH Scale

Some foods, that are on the fence and have an average level of acidity including tomatoes & figs, can be canned as acid foods (therefore through water bath canning) but first, their acidity must be increased, and they need to be treated with citric acid or lemon juice since their pH values may be somewhat higher than 4.6. Low-acid items, such as vegetables can be made acidic as well during the pickling process by adding vinegar.

Tomatoes, papaya, figs, melons, white peaches, bananas, and white nectarines fall into the category of food that needs to have their PH lowered through the addition of compounds such as acid citric, lemon, and vinegar.

It's crucial to remember that what matters is the pH of the whole jar. This is why it's so important to stick to tried-and-true recipes. For example, when making items like tomato sauce or salsa, which can include onions, basil & garlic in the sauce, the overall acidity of the mix is what counts.

## Section 2: Water Bath Canning Intro

Only store high-acid items like fruits, pickles & acidic tomatoes using the boiling water bath technique.

**General Process**

Here we will explain the general process so that you can familiarize yourself with it, if something feels vague do not worry in each of the recipes you will find detailed and step-by-step instructions. Without further ado let's dive in.

1) With heated water, fill the canner almost halfway. Heat the water by placing it on the fire. To avoid jar breakage, raw-packed jars are put in the canner, making sure the water is hot but not boiling.

2) Fill the jar with the heated meal, leaving the required headspace. The headspace is the distance between the produce/meal within the jar and the jar's rim. Each canning jar naturally allows 1/4", half-inch, or one-inch space. Put the food in the jars.

3) Place the lids; create a barrier between the jars and the canner's bottom by placing a stand.

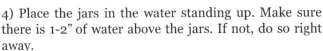

4) Place the jars in the water standing up. Make sure there is 1-2" of water above the jars. If not, do so right away.

5) Place the canner cover on it.

You only begin timing after the water has reached a rolling boil. If the water was already boiling when the jars were added, this refers to the moment the water starts to boil again fully. The processing time does not include the time it takes to heat the water in the canner. (You'll need to constantly open the lid to examine to see when complete boiling has started)

6) Boil the canner for the allotted amount of time. It is most practical to cover the canner at this time.

7) Remove the canner top and turn off the flame when the time is up. Or leave the top as it is. Keep the jars in the canner exactly as they are.

8) Set a five-minute timer (indicative time, which may change for specific recipes).

9) After five minutes, take the jars out and set them someplace warm and dry, preferably on a wire rack.

10) Avoid touching the rings, covering the jars, turning them upside down, or attempting to clean or dry them during this time. Any moisture will soon evaporate from them.

11) The Jars should be left undisturbed for 12-24 hours.

12) Loosen the screw bands and make sure the flat lid is well sealed.

13) Treat those that didn't seal and store them in the refrigerator.

14) Clean the jars, date them, and then store them without the screw bands in a cold, dark area.

## Section 3: Pressure Canning Intro

### How does pressure canning work?

Pressure canning might sound intimidating and make you want to stick to water bath canning only, however, it's actually much simpler than you think. Once you try it out for the first time and get over that scary first time it will quick quickly become one of your favorite methods to can, but unlike water bath canning, this method will open a big door of options for you to be able to can low acid vegetables, meats, seafood, and all these things that you are missing on because it's not safe to can them in a water bath canner.

When boiling water in a pot, your water temperature will be linked to your altitude. The basic temperature is 215 F for an altitude that is less than 1000 ft.

Whole high acid food can be canned safely in water bath canner thanks to their acidity that kills the bacteria and keeps them safe, meats along with soups, stews, low acid vegetables, and fruits require a temperature of 240° to 250°F to be canned safely, which is a temperature that you won't be able to get by boiling the water in a pot. That's where the pressure canner's role comes in. A pressure canner uses pressure to increase the temperature inside it to reach high degrees of temperatures that will kill the bacteria in your foods, and thus allow you to store them safely for a long time.

## What food needs to be pressured?

The only foods that you must can in a pressure canner are low acid ones since they can basically can't protect themselves. High-acid foods like can be safely canned in a simple water bath and stored for a long time without having to worry about them going bad.

Low acid foods that need to be pressure canned are the following:

- Low acid vegetables
- Soups and Stews
- Stocks and Broths
- Beef
- Poultry
- Fish
- Wild Game Meat
- Chili
- Baked, dry, and fresh Beans

All these foods must be pressure canned if you wish to store them because water bath canning will not be able to kill all the bacteria in them, which causes a toxin called botulism to build up over time, and create danger for food poisoning.

## Foods that can't be processed in the pressure canner?

Just like there are foods that must be processed in a pressure canner, there are some foods that must not be processed in the pressure canner at all such as:

- **Dairy products (butter, milk, cheese...) and coconut milk:** All dairy products are known to support the growth of Clostridium botulinum spores at room temperature. So pressure canning them, and storing them in a pantry is not safe at all.

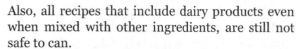
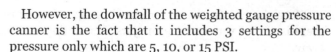

Also, all recipes that include dairy products even when mixed with other ingredients, are still not safe to can.

- **Eggs:** There is no available research to support canning eggs, so it's better to avoid canning altogether. You can pickle them instead and store them in the fridge.
- **All type of oils:** Oils are known to interfere with proper heat penetration when processing the food, which means that fat molecules in the oil coat the bacterial spores and protects them from destruction, allowing their survival. So do not can any oils, fats, or any recipes that require oil in them like pesto sauce except small dose used in sauces, and salsas...that are cooked.
- **Flour, Corn Starch, and starchy foods (rice, pasta...):** These foods are also known to interfere with the heating process which prevents the bacteria in them from dying.

Always make your research before canning certain ingredients to make sure they are safe, and stay away from this list completely. This doesn't mean though that you can't store them at all, they are plenty of ways to do it safely that don't require canning.

## Types of Pressure Canners

There are two types of pressure canners that almost all canning lovers use. They function a bit differently from each other, but their role is the same and they yield the same results. You just have to choose which one you prefer to work with.

### Weighted Gauge Pressure Canner:

This pressure canner is very easy to use as it is equipped with a steam valve that jiggles when the canner reaches the desired temperature.

Once it reaches the temperature that you selected for it, you just have to lower the heat and process your food for the recommended amount of time. During the process, the valve keeps making noises to confirm that it's still maintaining pressure, which is perfect because it means that you don't have to monitor it the whole time. You can leave it, and go on with your day and chores until the processing time is up.

When done, you just have to release the pressure gently accordingly to your recipe instructions and store your canned goods.

However, the downfall of the weighted gauge pressure canner is the fact that it includes 3 settings for the pressure only which are 5, 10, or 15 PSI.

It's perfect if you are living at an altitude that is at or less than 1000 ft because most foods can be canned at that altitude at 10 PSI, but if you are living at a higher altitude, you will need to increase the pressure, and the only possible setting is 15 PSI which is typically too high for the good.

### Dial Gauge Pressure Canner:

Unlike the weighted gauge pressure canner, the dial gauge pressure canner requires more attention. This canner's pressure can be increased or decreased by heat which makes stabilizes the pressure inside. This means that you have to stay close to it, and constantly check its dial to make sure it has the right pressure by adjusting it every time it starts to change.

What's amazing about it though, and makes it perfect if you are living at a higher altitude is that it has more PSI selections, which means that you don't have to increase the PSI like the weighted gauge pressure canner from 10 to 15 PSI and endanger the quality of your foods, you can increase it to 12 PSI only.

## Pressure Cooker VS Pressure Canner

The pressure cooker and pressure canner might have similar names, but they are actually completely different. The pressure canner was made for canning, while the pressure cooker was made to cook foods with very few exceptions for canning. If you wish to use a pressure cooker for canning, you will have to check with your manufacturer first to confirm if the model you have is approved for canning or not.

If it's not approved, it means you cannot use it at all for canning.

If it is approved, then you have to check and make sure your pressure canner has PSIG settings, that you can actually choose to pressure at 10 Psi, 5 Psi, and 15 Psi. You cannot use low and high-pressure settings only because you need to be able to set it to a certain pressure in order to can your food safely.

## How to use the pressure Canner?

Now that we have talked about how pressure canning works, what food is safe to can, what food is not safe, and the types of pressure canners available, it's time to know how to use one. It can be intimidating at first while you try to read the instructions and implement them, but with a few tries, you will quickly remember, and it's gonna become a piece of cake.

### Pressure canning prep

The first thing to do is to prepare all your pressure canner supplies and place them in one place, so when you start the canning process, and want to add the jars to the canner, you can find everything in one place next to you instead of having to look for them.

If your pressure canner doesn't have a gasket, brush the edges with some olive oil, it will help the lid go on smoothly, and make sure the pressure canner is sealed properly.

### Preparing food for pressure canning

Preparing the food for pressure canning will depend on the instructions of the recipe you are using, and the packing method you are using.

### Pre-heating the pressure canner

Contrary to a water bath canner, the pressure canner doesn't require a lot of water for canning because the sealed lid traps the steam inside. The amount of water that you need to add to it depends on the model of your pressure canners. Read the manual, and see how much water it requires.

Next, just like the water bath canning method, you must place a trivet/rack in the pressure canner, then you can put the jars on top because putting the jars directly at the bottom will put directly on top of heat which will cause the jars to break and crack open.

After you add the water, heat it depending on the packing method that you are using. If you are using the cold pack method, where the food that you are canning is not cooked, heat the water over medium heat until it becomes hot and registers around 140 F.

If you are using the hot pack method instead, bring the water to a gentle simmer, or until it registers around 180 F.

For both methods, do not bring the water to a boil, at all. The temperatures used for the two packing methods help put heat in the pressure canners to match the temperature of the jars, so when you process them, they don't break.

### Bringing pressure canner up to pressure

To bring the pressure canner to pressure, place the jars on top of the trivet/rack, then put on the lid and make sure it's sealed tightly. Leave the steam valve open, and bring the water in it to a boil over high heat. This is a very important step because it will make sure that the pressure canner is full of steam to be able to process your food properly. You will know when the water is boiling when steam starts to come out from the vent.

When that happens, allow the pressure canner to steam for 10 full minutes to make sure there are no air pockets left inside it.

If you are using a weighted gauge pressure canner, you can then seal the steam vent with the canning weight, and adjust the pressure needed depending on your altitude and the recipe you are using.

If you are using a dial gauge pressure canner, you have to read the manual that comes with the model and apply the instructions in it, then adjust the pressure needed for it as well depending on your altitude and the recipe you are using.

**Processing food in a pressure canner:** In this next step, it's very important to note that recipes give the processing time needed for the food only, it doesn't include the time that it requires for the pressure canner to come up to pressure because it varies from one model to another.

So first, bring your pressure canner up to pressure, it can take from up to 10 to 45 minutes, again depending on your model, and then you can start timing the processing time required for your food.

**Unloading a pressure canner:** This is the easier part. Once the processing time is over, you just have to turn off the heat and let your pressure canner sit where it is, without moving or touching it until its pressure setting reaches its own. You can also just leave it there overnight, and check it in the morning. Once the pressure reaches 0, you can then release the valve to allow the remaining pressure to escape, and open the lid.

It's essential that you follow these steps, because if you try to open the pressure canner before its pressure reaches 0, it will cause your jars to break, and all your work will be in vain.

## Section 4: Avoid Unsafe Canning Methods

Some canning techniques from decades past are no longer regarded as safe. Don't use these techniques to can food at home.

The "open kettle technique" or "hot-fill" is putting hot food into jars and waiting for the jars to seal as a result of the food's heat. This is dangerous! Heat levels are insufficient to kill rotting germs. Pickles, jellies, and

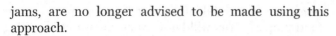

jams, are no longer advised to be made using this approach.

It may be risky to treat jars in the oven since heat may not be uniformly distributed within the jars, and they might burst, hurting you. Jars are not intended for use in an oven. Oven canning may be described in certain vintage cookbooks, although it is no longer advised.

Although dishwashers, slow cookers, sunlight, crock pots, microwaves, and slow cookers may include instructions for canning. These techniques are not advised since they might be quite risky. Avoid using chemicals or canning powders that aim to substitute heat treatment.

## Section 5: Handling the processed jars

Check the Lid for a Good Seal: As 2-piece lids cool, they often seal with a "pop" effect. Test the lid once it has totally cooled. It ought to have a downward curvature and be immobile when touched with a finger. If a jar is not tightly closed, store it in the refrigerator and utilize any undamaged food within two to three days, reprocess it within twenty-four hours, or keep it in the freezer.

Do not open sealed jars containing lost liquid; instead, make plans to utilize them first. Although the food may get discolored, it is still safe provided it is sealed and the liquid is just below the food.

Labeling and Storing Jars: To prevent the screw bands from rusting, take them off. Screw bands should be washed, dried, and kept in storage. The jars' outside food residue should be cleaned, then rinsed. The label should display the contents, the date, and the lot number. Store in a spot that's tidy, cool, dark, and dry. The ideal range of temperatures is 50 to 70 °F. Store canned goods away from hot appliances, such as a stove or furnace, and direct sunlight. Dry off any canned items. Food may deteriorate if dampness corrodes metal covers and causes leaks. Utilize canned foods within a year for the highest quality.

### Reprocess the unsealed jars

Food from jars that didn't seal should only be processed again if you choose to do so within 24 hours. To accomplish this, take off the lid and look for any little nicks on the jar's sealing surface. If required, replace the jar, add a fresh, treated lid, and repeat the procedure following the previous processing time. Use the goods that have been re-canned first, and mark the jars with

this information. They won't have as many nutrients as food that has just been processed once, and their texture will be softer.

When there is rotting: Foods in cans that exhibit any signs of rotting shouldn't be tasted or used. Before opening any jars, give them a careful inspection. A jar with a bulging lid or one that leaks indicate deterioration. When you remove the lid, check for further symptoms like spurting liquid, an unpleasant odor, or mold. Canned foods that have gone bad should be thrown away wherever neither people nor animals will consume them.

All questionable containers of low-acid, damaged items, including fruits, vegetables, meat, fish, and tomatoes, should be handled like this.

Put the cans in a thick rubbish bag if they are still sealed. Seal the bag, then either bury it in a local landfill or put it in an ordinary garbage can. Before being thrown away, the cans must be detoxified if they are open, leaking, or not properly sealed.

Low-acid foods that are poorly canned may retain the toxin that produces botulism without displaying any indications of deterioration. Even if there are no visible symptoms of deterioration, cans of food that have not been adequately processed must also be thrown away. Likewise, if they are cracked, open, or leaking, they must be detoxified and thrown away as instructed above. If any of the below holds true, low-acid foods are deemed incorrectly canned:

- The meal was not canned under pressure.
- The gauge was incorrect.
- The jar size, kind of pack, or type of food processed did not employ current studied processing periods or pressures.
- The food was canned at an incorrect altitude for the processing duration and pressure.

## Section 6: Ways to Detoxify Low-Acid Canned Foods

Either botulinum toxin enters via the skin or is eaten; either way, it may be a lethal contact. Avoid contact or splashing with any questionable food or drink at all costs. Put on strong plastic rubber gloves. Put on aprons and garments that may be thrown away or cleaned if they get polluted.

## Detoxification Guidelines

1) In an 8-quart saucepan or bigger pot, carefully set the jars on their sides with their lids still on.

2) Gloved hands should be properly cleaned.

3) Carefully, without sputtering, add boiling water to the pot until it is full and at least one *inch* of water is visible over the jars.

4) When the water is boiling, cover the saucepan with a lid.

5) To ensure that the food & containers are detoxified, boil for half an hour.

6) Cool the jars, their lids, and the food before throwing them away or disposing of them in a local landfill.

## How to Clean Polluted Surfaces

1) Put on rubber or thick plastic gloves to wipe up contaminated surfaces, tools, can openers, and clothes that may have come into touch with questionable foods or liquids

2) Use a new mixture of 5 parts water to one-part liquid home chlorine bleach (5-6 percent sodium hypochlorite).

3) Spray the bleach solution over the surfaces, then leave for half an hour. Avert breathing bleach or skin contact.

4) When cleaning up spills, use paper towels and put them in a plastic bag before throwing them away.

5) Reapply the bleach solution. After 30 minutes, rinse.

6) Clean any decontaminated surfaces, containers, tools, outfits, etc.

As soon as the cleaning is finished, throw away the gloves.

## Section 7: Canning Equipment

- Jars, screw bands & lids for canning: Only use spotless jars free of nicks or fractures
- If you have a pot with a fitting lid that is big enough just to completely submerge the jars in water by two"—and that will enable the water to boil when covered—you don't need to buy a specific water-bath canner for water-bath canning. A cake cooling rack will work as inside the or inside-the-canner rack. Fruits, jams, chutney, jellies, salsa, & other high-acid foods may be preserved in a water bath canner.
- Pressure canner for low acid items like broths, green beans, & meats. Use only a pressure canner designed exclusively for canning never a pressure cooker.
- The steam canner Jars in conventional and wide mouth sizes (half a pint, 1 pint, 1 1/2 pint, half a gallon & quart).
- Lids (should be new)
- A jar lifter, big "tongs" that make it easier to pick up hot jars, put them securely in a pot with boiling water, and then remove them from the hot water.
- Hot pads for hand protection
- Bands (old in good condition or new)
- Towels for cooling hot jars on
- Bottle Labels
- Timer to monitor processing duration
- Mouth funnel sizes
- Ladle: Using a ladle makes loading food into canning jars easier.
- Wide-mouth canning funnels that let you fill jars more easily and without spilling.
- Measuring device & spatula as Bubble Popper
- Measuring Cups

### Others good to have

- Pectin
- Juicer steam
- Food processor
- Lid Rack
- A manual food mill
- Salt for pickling

## Section 8: Mind your Altitude, how to find it

If you are a canning expert and just looking for extra recipes to try, then you must already know your altitude and how important it is when canning. If you are new to homemade canning, don't let the Altitude word and big numbers scare you off, this is actually a very simple topic to understand and implement, and it's essential that you understand it before you attempt homemade canning because it will affect your results.

Whether you want to can meats, vegetables, fruits, or jams...you have to take into consideration your Altitude because it will affect the processing time and pressure depending on the canning method you are using. The increase of the altitude especially if it's more than 1,000 feet above sea level causes the atmospheric pressure to reduce which means that the air becomes thinner, which

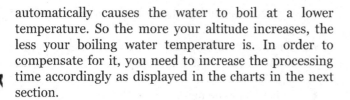

automatically causes the water to boil at a lower temperature. So the more your altitude increases, the less your boiling water temperature is. In order to compensate for it, you need to increase the processing time accordingly as displayed in the charts in the next section.

### How Can I Find My Altitude?

Finding your altitude is very easy, a simple research on google can give it to you. You can find it on google maps, or Wikipedia.

### How Does High Altitude Affect Water Bath Canning?

Since high altitude causes the air to thin, it also causes the temperature of your boiling water to decrease. The only way to compensate for it is by increasing the processing time to ensure that the heat eradicates all the bacteria in the food. If you fail to do that, this action might cause your canned food to go bad, and build up some very dangerous toxins such as botulism.

### How Does High Altitude Affect Pressure Canning?

High altitude affects pressure canning differently than water bath canning. Both canners' temperature decreases with high altitude, however, while the water bath method requires the processing time to be increased, you don't need to change anything for the processing time for the pressure canner, but you do need to increase the pressure to make sure the temperature is high enough to eradicate all the bacteria in the food.

| 1,001-3,000 | Add 5 minutes to the processing time |
| 3,001-6,000 | Add 10 minutes to the processing time |
| 6,001-8,000 | Add 15 minutes to the processing time |
| 8,001-10,000 | Add 20 minutes to the processing time |

## Section 9: Altitude Adjustments

## Altitude Adjustments for Boiling Water Bath Canner

If you are using a water bath canning method, these general recommendations for altitude adjustments will help you safely can your foods.

| Altitude in Feet | Increase The Original Processing Time |
| --- | --- |
| 0 – 1000 | 0 minutes |

## Altitude Adjustments for dial gauge Pressure Canner

If you are using a dial gauge pressure canner, these general recommendations for pressure adjustments will help you safely can your foods.

| Altitude in Feet | Pressure to Be Used |
| --- | --- |
| 0 – 1000 | 11 Psi/lb |
| 1001-2000 | 11 Psi/lb |
| 2001-4000 | 12 Psi/lb |
| 4001-6000 | 13 Psi/lb |
| 6001-8000 | 14 Psi/lb |
| 8001-10,000 | 15 Psi/lb |

## Altitude Adjustments for weighted gauge Pressure Canner

If you are using a weight gauge pressure canner, these general recommendations for pressure adjustments will help you safely can your foods.

| Altitude in Feet | Pressure to Be Used |
| --- | --- |
| 0 – 1000 | 10 Psi/lb |

| | |
|---|---|
| 1001-2000 | 15 Psi/lb |
| 2001-4000 | 15 Psi/lb |
| 4001-6000 | 15 Psi/lb |
| 6001-8000 | 15 Psi/lb |
| 8001-10,000 | 15 Psi/lb |

## Section 10: Key things to remember

- Low-acid foods should be canned using a pressure canner.
- Utilize scientifically validated recipes and apply the appropriate amount of time and pressure.
- Organize and clean the necessary tools, vegetables, fruits, or other foods.
- Handle little bits of the product at a time while washing it, if uncooked. Some of the most difficult-to-kill microorganisms are found in dirt.
- The canning process works better with cleaner raw materials
- Don't can food that has gone bad or been harmed
- Getting the Jars & Lids ready: Inspect the jars and eliminate the jars with nicks, fractures, or jagged edges. Food spoiling will occur as a consequence of these flaws since they prevent the jar from having an airtight seal. Every canning jar has to be thoroughly cleaned with soapy water, washed, and then kept hot. The jars might be cleaned with soap or by putting them in the canner's water while it's heating. As the jars are loaded with hot food and put in the canner, they must be maintained hot to avoid breaking.
- Boiling the jars for ten minutes is required to sterilize them before filling them with food and processing them in the canner (water bath) for less than ten minutes.
- Adjust processing time and pressure according to your altitude
- Jars boiled in a pressure canner or a water bath for at least ten minutes will sterilize the contents as they process.
- Use only brand-new two-piece lids, please. Treat them according to the manufacturer's directions. Others must be boiled, while others must be nearly brought to a boil and then keep them in hot water.
- Use only the freshest, best-quality vegetables. Overripe fruits and vegetables should not be canned since they are on the verge of becoming bad.
- Make absolutely sure you have everything you need before beginning by gathering your supplies and ingredients. It's not time to go to the store at this point in the procedure.
- Observe instructions and recipes to the letter. Your family's safety relies on you executing things right, so don't improvise.
- When you're prepared to fill the jars, sterilize them by cleaning them and then keeping them hot in a saucepan of boiling water. Even without a boiling water pot, the task may easily be completed by using the dishwasher!
- Don't fill the jars all the way to the top.
- Before attaching the lid and screw band, it's crucial to wipe the jar's threads & rims. Only finger tightening is used to tighten the band.
- As the containers cool, you may hear a "pinging" or popping sound, which is one indication that the lids have been sealed correctly. Jars that don't seal should be used right away
- As long as cans are kept in a cold, dry environment, your canned goods should generally remain fresh throughout the whole year. A damaged seal indicates that air has entered. Additionally, a bulging lid or one that seems rusted or rusty is a symptom of spoiling.
- If you ever open a processed can and see mildew, cloudiness, or bubbles, the seal has likely broken, and the contents are ruined. Eat nothing.

## Section 11: Canning FAQs

### Can anything be preserved by pressure canning?

No. One wouldn't know the safe time needed as so many foods intended for water bathing lack suggested pressure canning times. A key rule of safe canning is to never assume the processing times, no matter how much "over calculating" one thinks they are allowing for good measure.

And once again, no, you really don't want to. It's much more of a quality problem than a safety one. Jams, pickles, relishes, chutneys & jellies would be destroyed by pressure canning. Pickled beets will come out so spongy if one pressure can them (for half an hour, the same length of time as a water bath). Thus, no taste is gained.

As you get your pressure canner, you will want to pressure can everything because you believe it will somehow offer an additional margin of safety. And it simply appears more effective since it consumes less water. However, you truly do need to have both processing techniques in your toolbox.

## Why, despite having an acidic pH, is lemon juice and other food considered alkalizing for health reasons?

The pH of a meal before it is digested has very little impact on whether it will have an alkaline or acidic impact on the body.

Rather, it depends on whether the body processes it after digestion and produces alkaline or acidic byproducts.

The kidneys typically maintain the blood's pH balance by eliminating excess alkali or acid via urine.

Lemon juice creates alkaline byproducts once it is metabolized, which raises the pH of the urine. Despite having an acidic pH before it is digested.

## What safety standards apply to canning?

Ensure that your jars and lids are in excellent condition.

Usage (or repurpose) canning jars designed for household use. Look for cracks, then discard any jars that are damaged.

Check to see whether the jar rings are rusted or damaged.

Purchase new jar lids. Ensure the supply is brand new or no older than a year old since the bonding compound may degrade over time, particularly in damp basements. Never use an old lid again.

Follow the most recent canning instructions. A recipe that is older than 1997, apart from jellies & jams, should be stored in the family album.

Select the appropriate canner for the task.

Jams, relishes, pickles, fruits, & jellies, including apples, peaches, tomatoes & apple sauce, are all canned in water baths. Vegetables, fish, broth, meats, and certain tomato products should be canned using a pressure canner, particularly if they include a lot of low-acid vegetables like celery, onions, or peppers. Because it takes significantly less time and requires less energy, some choose to can tomatoes with a pressure canner.

Have the dial gauge on a pressure canner that has one checked yearly to ensure it is reading correctly. Inquire about gauge testing from the manufacturer.

Check that the gasket is still malleable & soft before pressure canning. You must change it if it is broken or dry.

For canning, always use premium, perfectly ripe food. The produce in the can you start with will never be greater than what you finish up with. Strawberries that are too ripe might result in a sloppy jam. Tomatoes that are mushy, decayed, or overripe can have a higher pH, attempting to make the processing time insufficient for safety. Some tomatoes are frequently sold in baskets labeled "canning tomatoes" when they are actually no good tomatoes for canning.

Before you begin, make sure everything is tidy. Keep your home clean:

Canners should be absolutely clean

Worktops or other surfaces - jar lifters, jars, & screw bands.

Fresh vegetables (just wash under cool running water without using soap or bleach).

Adhere strictly to the instructions in authorized recipes. You run the danger of disrupting the equilibrium that would produce a safe, good-quality end result when you alter the quantity or type of a component. Jams will get too soft if there isn't enough sugar, and pickles may become dangerous if there isn't enough acid or sodium. Tomato sauce may become more susceptible to botulism if there are too many peppers & onions added.

Follow processing deadlines, even if they appear lengthy. Foods that have been processed in a pressure canner or water bath are safe for long-term storage. Jellies & jams are processed quickly, killing yeasts, mildew & mold that would otherwise grow when the items weren't water-bathed but rather coated in paraffin.

Let the jars naturally cool for at least 12 hours with the correct side up before checking the seals. Testing sooner might result in the new seal breaking.

Cold jars should be kept away from open windows to avoid breaking from chilly night winds on hot jars.

When a jar is opened, it needs to be kept in the fridge for leftovers.

## How to Determine whether a Canning Jar Has Properly Sealed?

Use your finger or thumb to press the center of the lid. The lid is not sealed if it pops up when the finger is released.

Or Use the bottom of a spoon to tap the lid. The cover is not sealed if it just produces a faint noise. A dull sound will also result if the food comes in touch with the bottom of the lid. The jar will emit a ringing, rising sound if it is properly sealed

Or, look over the lid while holding the jar at eye level. The top should be curled downwards a little. The lid may not be shut if the middle is either flat or bulging.

# |Part 2| Water Bath Canning Recipes

## Section 1: Canned Fruits

### Homemade Canned Peaches

|Intro|: Peaches are one of the easiest canned recipes to try at home, especially if you are a beginner. They are also great to use all year round to make peach cobbler, and they taste even better with some simple vanilla ice cream. A recent study also confirmed recently that peaches are as loaded with nutrients and in some cases, they have more nutrition than fresh peaches.

### Equipment:
- StockPot
- Rack
- Thongs
- Towel
- Saucepan
- 14 quarts jars
- Large Bowl
- Funnel

**Nutrition Facts** per 14 quarts

| Calories | 430kcal |
|----------|---------|
| Carbs    | 105g    |
| Protein  | 10g     |
| Fats     | 3g      |

### Core Ingredients
- 34 pounds of fresh peaches

### Ingredients for The Syrup
- 6 cups of boiling water
- 3 cups of granulated sugar

### Step 1 - Preparation
- Start by sterilizing the jars where you will be storing the peaches, and make sure the rings are wiped clean.
- To sterilize the jars, bring a large pot of water to a boil, then turn off the heat, place the jars in it, and let them sit in it for 5 to 10 minutes.
- Use thongs to pull them out then place them with the lid down on a towel to dry.

### Step 2 – Bath water Canning
- To prepare for the canning process, fill a large stockpot with enough water to cover the jars by 1.5 to 2 inches.
- Bring it to a boil on high heat, then lower the heat and let it simmer while preparing the peaches.

### Step 3 – Preparing The Peaches
- Fill a large pot with water and bring it to a boil.
- Add to it the peaches and blanch them for 1 minute, then drain them and transfer them to a large bowl filled with water and ice.
- Allow the peaches to sit in the ice bath for a minute to cool down a bit, then peel them, cut them in half, remove the pit, and cut them into thick slices.

### Step 4 – Making The Syrup
- Combine the sugar with hot water in a saucepan and stir them well over medium heat until the sugar dissolves.
- Pour the syrup gently over the peaches until they are covered, then tap the jars gently on the countertop to remove the air bubbles.

### Step 5 – Canning The Peaches
- Wipe the sides of the jars with a clean and slightly wet rag, then put on the lids and secure them tightly. Press the center of the lids to ensure they are sealed properly.
- Place the jars in a rack and lower them to the boiling water in the water bath canner.
- If you don't have a rack to use with your stockpot, you can make one using aluminum foil. Get 7 pieces of aluminum that are 6 inches tall, and roll them into stripes.
- Shape 3 stripes into circles by cramping their ends together, then use the remaining 4 pieces to make a net inside of the circle in a zig-zag pattern by cramping the ends of each stripe into the circle.
- Make sure all the jars are immersed and completely covered with water, if they are not, add more water until they are covered.
- Bring the water to a boil one more on medium to high heat, then put on the lid and let them process for 25 minutes at an altitude that is less than 1000. If you have a higher altitude, adjust your processing time according to your altitude, check the dedicated section.

### Step 6 – Letting The Jars Rest

- Once the time is up, wet a large towel with some water then place it on a countertop.
- Gently remove the peach jars from the pot then place them on the wet towel, and let them rest until they completely cool down.

### Step 7 – Storing The Canned Peaches

- Double check the peach jars to make sure they are sealed then you can store them in a dark and cool place for 12 to 16 months.
- If you find some jars that are not sealed properly, you won't be able to store them. You can let them sit in the fridge instead and serve them in the next day or two and enjoy!

## Homemade Canned Blueberries

|Intro|: Canning Blueberries for the summer or winter is a very simple task that will save you a lot of space in the freezer, and add a very delicious and unique flavor to your blueberry pies, and cakes...Water bath canning is the best method to go about it, and will make it last for up to 18 months.

### Equipment:

- StockPot
- Rack
- Thongs
- Towel
- Saucepan
- 9 Pints jars
- Funnel

#### Nutrition Facts per 1 Pint

| Calories | 294.29kcal |
|----------|------------|
| Carbs    | 75.08g     |
| Protein  | 2.98g      |
| Fats     | 1.33g      |

### Core Ingredients

- 8 pounds of fresh blueberries, dark blue or dark black

### Ingredients for Blueberry Syrup

- 6 ½ cups of water
- ¾ cup of granulated sugar

### Step 1 - Preparation

- Start by washing the blueberries and removing their stems.
- Transfer them to a colander and let them drain while preparing the water bath canner.

### Step 2 – Sterilizing The Jars

- Start by sterilizing the jars where you will be storing the blueberries, and make sure the rings are wiped clean.
- To sterilize the jars, bring a large pot of water to a boil, then turn off the heat, place the jars in it, and let them sit in it for 5 to 10 minutes.
- Use thongs to pull them out then place them with the lid down on a towel to dry.

### Step 3 – Preparing The Water Bath Canner

- To prepare for the canning process, fill a large stockpot with enough water to cover the jars by 1.5 to 2 inches.
- Bring it to a boil on high heat, then lower the heat and let it simmer while preparing the blueberries.

### Step 4 – Blueberry Syrup

- Combine the water with sugar in a large saucepan then bring them to a boil over high heat while stirring the whole time.
- Spoon ½ cup of blueberry syrup into each jar.
- Next, you can decide if you want to proceed with the raw pack method or the hot pack method. Both methods are good, but each one has its advantages.

### Step 5 – Raw Pack Method

- The raw pack method means canning the blueberries without cooking them first. It's a very easy and fast method to use, however, the berries in this case are more susceptible to discoloration after a certain amount of storage.
- Add the blueberries into the jars and pack them tightly while leaving ½ inch of space.
- Pour the remaining syrup on top of the blueberries until they are covered, then add the lids and seal the jars tightly.
- Wipe the sides of the jars with a clean and slightly wet rag, then put on the lids and secure them tightly. Press the center of the lids to ensure they are sealed properly.

### Step 6 – Hot Pack Method

- The hot pack method means canning the blueberries after cooking them for a bit. This method helps the berries retain more flavor, and prevent them from floating or discolorating.
- Bring a large saucepan or a pot to a boil, and blanch in it the blueberries for 15 seconds.
- Once the time is up, drain them and transfer them to the jars and pack them tightly while leaving ½ inch of space.
- Pour the remaining syrup on top of the blueberries until they are covered, then add the lids and seal the jars tightly.
- Wipe the sides of the jars with a clean and slightly wet rag, then put on the lids and secure them tightly. Press the center of the lids to ensure they are sealed properly.

### Step 7 - Canning

- Place the jars in a rack and lower them to the boiling water in the water bath canner.
- If you don't have a rack to use with your stockpot, you can make one using aluminum foil. Get 7 pieces of aluminum that are 6 inches tall, and roll them into stripes.
- Shape 3 stripes into circles by cramping their ends together, then use the remaining 4 pieces to make a net inside of the circle in a zig-zag pattern by cramping the ends of each stripe into the circle.
- Make sure all the jars are immersed and completely covered with water, if they are not, add more water until they are covered.
- Bring the water to a boil one more on medium to high heat, then put on the lid and let them process for 15 minutes at an altitude that is less than 1000. If you have a higher altitude, adjust your processing time according to your altitude, check the dedicated section. .

### Step 8 – Letting the Jars Rest

- Once the time is up, turn off the heat and remove the lid, then allow the jar to sit in the hot water for 5 few minutes.
- Gently remove the jars and place them on a large towel, then let them cool down completely for at least 24 hours.

### Step 9- Storing

- Double check the jars to make sure they are sealed then you can store them in a dark and cool place for 18 months.

- If you find some jars that are not sealed properly, you won't be able to store them. You can let them sit in the fridge instead and serve them in the next day or two and enjoy!

## Homemade Canned Strawberries

**|Intro|**: Canning strawberries in whole is the perfect way to preserve them as it is a versatile method that will enable you to use them for various recipes, from cakes, to pies, and salads. The syrup the strawberries create when canned makes for a very delicious topping for your ice cream or pancakes as well. You can enjoy your canned strawberries and syrup for a whole year.

### Equipment:

- StockPot
- Rack
- Thongs
- Towel
- Saucepan
- 4 Pint jars
- Funnel
- Bowl

#### Nutrition Facts per 1-pint jar

| Calories | 292.07kcal |
|----------|------------|
| Carbs | 73.65g |
| Protein | 2.07g |
| Fats | 0.93g |

### Core Ingredients

- 8 cups of fresh and firm strawberries, rinsed and hulled
- 1 cup of sugar
- 1 teaspoon of citric acid

### Step 1 - Preparation

- Start by washing and hulling the strawberries, then toss them in a large bowl with sugar, and let them sit for 6 to 7 hours.
- The sugar will extract the strawberries' juice and this will add more flavor to them when canned.

### Step 2 - Sterilizing The Jars

- Start by sterilizing the jars where you will be storing the strawberries, and make sure the rings are wiped clean.

- You can sterilize them by placing them in a boiling pot of water and letting them sit in it for 5 to 10 minutes with the heat turned off.
- Use thongs to pull them out then place them with the lid down on a towel to dry.

## Step 3 – Preparing The Water Bath Canner

- To prepare for the canning process, fill a large stockpot with enough water to cover the jars by 1.5 to 2 inches.
- Bring it to a boil on high heat, then lower the heat and let it simmer while preparing the strawberries.

## Step 4 – Heating the Strawberries

- Transfer the strawberries with the released juice into a large saucepan.
- Cook them on low heat for 60 seconds while stirring them slightly to mash them.

## Step 5 - Packing

- Once the time is up, gently transfer the whole strawberries to the jars and pack them, but leave a ½ inch of space in each jar.
- Make sure to pack as many as you can because they shrink with time, if you don't, you will end up with half-filled jars after you store them.
- Cover the strawberries completely with water, add ¼ teaspoon of citric acid to each jar then add the lids and seal the jars tightly.
- The acid will help the strawberries maintain their color longer because they tend to start losing it in the first few months of storage and will also help improve their flavor.
- Wipe the sides of the jars with a clean and slightly wet rag, then put on the lids and secure them tightly. Press the center of the lids to ensure they are sealed properly.

## Step 6 - Canning

- Place the jars in a rack and lower them to the boiling water in the water bath canner.
- If you don't have a rack to use with your stockpot, you can make one using aluminum foil. Get 7 pieces of aluminum that are 6 inches tall, and roll them into stripes.
- Shape 3 stripes into circles by cramping their ends together, then use the remaining 4 pieces to make a net inside of the circle in a zig-zag pattern by cramping the ends of each stripe into the circle.

- Make sure all the jars are immersed and completely covered with water, if they are not, add more water until they are covered.
- Bring the water to a boil one more on medium to high heat, then put on the lid and let them process for 10 minutes at an altitude that is less than 1000. If you have a higher altitude, adjust your processing time according to your altitude, check the dedicated section. .

## Step 7 – Letting the Jars Rest

- Once the time is up, turn off the heat and remove the lid gently remove the jars from the pot.
- Place them on a large towel, then let them cool down completely for at least 12 to 24 hours.

## Step 8- Storing

- Double check the jars to make sure they are sealed then you can store them in a dark and cool place for 12 months.
- If you find some jars that are not sealed properly, you won't be able to store them. You can let them sit in the fridge instead and serve them in the next two to 3 days or drain them, and use them in a pie filling and enjoy!

## Homemade Canned Apples

|Intro|: Apples are arguably the only fruit that everyone loves. Water bath canning them at home makes it that much more delicious, and a perfect filling for your pies, turnovers, and cakes...that will save you time, and money, and add more flavors to your dishes. You can store and enjoy your apples for up to 2 years.

### Equipment:

- StockPot
- Rack
- Thongs
- Towel
- Saucepan
- 9 Pint Jars
- Large Bowl
- Funnel

**Nutrition Facts** per ½ cup

| Calories | 90kcal |
|----------|--------|
| Carbs | 23g |
| Protein | 0.5g |

| Fats | 0.3g |
|------|------|

## Core Ingredients

- 13.5 pounds of fresh and crisp apples
- 5 ¾ cups of water
- 1 ½ cup of white granulated sugar

## Step 1 - Preparation

- Wash the apples and peel them, then cut them into slightly thick slices.

## Step 2 - Sterilizing The Jars

- Start by sterilizing the jars where you will be storing the apples, and make sure the rings are wiped clean.
- You can sterilize them by placing them in a boiling pot of water and letting them sit in it for 5 to 10 minutes with the heat turned off.
- Use thongs to pull them out then place them with the lid down on a towel to dry.

## Step 3 – Preparing The Water Bath Canner

- To prepare for the canning process, fill a large stockpot with enough water to cover the jars by 1.5 to 2 inches.
- Bring it to a boil on high heat, then lower the heat and let it simmer while preparing the apple jars.

## Step 4 – Preparing the Syrup

- Combine the sugar with water in a large saucepan then bring them to a boil while stirring until the sugar dissolves completely.

## Step 5 – Cooking the Apples

- Add the apple slices to the syrup, then put on the lid and bring them to a rolling boil for 5 minutes.

## Step 6 - Packing

- Once the time is up, turn off the heat and gently transfer the apple slices to the jars and pack them, but leave a ½ inch of space in each jar.
- Pour the remaining syrup over the apples, then add the lids and secure them tightly.
- Wipe the sides of the jars with a clean and slightly wet rag, then put on the lids and secure them tightly. Press the center of the lids to ensure they are sealed properly.

## Step 7 - Canning

- Place the jars in a rack and lower them to the boiling water in the water bath canner.
- If you don't have a rack to use with your stockpot, you can make one using aluminum foil. Get 7 pieces of aluminum that are 6 inches tall, and roll them into stripes.
- Shape 3 stripes into circles by cramping their ends together, then use the remaining 4 pieces to make a net inside of the circle in a zig-zag pattern by cramping the ends of each stripe into the circle.
- Make sure all the jars are immersed and completely covered with water, if they are not, add more water until they are covered.
- Bring the water to a boil one more on medium to high heat, then put on the lid and let them process for 20 minutes at an altitude that is less than 1000. If you have a higher altitude, please refer to altitude adjustments to see how you can adjust your processing time.

## Step 8 – Letting the Jars Rest

- Once the time is up, turn off the heat and remove the lid gently remove the jars from the pot.
- Place them on a large towel, then let them cool down completely for at least 12 to 24 hours.

## Step 9 - Storing

- Double check the jars to make sure they are sealed then you can store them in a dark and cool place for up to 2 years.
- If you find some jars that are not sealed properly, you won't be able to store them. You can let them sit in the fridge instead and serve them in the next two to 3 days or drain them, and use them in a pie filling and enjoy!

## Homemade Canned Pears

|Intro|: Pears are yet another perfect and easy fruit to can as it turns out very delicious, and versatile as you can use them with so many dishes and baked goods. This also makes this recipe perfect for beginners to try it portrays exactly what you get with homemade canned foods which are very delicious food with a long shelf life that can last up to 12 months like these pears.

## Equipment:

- StockPot
- Rack
- Thongs

- Towel
- Saucepan
- 14 Pint Jars
- Funnel

**Nutrition Facts** per 1 cup

| Calories | 212kcal |
|----------|---------|
| Carbs | 56g |
| Protein | 1g |
| Fats | 1g |

## Core Ingredients

- 17 pounds of fresh pears
- 6 cups of water
- 1 cup of granulated sugar

## Step 1 - Sterilizing The Jars

- Start by sterilizing the jars where you will be storing the pears, and make sure the rings are wiped clean.
- You can sterilize them by placing them in a boiling pot of water and letting them sit in it for 5 to 10 minutes with the heat turned off.
- Use thongs to pull them out then place them with the lid down on a towel to dry.

## Step 2 – Preparing The Water Bath Canner

- To prepare for the canning process, fill a large stockpot with enough water to cover the jars by 1.5 to 2 inches.
- Bring it to a boil on high heat, then lower the heat and let it simmer while preparing the pears.

## Step 3 - Preparation

- Start by washing the pears, peeling them, coring them, and cutting them into 4 halves.

## Step 4 – Preparing the Syrup

- Combine the sugar with water in a large saucepan then bring them to a boil while stirring until the sugar dissolves completely.

## Step 5 – Cooking the Pears

- Add the pear slices to the syrup, then put on the lid and bring them to a rolling boil for 5 minutes.

## Step 6 - Packing

- Once the time is up, turn off the heat and gently transfer the pears slices to the jars and pack them, but leave a ½ inch of space in each jar.
- Pour the remaining syrup over the pears, then add the lids and secure them tightly.
- Wipe the sides of the jars with a clean and slightly wet rag, then put on the lids and secure them tightly. Press the center of the lids to ensure they are sealed properly.

## Step 7 - Canning

- Place the jars in a rack and lower them to the boiling water in the water bath canner.
- If you don't have a rack to use with your stockpot, you can make one using aluminum foil. Get 7 pieces of aluminum that are 6 inches tall, and roll them into stripes.
- Shape 3 stripes into circles by cramping their ends together, then use the remaining 4 pieces to make a net inside of the circle in a zig-zag pattern by cramping the ends of each stripe into the circle.
- Make sure all the jars are immersed and completely covered with water, if they are not, add more water until they are covered.
- Bring the water to a boil one more on medium to high heat, then put on the lid and let them process for 20 minutes at an altitude that is less than 1000. If you have a higher altitude, please refer to altitude section to see how you can adjust your processing time.

## Step 8 – Letting the Jars Rest

- Once the time is up, turn off the heat and remove the lid gently remove the jars from the pot.
- Place them on a large towel, then let them cool down completely for at least 12 to 24 hours.

## Step 9- Storing

- Double check the jars to make sure they are sealed then you can store them in a dark and cool place for up to 12 months.
- If you find some jars that are not sealed properly, you won't be able to store them. You can let them sit in the fridge instead for up to 4 days, or you can use them to make a delicious pear pie filling and enjoy!

## Homemade Canned Cherries

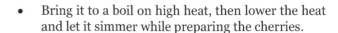

**|Intro|:** Canning cherries give you accessible cherries for several occasions. It's a delicacy that will last you for up to 12 months.

## Equipment:

- StockPot
- Rack
- Thongs
- Towel
- Saucepan
- 4 Pint Jars
- Cherry Pitter
- Funnel

### Nutrition Facts per 1 cup

| Calories | 411.07kcal |
|----------|-----------|
| Carbs | 104.89g |
| Protein | 1.77g |
| Fats | 0.53g |

## Core Ingredients

- 4 pounds of fresh cherries

## Ingredients for Syrup

- 8 ¼ cup of water
- 3 ¾ cups of white granulated sugar

## Step 1 - Preparation

- Start by washing the cherries and removing their stems.
- Give them to your kids or family members to pit them. If you wish, you can use them whole, but they taste much better when pitted.

## Step 2 – Sterilizing The Jars

- In the meantime, start sterilizing the jars where you will be storing the cherries, and make sure the rings are wiped clean.
- To sterilize the jars, bring a large pot of water to a boil, then turn off the heat, place the jars in it, and let them sit in it for 5 to 10 minutes.
- Use thongs to pull them out then place them with the lid down on a towel to dry.

## Step 3 – Preparing The Water Bath Canner

- To prepare for the canning process, fill a large stockpot with enough water to cover the jars by 1.5 to 2 inches.

- Bring it to a boil on high heat, then lower the heat and let it simmer while preparing the cherries.

## Step 4 – Packing Syrup

- Combine the water with sugar in a large saucepan then bring them to a boil over high heat while stirring the whole time.
- Spoon ½ cup of the syrup into each jar.
- Next, you can decide if you want to proceed with the raw pack method or the hot pack method. Both methods are good, but each one has its advantages.

## Step 5 – Raw Pack Method

- The raw pack method means canning the cherries without cooking them first. It's a very easy and fast method to use, however, the cherries in this case are more susceptible to discoloration after a certain amount of storage just like cherries.
- Add the cherries into the jars and pack them tightly while leaving ½ inch of space.
- Pour the remaining syrup on top of the cherries until they are covered, then add the lids and seal the jars tightly.
- Wipe the sides of the jars with a clean and slightly wet rag, then put on the lids and secure them tightly. Press the center of the lids to ensure they are sealed properly.

## Step 6 – Hot Pack Method

- The hot pack method means canning the cherries after cooking them for a bit. This method helps the cherries retain more flavor, and prevent them from floating or discolorating like berries.
- Bring the syrup to a boil, then stir into it the cherries and simmer them over low heat for 5 minutes, long enough to heat the cherries but not cook them.
- Once the time is up, transfer the cherries and syrup mixture into the jars and pack them tightly.
- Wipe the sides of the jars with a clean and slightly wet rag, then put on the lids and secure them tightly. Press the center of the lids to ensure they are sealed properly.

## Step 7 - Canning

- Place the jars in a rack and lower them to the boiling water in the water bath canner.
- If you don't have a rack to use with your stockpot, you can make one using aluminum foil. Get 7 pieces of aluminum that are 6 inches tall, and roll them into stripes.

- Shape 3 stripes into circles by cramping their ends together, then use the remaining 4 pieces to make a net inside of the circle in a zig-zag pattern by cramping the ends of each stripe into the circle.
- Make sure all the jars are immersed and completely covered with water, if they are not, add more water until they are covered.
- Bring the water to a boil one more on medium to high heat, then put on the lid and let them process for 25 minutes if you are using the raw pack method, and 20 minutes if you are using the hot pack method at an altitude that is less than 1000. If you have a higher altitude, please refer to the altitude adjustment to tune your processing time.

## Step 8 – Letting the Jars Rest

- Once the time is up, turn off the heat and remove the lid, then allow the jar to sit in the hot water for 5 few minutes.
- Gently remove the jars and place them on a large towel, then let them cool down completely for at least 24 hours.

## Step 9- Storing

- Double check the jars to make sure they are sealed then you can store them in a dark and cool place for 12 months.
- If you find some jars that are not sealed properly, you won't be able to store them. You can let them sit in the fridge instead and serve them in the 3 or 4 days, or simmer them until the cherries become soft, and use them for a pie filling and enjoy!

## Homemade Canned Grapefruit

|Intro|: Canning grapefruit provides a flavorful and preservative-free fruit in a jar, that you can enjoy all year round. This water bath canning recipe is very simple, and you can use it with a variety of citrus fruits like oranges, and mandarines...

## Equipment:

- StockPot
- Rack
- Thongs
- Towel
- Saucepan
- 9 Pint Jars
- Large Bowl
- Funnel

**Nutrition Facts** per 1-pint jar

| Calories | 200.56kcal |
|----------|------------|
| Carbs | 51.41g |
| Protein | 2.4g |
| Fats | 0.35g |

## Core Ingredients

- 13 pounds of ripe grapefruit

## Ingredients for The Syrup

- 4 cups of water
- 1 cup of white granulated sugar

## Step 1 - Preparation

- Start by peeling the grapefruits, then slice them into segments and remove from them the pit and white stuff completely.
- Leaving the membrane and the white tissue on the grapefruit segments will cause their taste to become bitter.

## Step 2 - Sterilizing The Jars

- Start sterilizing the jars where you will be storing the grapefruit, and make sure the rings are wiped clean.
- You can sterilize them by placing them in a boiling pot of water and letting them sit in it for 5 to 10 minutes with the heat turned off.
- Use thongs to pull them out then place them with the lid down on a towel to dry.

## Step 3 – Preparing The Water Bath Canner

- To prepare for the canning process, fill a large stockpot with enough water to cover the jars by 1.5 to 2 inches.
- Bring it to a boil on high heat, then lower the heat and let it simmer while preparing the grapefruit jars.

## Step 4 – Preparing the Syrup

- Combine the sugar with water in a large saucepan then bring them to a boil while stirring until the sugar dissolves completely.

## Step 5 - Packing

- Pack the grapefruit slices into the jars, but leave a ½ inch of space in each jar.
- Pour the syrup over the grapefruit segments, then add the lids and secure them tightly.

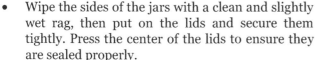

- Wipe the sides of the jars with a clean and slightly wet rag, then put on the lids and secure them tightly. Press the center of the lids to ensure they are sealed properly.

## Step 6 - Canning

- Place the jars in a rack and lower them to the boiling water in the water bath canner.
- If you don't have a rack to use with your stockpot, you can make one using aluminum foil. Get 7 pieces of aluminum that are 6 inches tall, and roll them into stripes.
- Shape 3 stripes into circles by cramping their ends together, then use the remaining 4 pieces to make a net inside of the circle in a zig-zag pattern by cramping the ends of each stripe into the circle.
- Make sure all the jars are immersed and completely covered with water, if they are not, add more water until they are covered.
- Bring the water to a boil one more on medium to high heat, then put on the lid and let them process for 10 minutes at an altitude that is less than 1000. If you have a higher altitude, adjust your processing time according to your altitude, check the dedicated section.

## Step 7 – Letting the Jars Rest

- Once the time is up, turn off the heat and remove the lid gently, then remove the jars from the pot.
- Place them on a large towel, then let them cool down completely for at least 12 hours.

## Step 8 - Storing

- Double check the jars to make sure they are sealed then you can store them in a dark and cool place for up to 18 months.
- If you find some jars that are not sealed properly, you won't be able to store them. You can let them sit in the fridge instead and serve them in the next two to 3 to 4 days or you can use them instead for a cake or pie and enjoy!

## Homemade Canned Pineapple

|Intro|: Pineapples are one of the most perfect fruits to can since they are high in both sugar and acid. Also, it's one of the canned fruits that everyone purchases canned. This water bath canning method will easily allow you to can it in your home and get a much more delicious result that you can use for up to 12 months.

## Equipment:

- StockPot
- Rack
- Thongs
- Towel
- Saucepan
- 4 Pints Jars
- Large Bowl
- Funnel

### Nutrition Facts per 1-pint jar

| Calories | 292.69kcal |
|----------|------------|
| Carbs | 76.55g |
| Protein | 2.49g |
| Fats | 0.55g |

## Core Ingredients

- 4 fresh pineapples
- 2 cups of water

## Ingredients for the syrup

- 3 cups of water
- 1/3 cup of white granulated sugar

## Step 1 - Preparation

- Start by washing and peeling the pineapples.
- Remove the core of the pineapples and place them aside, then slice the remaining flesh.
- You can choose to slice or mash the pineapples, but I highly recommend slicing them because it stores and tastes better.

## Step 2 – To prepare the Pineapple Syrup

- Combine 2 cups of water with the pineapple cores in a large saucepan, then bring them to a rolling boil for 10 minutes.
- Once the time is up, turn off the heat and place it aside.
- You can strain the pineapple cores and use them however you wish.

## Step 3 – Sterilizing The Jars

- In the meantime, start sterilizing the jars where you will be storing the pineapples, and make sure the rings are wiped clean.
- To sterilize the jars, bring a large pot of water to a boil, then turn off the heat, place the jars in it, and let them sit in it for 5 to 10 minutes.

- Use thongs to pull them out then place them with the lid down on a towel to dry.

## Step 4 – Preparing The Water Bath Canner

- To prepare for the canning process, fill a large stockpot with enough water to cover the jars by 1.5 to 2 inches.
- Bring it to a boil on high heat, then lower the heat and let it simmer while preparing the pineapples.

## Step 5 – Packing Syrup

- Combine the water with sugar in a large saucepan then bring them to a boil over high heat while stirring the whole time.
- Next, you can decide if you want to proceed with the raw pack method or the hot pack method. Both methods are good, but each one has its advantages.

## Step 6 – Raw Pack Method

- The raw pack method means canning the pineapples without cooking them first. It's a very easy and fast method to use.
- Pour ½ cup of the pineapple syrup into each jar.
- Add the pineapples into the jars and pack them tightly while leaving ½ inch of space.
- Pour the packing sugar syrup on top of the pineapples until they are covered, then add the lids and seal the jars tightly.
- Wipe the sides of the jars with a clean and slightly wet rag, then put on the lids and secure them tightly. Press the center of the lids to ensure they are sealed properly.

## Step 7 – Hot Pack Method

- The hot pack method means canning the pineapples after cooking them for a bit. This method helps the pineapples retain more flavor, and is just known to taste better than the hot pack method. pack method.
- Pour ½ cup of the pineapple syrup into each jar.
- Bring the sugar syrup to a boil, then stir into it the pineapples and simmer them over low heat for 10 minutes
- Once the time is up, transfer the pineapples and syrup mixture into the jars and pack them tightly.
- This process tends to be a little bit messy because the pineapples are mushy and hot, and you won't be able to pack them tightly, so you might need an extra jar.
- Wipe the sides of the jars with a clean and slightly wet rag, then put on the lids and secure them

tightly. Press the center of the lids to ensure they are sealed properly.

## Step 8 - Canning

- Place the jars in a rack and lower them to the boiling water in the water bath canner.
- If you don't have a rack to use with your stockpot, you can make one using aluminum foil. Get 7 pieces of aluminum that are 6 inches tall, and roll them into stripes.
- Shape 3 stripes into circles by cramping their ends together, then use the remaining 4 pieces to make a net inside of the circle in a zig-zag pattern by cramping the ends of each stripe into the circle.
- Make sure all the jars are immersed and completely covered with water, if they are not, add more water until they are covered.
- Bring the water to a boil one more on medium to high heat, then put on the lid and let them process for 25 minutes if you are using the raw pack method, and 20 minutes if you are using the hot pack method at an altitude that is less than 1000. If you have a higher altitude, adjust your processing time according to your altitude, check the dedicated section.

## Step 9 – Letting the Jars Rest

- Once the time is up, turn off the heat and remove the lid, then remove the jars from the hot water and place them on a kitchen towel.
- Allow the jars to cool down completely with might take 6 to 8 hours.

## Step 10- Storing

- Double check the jars to make sure they are sealed then you can store them in a dark and cool place for 12 months.
- If you find some jars that are not sealed properly, you won't be able to store them. You can let them sit in the fridge instead and serve them in 1 to 2 days, and enjoy!

## Homemade Canned Lemons

|Intro|: Lemon is generally served as an incredibly rejuvenating drink. Its slices or wedges are frequently served with salads or added to tea, or they can be squeezed over other raw fruits to add flavor while precluding them from turning brown. Another thing that makes this fruit perfect, is canning it. You can store it for

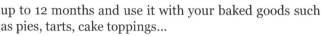

up to 12 months and use it with your baked goods such as pies, tarts, cake toppings...

## Equipment:
- StockPot
- Rack
- Thongs
- Towel
- Saucepan
- 6 Pint Jars
- Large Bowl
- Funnel

### Nutrition Facts per 1-pint jar

| Calories | 450kcal |
|----------|---------|
| Carbs | 120g |
| Protein | 2g |
| Fats | 1g |

## Core Ingredients
- 13 pounds of fresh lemons
- 10 ½ cups of water
- 1 ¼ cup of white granulated sugar

## Step 1 - Preparation
- Start by peeling the lemons, then slice them into segments and remove from them the pits and white tissue completely.
- Leaving the membrane and the white tissue on the lemon's segments will cause their taste to become bitter.

## Step 2 - Sterilizing The Jars
- Start sterilizing the jars where you will be storing the lemons, and make sure the rings are wiped clean.
- You can sterilize them by placing them in a boiling pot of water and letting them sit in it for 5 to 10 minutes with the heat turned off.
- Use thongs to pull them out then place them with the lid down on a towel to dry.

## Step 3 – Preparing The Water Bath Canner
- To prepare for the canning process, fill a large stockpot with enough water to cover the jars by 1.5 to 2 inches.

- Bring it to a boil on high heat, then lower the heat and let it simmer while preparing the lemons jars.

## Step 4 – Preparing the Syrup
- Combine the sugar with water in a large saucepan then bring them to a boil while stirring until the sugar dissolves completely.

## Step 5 - Packing
- Pack the lemons slices into the jars, but leave a ½ inch of space in each jar.
- Pour the syrup over the lemons segments, then add the lids and secure them tightly.
- Wipe the sides of the jars with a clean and slightly wet rag, then put on the lids and secure them tightly. Press the center of the lids to ensure they are sealed properly.

## Step 6 - Canning
- Place the jars in a rack and lower them to the boiling water in the water bath canner.
- If you don't have a rack to use with your stockpot, you can make one using aluminum foil.  Get 7 pieces of aluminum that are 6 inches tall, and roll them into stripes.
- Shape 3 stripes into circles by cramping their ends together, then use the remaining 4 pieces to make a net inside of the circle in a zig-zag pattern by cramping the ends of each stripe into the circle.
- Make sure all the jars are immersed and completely covered with water, if they are not, add more water until they are covered.
- Bring the water to a boil one more on medium to high heat, then put on the lid and let them process for 10 minutes at an altitude that is less than 1000. If you have a higher altitude, adjust your processing time according to your altitude, check the dedicated section. .

## Step 7 – Letting the Jars Rest
- Once the time is up, turn off the heat and remove the lid gently, then remove the jars from the pot.
- Place them on a large towel, then let them cool down completely for at least 12 hours until they cool down completely.

## Step 8 - Storing
- Double check the jars to make sure they are sealed then you can store them in a dark and cool place for up to 18 months.

- If you find some jars that are not sealed properly, you won't be able to store them. You can let them sit in the fridge instead and serve them in the next two to 4 days or you can use them instead for a cake or pie and enjoy!

## Homemade Canned Raspberries

**|Intro|:** Raspberries are a very lovely fruit to can as it turns into a unique delicacy that you can serve with baked goods and ice cream, and you can serve them on their own as well. Water bath canning it will make last for up to 12 months.

### Equipment:

- StockPot
- Rack
- Thongs
- Towel
- Saucepan
- 6 Pint jars
- Large Bowl
- Funnel

#### Nutrition Facts per 1 Pint jar

| Calories | 345kcal |
|----------|---------|
| Carbs | 87g |
| Protein | 2g |
| Fats | 1g |

### Core Ingredients

- 2 ¼ pounds of fresh raspberries

### Ingredients for Syrup

- 4 ¼ cups of water
- 1 ½ cup of white granulated sugar

### Step 1 - Preparation

- Start by washing the raspberries thoroughly, and remove any spoiled ones because they could ruin the whole jar.

### Step 2 - Sterilizing The Jars

- Start sterilizing the jars where you will be storing the raspberries, and make sure the rings are wiped clean.

- You can sterilize them by placing them in a boiling pot of water and letting them sit in it for 5 to 10 minutes with the heat turned off.
- Use thongs to pull them out then place them with the lid down on a towel to dry.

### Step 3 – Preparing The Water Bath Canner

- To prepare for the canning process, fill a large stockpot with enough water to cover the jars by 1.5 to 2 inches.
- Bring it to a boil on high heat, then lower the heat and let it simmer while preparing the raspberry jars.

### Step 4 – Preparing the Syrup

- Combine the sugar with water in a large saucepan then bring them to a boil while stirring until the sugar dissolves completely.

### Step 5 - Packing

- Pack the raspberries into the jars, but leave a ½ inch of space in each jar.
- Pour the syrup over the raspberries, then add the lids and secure them tightly.
- Wipe the sides of the jars with a clean and slightly wet rag, then put on the lids and secure them tightly. Press the center of the lids to ensure they are sealed properly.

### Step 6 - Canning

- Place the jars in a rack and lower them to the boiling water in the water bath canner.
- If you don't have a rack to use with your stockpot, you can make one using aluminum foil. Get 7 pieces of aluminum that are 6 inches tall, and roll them into stripes.
- Shape 3 stripes into circles by cramping their ends together, then use the remaining 4 pieces to make a net inside of the circle in a zig-zag pattern by cramping the ends of each stripe into the circle.
- Make sure all the jars are immersed and completely covered with water, if they are not, add more water until they are covered.
- Bring the water to a boil one more on medium to high heat, then put on the lid and let them process for 10 minutes at an altitude that is less than 1000. If you have a higher altitude, adjust your processing time according to your altitude, check the dedicated section. .

### Step 7 – Letting the Jars Rest

- Once the time is up, turn off the heat and remove the lid gently, then remove the jars from the pot.
- Place them on a large towel, then let them cool down completely for at least 12 hours until they cool down completely.

### Step 8 - Storing

- Double check the jars to make sure they are sealed then you can store them in a dark and cool place for up to 12 months.
- If you find some jars that are not sealed properly, you won't be able to store them.
- You can still store them though in the fridge for up to 3 weeks and enjoy!

## Homemade Canned Oranges

|Intro|: When in season, oranges are a fan favorite and a nice treat for both kids and grown up. Water bath canning them will enable you to enjoy them throughout the year by serving them on their own, or by adding to your baked goods for they make great cake toppings.

### Equipment:

- StockPot
- Rack
- Thongs
- Towel
- Saucepan
- 7 Pint jars
- Large Bowl
- Funnel

#### Nutrition Facts per 1-pint jar

| Calories | 348.97kcal |
|----------|-----------|
| Carbs | 89.09g |
| Protein | 2.56g |
| Fats | 0.33g |

### Core Ingredients

- 6 pounds of fresh and firm oranges

### Ingredients for Syrup

- 4 cups of water
- 2 cups of white granulated sugar

### Step 1 - Preparation

- Start by peeling the oranges, then slice them into segments and remove from them the pits and white tissue completely.
- Leaving the membrane and the white tissue on the lemons' segments will cause their taste to become bitter.

### Step 2 - Sterilizing The Jars

- Start sterilizing the jars where you will be storing the orange segments, and make sure the rings are wiped clean.
- You can sterilize them by placing them in a boiling pot of water and letting them sit in it for 5 to 10 minutes with the heat turned off.
- Use thongs to pull them out then place them with the lid down on a towel to dry.

### Step 3 – Preparing The Water Bath Canner

- To prepare for the canning process, fill a large stockpot with enough water to cover the jars by 1.5 to 2 inches.
- Bring it to a boil on high heat, then lower the heat and let it simmer while preparing the oranges.

### Step 4 – Preparing the Syrup

- Combine the sugar with water in a large saucepan then bring them to a boil while stirring until the sugar dissolves completely.

### Step 5 - Packing

- Pack the orange segments into the jars, but leave a ½ inch of space in each jar.
- Pour the syrup over the oranges, then add the lids and secure them tightly.
- Wipe the sides of the jars with a clean and slightly wet rag, then put on the lids and secure them tightly. Press the center of the lids to ensure they are sealed properly.

### Step 6 - Canning

- Place the jars in a rack and lower them to the boiling water in the water bath canner.
- If you don't have a rack to use with your stockpot, you can make one using aluminum foil. Get 7 pieces of aluminum that are 6 inches tall, and roll them into stripes.
- Shape 3 stripes into circles by cramping their ends together, then use the remaining 4 pieces to make a net inside of the circle in a zig-zag pattern by cramping the ends of each stripe into the circle.

- Make sure all the jars are immersed and completely covered with water, if they are not, add more water until they are covered.
- Bring the water to a boil one more on medium to high heat, then put on the lid and let them process for 10 minutes at an altitude that is less than 1000. If you have a higher altitude, adjust your processing time according to your altitude, check the dedicated section.

### Step 7 – Letting the Jars Rest
- Once the time is up, turn off the heat and remove the lid gently, then remove the jars from the pot.
- Place them on a large towel, then let them cool down completely for at least 12 hours until they cool down completely.

### Step 8 - Storing
- Double check the jars to make sure they are sealed then you can store them in a dark and cool place for up to 12 months.
- If you find some jars that are not sealed properly, you won't be able to store them.
- You can still store them though in the fridge for up to 4 weeks and enjoy!

## Homemade Canned Plums

|Intro|: Water bath canning plums are the perfect way to enjoy them all year. You can them whole, or slice them in half. You can also feel free to experiment with them by adding certain spices like cinnamon, cloves...

### Equipment:
- StockPot
- Rack
- Thongs
- Towel
- Saucepan
- 14 Pint jars
- Large Bowl
- Funnel

### Nutrition Facts per 1 Pint jar

| Calories | 302.49kcal |
|----------|-----------|
| Carbs | 76.21g |
| Protein | 2.92g |
| Fats | 1.17g |

### Core Ingredients
- 14 pounds of plums

### Ingredients for the Syrup
- 16 cups of water
- 2 cups of white granulated sugar

### Step 1 - Preparation
- Start by wishing the plums, remove their stem, then slice them in half and discard the pits.

### Step 2 – Sterilizing The Jars
- In the meantime, start sterilizing the jars where you will be storing the plums, and make sure the rings are wiped clean.
- To sterilize the jars, bring a large pot of water to a boil, then turn off the heat, place the jars in it, and let them sit in it for 5 to 10 minutes.
- Use thongs to pull them out then place them with the lid down on a towel to dry.

### Step 3 – Preparing The Water Bath Canner
- To prepare for the canning process, fill a large stockpot with enough water to cover the jars by 1.5 to 2 inches.
- Bring it to a boil on high heat, then lower the heat and let it simmer while preparing the plums.

### Step 4 – Packing Syrup
- Combine the water with sugar in a large saucepan then bring them to a boil over high heat while stirring the whole time.
- Next, you can decide if you want to proceed with the raw pack method or the hot pack method. Both methods are good, but each one has its advantages.

### Step 5 – Raw Pack Method
- The raw pack method means canning the plums without cooking them first. It's a very easy and fast method to use, however, the plums in this case are more susceptible to discoloration after a certain amount of storage just like cherries and berries
- Add the plums into the jars and pack them tightly while leaving ½ inch of space.
- Pour the remaining syrup on top of the plums until they are covered, then add the lids and seal the jars tightly.
- Wipe the sides of the jars with a clean and slightly wet rag, then put on the lids and secure them

tightly. Press the center of the lids to ensure they are sealed properly.

### Step 6 – Hot Pack Method

- The hot pack method means canning the plums after cooking them for a bit. This method helps the plums retain more flavor, prevent them from floating or discoloration and also helps them retain their texture and not get soft quickly.
- Bring the syrup to a boil, then stir into it the plums and boil them over low heat for 2 minutes, long enough to heat the plums but not cook them.
- Once the time is up, turn off the heat, and allow them to sit for 25 to 30 minutes.
- Transfer the plums and syrup mixture into the jars and pack them tightly while making sure to leave ½ inch of space empty.
- Wipe the sides of the jars with a clean and slightly wet rag, then put on the lids and secure them tightly. Press the center of the lids to ensure they are sealed properly.

### Step 7 - Canning

- Place the jars in a rack and lower them to the boiling water in the water bath canner.
- If you don't have a rack to use with your stockpot, you can make one using aluminum foil. Get 7 pieces of aluminum that are 6 inches tall, and roll them into stripes.
- Shape 3 stripes into circles by cramping their ends together, then use the remaining 4 pieces to make a net inside of the circle in a zig-zag pattern by cramping the ends of each stripe into the circle.
- Make sure all the jars are immersed and completely covered with water, if they are not, add more water until they are covered.
- Bring the water to a boil one more on medium to high heat, then put on the lid and let them process for 25 minutes if you are using the raw pack method, and 25 minutes if you are using the hot pack method at an altitude that is less than 1000. If you have a higher altitude, adjust your processing time according to your altitude, check the dedicated section.

### Step 8 – Letting the Jars Rest

- Once the time is up, gently remove the jars and place them on a large towel, then let them cool down completely for at least 24 hours.

### Step 9- Storing

- Double check the jars to make sure they are sealed then you can store them in a dark and cool place for 12 months.
- If you find some jars that are not sealed properly, you won't be able to store them. You can let them sit in the fridge instead and serve them in the 3 or 4 days, or simmer them until the plums become soft, and use them for a pie filling and enjoy!

## Section 2: Jams and Jellies

### Sweet Strawberry Lemonade Jam

**|Intro|:** This sweet strawberry lemonade jam is the perfect canning recipe for strawberry season. It's strawberry jam, with fresh lemon juice that gives it a nice kick, and a unique taste that elevates this jam and makes a perfect treat to enjoy all year round.

**Equipment:**
- StockPot
- Rack
- Thongs
- Towel
- Saucepan
- 3 Pint Jars
- Large Bowl
- Funnel

**Nutrition Facts** per 1 Pint Jar

| Calories | 370kcal |
|----------|---------|
| Carbs | 89.27g |
| Protein | 1.66g |
| Fats | 0.81g |

### Core Ingredients

- 4 cups of fresh and firm strawberries, crushed
- 7 cups of white granulated sugar
- 1 cup of fresh lemon juice
- 1 package of pectin powder (1.75 oz)

### Step 1 - Preparation

- Wash the strawberries thoroughly then remove their stems.

31

- Transfer them to a colander and let them drain for 10 to 15 minutes.

## Step 2 – Sterilizing The Jars
- In the meantime, start sterilizing the jars where you will be storing the lemonade jam, and make sure the rings are wiped clean.
- To sterilize the jars, bring a large pot of water to a boil, then turn off the heat, place the jars in it, and let them sit in it for 5 to 10 minutes.
- Use thongs to pull them out then place them with the lid down on a towel to dry.

## Step 3 – Preparing The Water Bath Canner
- To prepare for the canning process, fill a large stockpot with enough water to cover the jars by 1.5 to 2 inches.
- Bring it to a boil on high heat, then lower the heat and let it simmer while preparing the lemonade.

## Step 4 – Making The Lemonade
- To prepare the strawberry lemonade, place some of the strawberries in a large bowl, then use a potato masher to crush them completely until you measure 4 cups of crushed strawberries.
- Transfer the crushed strawberries to a large saucepan, then add to it the sugar with lemon juice.
- Sir them well until well combined, then add the pectin and mix them well.
- Bring the mixture to a rolling boil over high heat, then keep it boiling for 1 minute while stirring all the time.
- Once the time is up, turn off the heat then use a spoon or spatula to skim off the foam on top.

## Step 5 - Packing
- Quickly spoon the mixture while it's hot into the sterilized jars, and make sure to leave 1/8 of the space empty at the top of each jar.
- Wipe the sides of the jars with a clean and slightly wet rag, then put on the lids and secure them tightly. Press the center of the lids to ensure they are sealed properly.

## Step 6 - Canning
- Place the jars in a rack and lower them to the boiling water in the water bath canner.
- If you don't have a rack to use with your stockpot, you can make one using aluminum foil. Get 7 pieces of aluminum that are 6 inches tall, and roll them into stripes.

- Shape 3 stripes into circles by cramping their ends together, then use the remaining 4 pieces to make a net inside of the circle in a zig-zag pattern by cramping the ends of each stripe into the circle.
- Make sure all the jars are immersed and completely covered with water, if they are not, add more water until they are covered.
- Bring the water to a boil one more on medium to high heat, then put on the lid and let them process for 10 minutes at an altitude that is less than 1000. If you have a higher altitude, adjust your processing time according to your altitude, check the dedicated section. .

## Step 7 – Letting the Jars Rest
- Once the time is up, turn off the heat and remove the lid gently, then remove the jars from the pot.
- Place them on a large towel, then let them cool down completely for at least 12 hours until they cool down.

## Step 8 - Storing
- Double check the jars to make sure they are sealed then you can store them in a dark and cool place for up to 14 months.
- If you find some jars that are not sealed properly, you won't be able to store them in the pantry.
- You can still store them though in the fridge for up to 4 weeks and enjoy!

## Blackberry Jam

|Intro|: Blackberries are delicious on their own, so making blackberry jam makes them even better. This recipe makes a perfect low-sugar jam that will become a staple on your breakfast table, and also makes a great addition to your baked goods and cheesecakes.

### Equipment:
- StockPot
- Rack
- Thongs
- Towel
- Saucepan
- 9 Pint Jars
- Large Bowl
- Funnel

**Nutrition Facts** per 1 Pint Jar

| Calories | 266.47kcal |
|---|---|

| Carbs | 65.23g |
|---------|--------|
| Protein | 3.68g |
| Fats | 1.32g |

## Core Ingredients

- 5 pounds of fresh and firm blackberries
- 1 ½ cup of white granulated sugar
- ½ cup of fresh lemon juice
- ¼ cup of boiling water
- 4 teaspoons of pectin powder
- ½ teaspoon of calcium powder

## Step 1 - Preparation

- Start by preparing the calcium. Pour ¼ cup of boiling water into a small jar, then add to it ½ teaspoon of calcium.
- Shake the jar well until it dissolves, then place it aside to dissolve.

## Step 2 – Preparing The Jam

- Wash the berries nicely and let them sit in a colander to drain while preparing the water bath canner and jars.
- If you don't have fresh berries, frozen berries could also work.

## Step 3 – Sterilizing The Jars

- In the meantime, start sterilizing the jars where you will be storing the jam, and make sure the rings are wiped clean.
- To sterilize the jars, bring a large pot of water to a boil, then turn off the heat, place the jars in it, and let them sit in it for 5 to 10 minutes.
- Use thongs to pull them out then place them with the lid down on a towel to dry.

## Step 4 – Preparing The Water Bath Canner

- To prepare for the canning process, fill a large stockpot with enough water to cover the jars by 1.5 to 2 inches.
- Bring it to a boil on high heat, then lower the heat and let it simmer while preparing the jam.

## Step 5 – Making The Jam

- To prepare the jam, transfer the blackberries into a large bowl, then use a potato masher to mash them completely.
- Transfer the mashed blackberries to a large saucepan, then add 4 teaspoons of calcium water.
- Bring them to a boil over high heat, then add the sugar with pectin to them and stir them well.
- Bring the mixture to a boil again while stirring all the time, then turn off the heat.

## Step 6 - Packing

- Quickly spoon the jam while it's hot into the sterilized jars, and make sure to leave 1/8 of the space empty at the top of each jar.
- Wipe the sides of the jars with a clean and slightly wet rag, then put on the lids and secure them tightly. Press the center of the lids to ensure they are sealed properly.

## Step 7 - Canning

- Place the jars in a rack and lower them to the boiling water in the water bath canner.
- If you don't have a rack to use with your stockpot, you can make one using aluminum foil. Get 7 pieces of aluminum that are 6 inches tall, and roll them into stripes.
- Shape 3 stripes into circles by cramping their ends together, then use the remaining 4 pieces to make a net inside of the circle in a zig-zag pattern by cramping the ends of each stripe into the circle.
- Make sure all the jars are immersed and completely covered with water, if they are not, add more water until they are covered.
- Bring the water to a boil one more on medium to high heat, then put on the lid and let them process for 10 minutes at an altitude that is less than 1000. If you have a higher altitude, adjust your processing time according to your altitude, check the dedicated section.

## Step 8 – Letting the Jars Rest

- Once the time is up, turn off the heat and remove the lid gently, then remove the jars from the pot.
- Place them on a large towel, then let them cool down completely for at least 12 hours until they cool down.

### Step 9 - Storing

- Double check the jars to make sure they are sealed then you can store them in a dark and cool place for up to 12 months.
- If you find some jars that are not sealed properly, you won't be able to store them in the pantry.
- You can still store them though in the fridge for up to 4 weeks and enjoy!

---

## Pears Jam

|Intro|: This recipe macerates the pears in a mixture of lemon juice and sugar overnight, which gives the pears a very nice texture and flavor. The jam turns out amazing using this method and tastes like actual pear jam, not blended pears with sugar jam. This jam can last you for up to 18 months, so it's perfect for a large batch of pears that you easily double and triple.

### Equipment:

- StockPot
- Rack
- Thongs
- Towel
- Heavy Saucepan
- 5 Pint Jars
- Large Bowl
- Funnel

#### Nutrition Facts per 1 Pint Jar

| Calories | 586.74kcal |
|----------|------------|
| Carbs    | 153.51g    |
| Protein  | 1.3g       |
| Fats     | 0.52g      |

### Core Ingredients

- 4 pounds of fresh and firm pears, under ripped or just riped
- 3 cups of granulated white sugar
- ¼ cup of fresh lemon juice

### Step 1 - Preparation

- Wash the pears and remove the stems, then peel them and dice them.
- Transfer them to a large bowl, then add to them the sugar with lemon juice.

- Toss them well until all the pear pieces are coated to prevent them from oxidizing.
- Place the pears ball in the fridge and let them sit overnight. This step is essential because this recipe doesn't have pectin, the lemon and sugar in this case will draw out the juice of the pears which will make the jam gel naturally.

### Step 2 – Sterilizing The Jars

- In the meantime, start sterilizing the jars where you will be storing the jam, and make sure the rings are wiped clean.
- To sterilize the jars, bring a large pot of water to a boil, then turn off the heat, place the jars in it, and let them sit in it for 5 to 10 minutes.
- Use thongs to pull them out then place them with the lid down on a towel to dry.

### Step 3 – Preparing The Water Bath Canner

- To prepare for the canning process, fill a large stockpot with enough water to cover the jars by 1.5 to 2 inches.
- Bring it to a boil on high heat, then lower the heat and let it simmer while preparing the jam.

### Step 4 – Making The Jam

- To prepare the jam, transfer the pears mixture into a large heavy saucepan and cook them for 12 to 16 minutes over medium heat while stirring it all the time to prevent it from sticking to the bottom of the saucepan.
- If the pear pieces are too big, use a fork or a potato masher to mash them while cooking.
- Once time is up or the jam reaches the gel stage, turn off the heat, and quickly skim the foam on the top.
- You test the jam by using an instant-read thermometer, it should register 220 F, or you scoop some of it into a plate and place it in the freezer to cool down.

### Step 5 - Packing

- Quickly spoon the jam while it's hot into the sterilized jars, and make sure to leave 1/8 to ¼-inch of the space empty at the top of each jar.
- Wipe the sides of the jars with a clean and slightly wet rag, then put on the lids and secure them tightly. Press the center of the lids to ensure they are sealed properly.

### Step 6 - Canning

- Place the jars in a rack and lower them to the boiling water in the water bath canner.
- If you don't have a rack to use with your stockpot, you can make one using aluminum foil. Get 7 pieces of aluminum that are 6 inches tall, and roll them into stripes.
- Shape 3 stripes into circles by cramping their ends together, then use the remaining 4 pieces to make a net inside of the circle in a zig-zag pattern by cramping the ends of each stripe into the circle.
- Make sure all the jars are immersed and completely covered with water, if they are not, add more water until they are covered.
- Bring the water to a boil one more on medium to high heat, then put on the lid and let them process for 5 minutes at an altitude that is less than 1000. If you have a higher altitude, adjust your processing time according to your altitude, check the dedicated section.

### Step 7 – Letting the Jars Rest

- Once the time is up, turn off the heat and remove the lid gently, then remove the jars from the pot.
- Place them on a large towel, then let them cool down completely for at least 12 hours until they cool down.

### Step 8 - Storing

- Double check the jars to make sure they are sealed then you can store them in a dark and cool place for up to 18 months.
- If you find some jars that are not sealed properly, you won't be able to store them in the pantry.
- You can still store them though in the fridge for up to 4 weeks and enjoy!

## Orange Marmalade

|Intro|: Orange marmalade is a very fun and easy way to preserve your oranges in a different method instead of being stuck with the regular canned oranges and jam. The lemon rind used adds a very nice, different, and zesty flavor that gives it a nice kick.

### Equipment:

- StockPot
- Rack
- Thongs
- Towel
- 2 Saucepans
- 5 Pint Jars
- Large Bowl
- Funnel

**Nutrition Facts** per 1 tablespoon

| Calories | 48kcal |
|----------|--------|
| Carbs | 12g |
| Protein | 0g |
| Fats | 0g |

### Core Ingredients

- 2 pounds of fresh oranges
- 2 cups of water
- 2 cups of white granulated sugar

### Step 1 - Preparation

- Start by peeling the oranges, cut them into 4 pieces, then remove from them the pits and white flesh.
- It's essential to remove the white flesh and membrane because they will make the marmalade taste too bitter.

### Step 2 – Cooking The Rind and Oranges

- Start by placing the rind of the oranges in a saucepan, then cover them with water and bring them to a boil, then let them continue to cook until the ring becomes soft.
- In the meantime, place the orange pieces in a large saucepan with 2 cups of water and sugar then bring them to a boil over medium heat.
- Keep the orange mixture boiling over medium heat for 60 minutes while stirring it from time to time.
- Once the time is up and the rinds become soft, drain them, cut them into strips, then add them to the oranges mixture, and keep boiling them over medium heat for another 60 minutes while stirring them from time to time.

### Step 3 – Sterilizing The Jars

- In the meantime, start sterilizing the jars where you will be storing the marmalade, and make sure the rings are wiped clean.
- To sterilize the jars, bring a large pot of water to a boil, then turn off the heat, place the jars in it, and let them sit in it for 5 to 10 minutes.

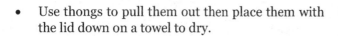

- Use thongs to pull them out then place them with the lid down on a towel to dry.

## Step 4 – Preparing The Water Bath Canner

- To prepare for the canning process, fill a large stockpot with enough water to cover the jars by 1.5 to 2 inches.
- Bring it to a boil on high heat, then lower the heat and let it simmer while preparing the marmalade.

## Step 5 - Packing

- Test the marmalade by placing some of it on a plate, and see if gels in 30 seconds. If it's not done, keep cooking it while stirring and test it every few minutes.
- Once it's done, quickly spoon the marmalade while it's hot into the sterilized jars, and make sure to leave 1/8 to ¼-inch of the space empty at the top of each jar.
- Wipe the sides of the jars with a clean and slightly wet rag, then put on the lids and secure them tightly. Press the center of the lids to ensure they are sealed properly.

## Step 6 - Canning

- Place the jars in a rack and lower them to the boiling water in the water bath canner.
- If you don't have a rack to use with your stockpot, you can make one using aluminum foil. Get 7 pieces of aluminum that are 6 inches tall, and roll them into stripes.
- Shape 3 stripes into circles by cramping their ends together, then use the remaining 4 pieces to make a net inside of the circle in a zig-zag pattern by cramping the ends of each stripe into the circle.
- Make sure all the jars are immersed and completely covered with water, if they are not, add more water until they are covered.
- Bring the water to a boil one more on medium to high heat, then put on the lid and let them process for 10 minutes at an altitude that is less than 1000. If you have a higher altitude, adjust your processing time according to your altitude, check the dedicated section. .

## Step 7 – Letting the Jars Rest

- Once the time is up, turn off the heat and remove the lid gently, then remove the jars from the pot.
- Place them on a large towel, then let them cool down completely for at least 12 hours until they cool down.

## Step 8 - Storing

- Double check the jars to make sure they are sealed then you can store them in a dark and cool place for up to 18 months.
- If you find some jars that are not sealed properly, you won't be able to store them in the pantry.
- You can still store them though in the fridge for up to 3 weeks and enjoy!

## Kiwi Jam

|Intro|: This Kiwi jam is one of the easiest jams that you can prepare in minutes. It tastes very tropical and fresh and makes for a nice jam to replace your regular jams. This jam includes kiwi seeds, but they are not bad at all. They actually add a very nice texture to the jam that makes it taste extra good.

## Equipment:

- StockPot
- Rack
- Thongs
- Towel
- Saucepan
- 5 Pint Jars
- Large Bowl
- Funnel

### Nutrition Facts per 14 quarts

| Calories | 1031.64kcal |
|----------|-------------|
| Carbs | 262.12g |
| Protein | 4.81g |
| Fats | 2.21g |

## Core Ingredients

- 4 pounds of fresh kiwis
- 4 cups of white granulated sugar
- ¼ cup of fresh lime juice

## Step 1 - Preparation

- Start by peeling and roughly chopping the kiwis.
- Transfer them to a large saucepan with sugar and lime juice and bring them to a boil over high heat.
- Lower the heat to medium heat then keep cooking the jam for 10 to 16 minutes while stirring it occasionally.

### Step 2 – Sterilizing The Jars

- In the meantime, start sterilizing the jars where you will be storing the jam, and make sure the rings are wiped clean.
- To sterilize the jars, bring a large pot of water to a boil, then turn off the heat, place the jars in it, and let them sit in it for 5 to 10 minutes.
- Use thongs to pull them out then place them with the lid down on a towel to dry.

### Step 3 – Preparing The Water Bath Canner

- To prepare for the canning process, fill a large stockpot with enough water to cover the jars by 1.5 to 2 inches.
- Bring it to a boil on high heat, then lower the heat and let it simmer while preparing the jam.

### Step 4 - Packing

- Test the jam to see if it's read by placing some of it on a plate, and letting it sit in the freezer for 30 seconds, then check if it's gelled. If it's not done, keep cooking it while stirring and test it every few minutes.
- Once the jam reaches a gel stage, quickly spoon it while it's hot into the sterilized jars, and make sure to leave 1/8 to ¼-inch of the space empty at the top of each jar.
- Wipe the sides of the jars with a clean and slightly wet rag, then put on the lids and secure them tightly. Press the center of the lids to ensure they are sealed properly.

### Step 5 - Canning

- Place the jars in a rack and lower them to the boiling water in the water bath canner.
- If you don't have a rack to use with your stockpot, you can make one using aluminum foil. Get 7 pieces of aluminum that are 6 inches tall, and roll them into stripes.
- Shape 3 stripes into circles by cramping their ends together, then use the remaining 4 pieces to make a net inside of the circle in a zig-zag pattern by cramping the ends of each stripe into the circle.
- Make sure all the jars are immersed and completely covered with water, if they are not, add more water until they are covered.
- Bring the water to a boil one more time on medium to high heat, then put on the lid and let them process for 5 minutes at an altitude that is less than 1000. If you have a higher altitude, adjust your

processing time according to your altitude, check the dedicated section. .

### Step 6 – Letting the Jars Rest

- Once the time is up, turn off the heat and remove the lid gently, then remove the jars from the pot.
- Place them on a large towel, then let them cool down completely for at least 12 hours until they cool down.

### Step 7 - Storing

- Double check the jars to make sure they are sealed then you can store them in a dark and cool place for up to 18 months.
- If you find some jars that are not sealed properly, you won't be able to store them in the pantry.
- You can still store them though in the fridge for up to 4 weeks and enjoy!

## Blueberry and Lavender Jam

|Intro|: Lavender transforms this simple blueberry jam into a nice and romantic jam. Delicate and flowery, it goes perfectly with any baked goods of your choice and adds a very nice taste and smell to them.

### Equipment:

- StockPot
- Rack
- Thongs
- Towel
- Saucepan
- 4 Pint Jars
- Large Bowl
- Funnel

### Nutrition Facts per 1 tablespoon

| Calories | 68kcal |
|----------|--------|
| Carbs    | 18g    |
| Protein  | 0g     |
| Fats     | 0g     |

### Core Ingredients

- 8 cups of fresh blueberries
- 4 ½ cup of white granulated sugar
- ½ cup of boiling water
- 2 tablespoons of dry lavender buds

- 1.75 oz packet of powdered pectin
- The juice of 1 lemon
- ½ teaspoon of butter, unsalted

## Step 1 - Preparation

- Place the lavender buds in a medium bowl, then add to them the boiling water.
- Let them sit for 10 minutes, then drain them, discard the lavender buds and place the lavender water aside.
- Place the blueberries in batches in a food processor, then pulse them several times until they become crushed.
- Combine the pectin with ¼ cup of sugar in a small bowl then place it aside.

## Step 2 – Sterilizing The Jars

- In the meantime, start sterilizing the jars where you will be storing the jam, and make sure the rings are wiped clean.
- To sterilize the jars, bring a large pot of water to a boil, then turn off the heat, place the jars in it, and let them sit in it for 5 to 10 minutes.
- Use thongs to pull them out then place them with the lid down on a towel to dry.

## Step 3 – Preparing The Water Bath Canner

- To prepare for the canning process, fill a large stockpot with enough water to cover the jars by 1.5 to 2 inches.
- Bring it to a boil on high heat, then lower the heat and let it simmer while preparing the jam.

## Step 4 – Making The Jam

- To prepare the jam, combine the crushed blueberries in a large heavy saucepan with lemon juice and lavender water.
- Add in the butter with the sugar and pectin mix then stir them well and bring them to a boil over high heat while stirring all the time.
- Add the remaining sugar to the saucepan and stir it well, then bring them to a boil once more, and let them boil for a full minute.
- Once time is up, turn off the heat, and quickly skim the foam on the top.

## Step 5 - Packing

- Quickly spoon the jam while it's hot into the sterilized jars, and make sure to leave 1/8 to ¼-inch of the space empty at the top of each jar.

- Wipe the sides of the jars with a clean and slightly wet rag, then put on the lids and secure them tightly. Press the center of the lids to ensure they are sealed properly.

## Step 6 - Canning

- Place the jars in a rack and lower them to the boiling water in the water bath canner.
- If you don't have a rack to use with your stockpot, you can make one using aluminum foil. Get 7 pieces of aluminum that are 6 inches tall, and roll them into stripes.
- Shape 3 stripes into circles by cramping their ends together, then use the remaining 4 pieces to make a net inside of the circle in a zig-zag pattern by cramping the ends of each stripe into the circle.
- Make sure all the jars are immersed and completely covered with water, if they are not, add more water until they are covered.
- Bring the water to a boil one more on medium to high heat, then put on the lid and let them process for 10 minutes at an altitude that is less than 1000. If you have a higher altitude, adjust your processing time according to your altitude, check the dedicated section. .

## Step 7 – Letting the Jars Rest

- Once the time is up, turn off the heat and remove the lid gently, then remove the jars from the pot.
- Place them on a large towel, then let them cool down completely for at least 12 hours until they cool down.

## Step 8 - Storing

- Double check the jars to make sure they are sealed then you can store them in a dark and cool place for up to 12 months.
- If you find some jars that are not sealed properly, you won't be able to store them in the pantry.
- You can still store them though in the fridge for up to 3 weeks and enjoy!

## Golden Apricot Jam

|Intro|: This golden apricot jam is basically summer in a jar that you can pull out and enjoy in the fall, winter, and spring. It looks fantastic and tastes even better with bread, croissant, cheesecake, cake...

**Equipment:**

- StockPot

- Rack
- Thongs
- Towel
- Saucepan
- 5 Pint Jars
- Large Bowl
- Funnel

**Nutrition Facts** per 1 tablespoon

| Calories | 41kcal |
|----------|--------|
| Carbs | 10.6g |
| Protein | 0.1g |
| Fats | 0g |

## Core Ingredients

- 4 cups of golden apricots
- 6 cups of cane sugar
- ¼ cup of fresh lemon juice

## Step 1 – Sterilizing The Jars

- Start by sterilizing the jars where you will be storing the jam, and make sure the rings are wiped clean.
- To sterilize the jars, bring a large pot of water to a boil, then turn off the heat, place the jars in it, and let them sit in it for 5 to 10 minutes.
- Use thongs to pull them out then place them with the lid down on a towel to dry.

## Step 2 – Preparing The Water Bath Canner

- To prepare for the canning process, fill a large stockpot with enough water to cover the jars by 1.5 to 2 inches.
- Bring it to a boil on high heat, then lower the heat and let it simmer while preparing the jam.

## Step 3 - Preparation

- Start by peeling, pitting, and coarsely chopping the apricots until you measure 4 cups.
- Transfer them to a large heavy saucepan, then use a potato masher to mash them
- Add in the cane sugar with fresh lemon juice and stir them well.
- Attach a candy thermometer to the side of the saucepan, then turn on the heat o medium, and cook the jam while stirring all the time until reaches 220 F.
- If you don't have a thermometer, you can use the traditional way instead. Cook the jam for 10 minutes while stirring for 10 minutes, then start testing it after that every few minutes by spooning some of it onto a plate, and letting it sit in the freezer for 30 seconds to see if it gels.
- If doesn't gel, cook it for a few more minutes and continue to test it until it's done.

## Step 4 - Packing

- Quickly spoon the jam while it's hot into the sterilized jars, and make sure to leave 1/8 to ¼-inch of the space empty at the top of each jar.
- Wipe the sides of the jars with a clean and slightly wet rag, then put on the lids and secure them tightly. Press the center of the lids to ensure they are sealed properly.

## Step 5 - Canning

- Place the jars in a rack and lower them to the boiling water in the water bath canner.
- If you don't have a rack to use with your stockpot, you can make one using aluminum foil. Get 7 pieces of aluminum that are 6 inches tall, and roll them into stripes.
- Shape 3 stripes into circles by cramping their ends together, then use the remaining 4 pieces to make a net inside of the circle in a zig-zag pattern by cramping the ends of each stripe into the circle.
- Make sure all the jars are immersed and completely covered with water, if they are not, add more water until they are covered.
- Bring the water to a boil one more on medium to high heat, then put on the lid and let them process for 15 minutes at an altitude that is less than 1000. If you have a higher altitude, adjust your processing time according to your altitude, check the dedicated section. .

## Step 6 – Letting the Jars Rest

- Once the time is up, turn off the heat and remove the lid gently, then remove the jars from the pot.
- Place them on a large towel, then let them cool down completely for at least 24 hours until they cool down.

### Step 7 - Storing

- Double check the jars to make sure they are sealed then you can store them in a dark and cool place for up to 12 months.
- If you find some jars that are not sealed properly, you won't be able to store them in the pantry.
- You can still store them though in the fridge for up to 3 weeks and enjoy!

## Grape Jelly

|Intro|: Grape jelly price keeps on increasing constantly, so if you are a fan, this recipe will enable you to prepare it for yourself at home, save a lot of money, eat healthy but tasty jelly, and get to enjoy it all year round. You can serve it on its own, spread it on croissants, muffins, or bread...and enjoy!

### Equipment:

- StockPot
- Rack
- Thongs
- Towel
- Saucepan
- 3 Pint Jars
- Large Bowl
- Funncl
- Whisk

**Nutrition Facts** per 1 g

| Calories | 68 kcal |
|----------|---------|
| Carbs | 17g |
| Protein | 0.2g |
| Fats | 008g |

### Core Ingredients

- 4 cups of fresh grape juice
- 2 cups of granulated cane sugar
- ¼ cup of boiling water
- ¼ cup of fresh lemon juice
- 4 teaspoons of powdered pectin
- 4 teaspoons of calcium water

### Step 1 - Preparation

- Start by preparing the calcium. Pour ¼ cup of boiling water into a small jar, then add to it ½ teaspoon of calcium.
- Shake the jar well until it dissolves, then place it aside to dissolve.

### Step 2 – Sterilizing The Jars

- In the meantime, start sterilizing the jars where you will be storing the jam, and make sure the rings are wiped clean.
- To sterilize the jars, bring a large pot of water to a boil, then turn off the heat, place the jars in it, and let them sit in it for 5 to 10 minutes.
- Use thongs to pull them out then place them with the lid down on a towel to dry.

### Step 3 – Preparing The Water Bath Canner

- To prepare for the canning process, fill a large stockpot with enough water to cover the jars by 1.5 to 2 inches.
- Bring it to a boil on high heat, then lower the heat and let it simmer while preparing the jelly.

### Step 4 – Preparing The Jelly

- Combine the lemon juice with grape juice, and 4 teaspoons of calcium water in a large saucepan then bring them to a rolling boil over high heat.
- Mix the pectin with sugar to a medium boil, then add them to the jelly mixture.
- Keep the jelly boiling for 2 minutes while stirring all the time with a whisk until the pectin and sugar dissolve.
- Once the time is up, and the jelly starts boiling again, turn off the heat.

### Step 5 - Packing

- Quickly spoon the jam while it's hot into the sterilized jars, and make sure to leave 1/8 to ¼-inch of the space empty at the top of each jar.
- Wipe the sides of the jars with a clean and slightly wet rag, then put on the lids and secure them tightly. Press the center of the lids to ensure they are sealed properly.

### Step 5 - Canning

- Place the jars in a rack and lower them to the boiling water in the water bath canner.
- If you don't have a rack to use with your stockpot, you can make one using aluminum foil. Get 7

pieces of aluminum that are 6 inches tall, and roll them into stripes.

- Shape 3 stripes into circles by cramping their ends together, then use the remaining 4 pieces to make a net inside of the circle in a zig-zag pattern by cramping the ends of each stripe into the circle.
- Make sure all the jars are immersed and completely covered with water, if they are not, add more water until they are covered.
- Bring the water to a boil one more on medium to high heat, then put on the lid and let them process for 10 minutes at an altitude that is less than 1000. If you have a higher altitude, adjust your processing time according to your altitude, check the dedicated section. .

## Step 6 – Letting the Jars Rest

- Once the time is up, turn off the heat and remove the lid gently, then remove the jars from the pot.
- Place them on a large towel, then let them cool down completely for at least 24 hours until they cool down.

## Step 7 - Storing

- Double check the jars to make sure they are sealed then you can store them in a dark and cool place for up to 12 months.
- If you find some jars that are not sealed properly, you won't be able to store them in the pantry.
- You can still store them though in the fridge for up to 4 weeks and enjoy!

## Watermelon Jelly

|Intro|: Watermelon is such a juice, refreshing and messy fruit that is perfect for the summer. However, you can now enjoy it all seasons as a jelly. This recipe is very simple, and straightforward and you can store it for up to 1 year and enjoy its unique and delicious flavor.

## Equipment:

- StockPot
- Rack
- Thongs
- Towel
- Saucepan
- 8 Pint Jars
- Large Bowl
- Funnel
- Whisk

## Nutrition Facts per 1 Pint Jar

| Calories | 431.74kcal |
|----------|------------|
| Carbs | 110.8g |
| Protein | 0.7g |
| Fats | 0.19g |

## Core Ingredients

- 4 cups of fresh watermelon juice, strained
- 4 cups of white granulated sugar
- ¼ cup of fresh lemon juice
- 4 tablespoons of powdered pectin, low-sugar

## Step 1 – Sterilizing The Jars

- Start by sterilizing the jars where you will be storing the jelly, and make sure the rings are wiped clean.
- To sterilize the jars, bring a large pot of water to a boil, then turn off the heat, place the jars, and let them sit in it for 5 to 10 minutes.
- Use thongs to pull them out then place them with the lid down on a towel to dry.

## Step 2 – Preparing The Water Bath Canner

- To prepare for the canning process, fill a large stockpot with enough water to cover the jars by 1.5 to 2 inches.
- Bring it to a boil on high heat, then lower the heat and let it simmer while preparing the jelly.

## Step 3 – Preparing The Jelly

- Start by cutting the watermelon into chunks, then discard the ring and white flesh.
- Use a fork to remove the pits then juice it and strain it until you measure 4 cups.
- Mix the pectin with sugar in a medium ball then place it aside.
- Pour the watermelon juice and lemon juice into a large saucepan, and attach to it a candy thermometer.
- Bring the juice to a rolling boil over high heat and keep cooking for 20 to 30 minutes until reaches 220 F.
- Once the time is up, add in the pectin and sugar mixture, then stir them well and bring them to another rolling boil.

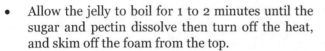

- Allow the jelly to boil for 1 to 2 minutes until the sugar and pectin dissolve then turn off the heat, and skim off the foam from the top.

## Step 4 - Packing

- Quickly spoon the jelly while it's hot into the sterilized jars, and make sure to leave 1/8 to ¼-inch of the space empty at the top of each jar.
- Wipe the sides of the jars with a clean and slightly wet rag, then put on the lids and secure them tightly. Press the center of the lids to ensure they are sealed properly.

## Step 5 - Canning

- Place the jars in a rack and lower them to the boiling water in the water bath canner.
- If you don't have a rack to use with your stockpot, you can make one using aluminum foil. Get 7 pieces of aluminum that are 6 inches tall, and roll them into stripes.
- Shape 3 stripes into circles by cramping their ends together, then use the remaining 4 pieces to make a net inside of the circle in a zig-zag pattern by cramping the ends of each stripe into the circle.
- Make sure all the jars are immersed and completely covered with water, if they are not, add more water until they are covered.
- Bring the water to a boil one more on medium to high heat, then put on the lid and let them process for 5 minutes at an altitude that is less than 1000. If you have a higher altitude, adjust your processing time according to your altitude, check the dedicated section. .

## Step 6 – Letting the Jars Rest

- Once the time is up, turn off the heat and remove the lid gently, then remove the jars from the pot.
- Place them on a large towel, then let them cool down completely for at least 12 hours until they cool down.

## Step 7 - Storing

- Double check the jars to make sure they are sealed then you can store them in a dark and cool place for up to 12 months.
- If you find some jars that are not sealed properly, you won't be able to store them in the pantry.
- You can still store them though in the fridge for up to 4 weeks and enjoy!

# Cranberry Pepper Jam

|Intro|: This is an Asian-inspired jam that creates the perfect marriage between the sweet and hot taste. The taste of cranberries tastes outstanding with the jalapeno peppers and makes for a delicious jam that goes very well with baked goods, to grilled meats, and makes a great addition to salsas and sauces as well.

## Equipment:

- 2 StockPots
- Rack
- Thongs
- Towel
- 6 Pint Jars
- Large Bowl
- Funnel

**Nutrition Facts** per 1 tablespoon

| Calories | 20kcal |
|----------|--------|
| Carbs | 5g |
| Protein | 1g |
| Fats | 1g |

## Core Ingredients

- 4 cups of white granulated sugar
- 2 cups of fresh and firm cranberries
- 2 cups of cider vinegar
- 1 cup of jalapeno pepper, finely chopped
- 1 cup of water
- 6 tablespoons of low sugar pectin powder

## Step 1 - Preparation

- Start by washing and sorting the cranberries, then place them in a colander and let them drain.
- Remove the seeds from the jalapenos, and chop them until you measure 1 cup.
- Mix the pectin with sugar in s a medium bowl, then place it aside.

## Step 2 – Sterilizing The Jars

- In the meantime, start sterilizing the jars where you will be storing the jelly, and make sure the rings are wiped clean.
- To sterilize the jars, bring a large pot of water to a boil, then turn off the heat, place the jars in it, and let them sit in it for 5 to 10 minutes.

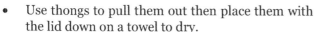

- Use thongs to pull them out then place them with the lid down on a towel to dry.

### Step 3 – Preparing The Water Bath Canner

- To prepare for the canning process, fill a large stockpot with enough water to cover the jars by 1.5 to 2 inches.
- Bring it to a boil on high heat, then lower the heat and let it simmer while preparing the jam.

### Step 3 – Preparing The Jam

- Combine the cranberries with chopped jalapeno and vinegar in a stockpot then bring them to a boil.
- Lower the heat, and let the cranberries and jalapeno mixture cook for 10 to 12 minutes until they become soft.
- Once the time is up, strain the cranberries and jalapeno using a fine mesh strainer, then transfer them to a food processor and process them until they become smooth.
- Discard the cooking liquid, then pour the cranberry mixture back into the pot, and bring it to a rolling boil.
- Add in the pectin and sugar mixture then bring them to another boil while stirring.
- Cook the jelly for 1 to 2 minutes while stirring them constantly with a whisk until the sugar and pectin dissolve, then turn off the heat.

### Step 4 - Packing

- Quickly spoon the jelly while it's hot into the sterilized jars, and make sure to leave 1/8 to ¼-inch of the space empty at the top of each jar.
- Wipe the sides of the jars with a clean and slightly wet rag, then put on the lids and secure them tightly. Press the center of the lids to ensure they are sealed properly.

### Step 5 - Canning

- Place the jars in a rack and lower them to the boiling water in the water bath canner.
- If you don't have a rack to use with your stockpot, you can make one using aluminum foil. Get 7 pieces of aluminum that are 6 inches tall, and roll them into stripes.
- Shape 3 stripes into circles by cramping their ends together, then use the remaining 4 pieces to make a net inside of the circle in a zig-zag pattern by cramping the ends of each stripe into the circle.

- Make sure all the jars are immersed and completely covered with water, if they are not, add more water until they are covered.
- Bring the water to a boil one more on medium to high heat, then put on the lid and let them process for 15 minutes at an altitude that is less than 1000. If you have a higher altitude, adjust your processing time according to your altitude, check the dedicated section. .

### Step 6 – Letting the Jars Rest

- Once the time is up, turn off the heat and remove the lid gently, then remove the jars from the pot.
- Place them on a large towel, then let them cool down completely for at least 12 hours until they cool down.

### Step 7 - Storing

- Double check the jars to make sure they are sealed then you can store them in a dark and cool place for up to 12 months.
- If you find some jars that are not sealed properly, you won't be able to store them in the pantry.
- You can still store them though in the fridge for up to 3 weeks and enjoy!

## Carrot Cake Jam

**|Intro|:** This carrot cake jam is such a delicacy that will warm up your kitchen and house with its spices and makes it feel like the holidays all over again, which makes also a great gift that will please your friends and family for sure.

### Equipment:

- 2 StockPots
- Rack
- Thongs
- Towel
- 4 Pint Jars
- Large Bowl
- Funnel

### Nutrition Facts per 1 tablespoon

| Calories | 110kcal |
|----------|---------|
| Carbs | 27g |
| Protein | 1g |
| Fats | 1g |

## Core Ingredients

- 6 ½ cup of white granulated sugar
- 2 cups of canned or fresh crushed pineapple with its juice
- 1 ½ cup of fresh apple, diced
- 1 ½ cup of fresh carrots, shredded
- ½ cup of pecans, finely chopped
- 6 tablespoons of pectin powder
- 3 tablespoons of fresh lemon juice
- 1 teaspoon of cinnamon powder
- ¼ teaspoon of nutmeg powder
- ¼ teaspoon of cloves powder

## Step 1 – Sterilizing The Jars

- Start by sterilizing the jars where you will be storing the jelly, and make sure the rings are wiped clean.
- To sterilize the jars, bring a large pot of water to a boil, then turn off the heat, place the jars in it, and let them sit in it for 5 to 10 minutes.
- Use thongs to pull them out then place them with the lid down on a towel to dry.

## Step 2 – Preparing The Water Bath Canner

- To prepare for the canning process, fill a large stockpot with enough water to cover the jars by 1.5 to 2 inches.
- Bring it to a boil on high heat, then lower the heat and let it simmer while preparing the jam.

## Step 3 – Preparing The jam

- Start by peeling and shredding the carrots until you measure 1 ½ cup.
- Peel and core enough apples to measure 1 ½ cup
- Mix the pectin powder with ½ cup of sugar in a small bowl then place it aside.
- Combine the shredded carrots, with apples, pineapple, pecans, lemon juice, cinnamon powder, nutmeg powder, and cloves powder then mix them well.
- Bring the mixture to a boil, then lower the heat, and cook them for 15 to 16 minutes until the apples, and carrots become soft while stirring them from time to time.
- Once the fruits are cooked, turn off the heat, then add the sugar and pectin mixture with the remaining sugar and stir them well.

- Bring the mixture back to a full rolling boil and let it cook for 1 to 2 minutes while stirring it constantly until the sugar and pectin dissolve.

## Step 4 - Packing

- Quickly spoon the jam while it's hot into the sterilized jars, and make sure to leave 1/8 to ¼-inch of the space empty at the top of each jar.
- Wipe the sides of the jars with a clean and slightly wet rag, then put on the lids and secure them tightly. Press the center of the lids to ensure they are sealed properly.

## Step 5 - Canning

- Place the jars in a rack and lower them to the boiling water in the water bath canner.
- If you don't have a rack to use with your stockpot, you can make one using aluminum foil. Get 7 pieces of aluminum that are 6 inches tall, and roll them into stripes.
- Shape 3 stripes into circles by cramping their ends together, then use the remaining 4 pieces to make a net inside of the circle in a zig-zag pattern by cramping the ends of each stripe into the circle.
- Make sure all the jars are immersed and completely covered with water, if they are not, add more water until they are covered.
- Bring the water to a boil one more on medium to high heat, then put on the lid and let them process for 10 minutes at an altitude that is less than 1000. If you have a higher altitude, adjust your processing time according to your altitude, check the dedicated section. .

## Step 6 – Letting the Jars Rest

- Once the time is up, turn off the heat and remove the lid gently, then remove the jars from the pot.
- Place them on a large towel, then let them cool down completely for at least 12 hours until they cool down.

## Step 7 - Storing

- Double check the jars to make sure they are sealed then you can store them in a dark and cool place for up to 12 months.
- If you find some jars that are not sealed properly, you won't be able to store them in the pantry.
- You can still store them though in the fridge for up to 3 weeks and enjoy!

## Peach Vanilla Jam

|Intro|: They are a lot of peach jams that you can at home, but this peach vanilla jam is the best one them. It's low on sugar, healthy, delicious, and the perfect way to preserve your peaches and use them all year round with some oatmeal, yogurt, and desserts.

### Equipment:

- StockPot
- Rack
- Thongs
- Towel
- Saucepan
- 2 Pint Jars
- Large Bowl
- Funnel

### Nutrition Facts per 1 tablespoon

| Calories | 32.64kcal |
|----------|-----------|
| Carbs | 8.37g |
| Protein | 0.08g |
| Fats | 0.04g |

### Core Ingredients

- 4 ½ cups of peaches, seeded and finely chopped
- 3 cups of granulated white sugar
- 1.75 ounces of powdered pectin
- 3 tablespoons of fresh lemon juice
- 1 teaspoon of vanilla extract

### Step 1 – Sterilizing The Jars

- Start by sterilizing the jars where you will be storing the jelly, and make sure the rings are wiped clean.
- To sterilize the jars, bring a large pot of water to a boil, then turn off the heat, place the jars in it, and let them sit in it for 5 to 10 minutes.
- Use thongs to pull them out then place them with the lid down on a towel to dry.

### Step 2 – Preparing The Water Bath Canner

- To prepare for the canning process, fill a large stockpot with enough water to cover the jars by 1.5 to 2 inches.
- Bring it to a boil on high heat, then lower the heat and let it simmer while preparing the jam.

### Step 3 – Preparing The jam

- Start by peeling and seeding, and roughly chop the peaches.
- Mix the pectin powder with ½ cup of sugar in a small bowl then place it aside.
- Transfer the chopped peaches to a large saucepan, then use a potato masher to crush them.
- Add the sugar and pectin mixture, lemon juice, and vanilla to the peaches then mix them well and bring them to a rolling boil while stirring.
- Add the remaining sugar mixture, then boil the jam for 1 to 2 minutes while stirring them constantly until the sugar dissolves.

### Step 4 - Packing

- Quickly spoon the jam while it's hot into the sterilized jars, and make sure to leave 1/8 to ¼-inch of the space empty at the top of each jar.
- Wipe the sides of the jars with a clean and slightly wet rag, then put on the lids and secure them tightly. Press the center of the lids to ensure they are sealed properly.

### Step 5 - Canning

- Place the jars in a rack and lower them to the boiling water in the water bath canner.
- If you don't have a rack to use with your stockpot, you can make one using aluminum foil. Get 7 pieces of aluminum that are 6 inches tall, and roll them into stripes.
- Shape 3 stripes into circles by cramping their ends together, then use the remaining 4 pieces to make a net inside of the circle in a zig-zag pattern by cramping the ends of each stripe into the circle.
- Make sure all the jars are immersed and completely covered with water, if they are not, add more water until they are covered.
- Bring the water to a boil one more on medium to high heat, then put on the lid and let them process for 5 minutes at an altitude that is less than 1000. If you have a higher altitude, adjust your processing time according to your altitude, check the dedicated section.

### Step 6 – Letting the Jars Rest

- Once the time is up, turn off the heat and remove the lid gently, then remove the jars from the pot.
- Place them on a large towel, then let them cool down completely for at least 12 hours until they cool down.

## Step 7 - Storing

- Double check the jars to make sure they are sealed then you can store them in a dark and cool place for up to 12 months.
- If you find some jars that are not sealed properly, you won't be able to store them in the pantry.
- You can still store them though in the fridge for up to 4 weeks and enjoy!

## Honey Cantaloupe Jam

|Intro|: This unique jam is perfect for the summer as you store it for up to 1 year, and enjoy it with toast, scones, and biscuits. It's also guaranteed to be a huge hit with the grown-ups and the kids alike.

### Equipment:

- StockPot
- Rack
- Thongs
- Towel
- Saucepan
- 4 Pint Jars
- Large Bowl
- Funnel

### Nutrition Facts per 1 Pint Jar

| Calories | 471.59kcal |
|----------|------------|
| Carbs | 119.57g |
| Protein | 1.82g |
| Fats | 0.92g |

### Core Ingredients

- 2 large firm and ripe cantaloupes (2 pounds each)
- 2 cups of granulated white sugar
- 6 ounces of liquid pectin
- ½ cup of fresh lemon juice
- ½ teaspoon of butter, unsalted

### Step 1 – Sterilizing The Jars

- Start by sterilizing the jars where you will be storing the jelly, and make sure the rings are wiped clean.
- To sterilize the jars, bring a large pot of water to a boil, then turn off the heat, place the jars in it, and let them sit in it for 5 to 10 minutes.

- Use thongs to pull them out then place them with the lid down on a towel to dry.

### Step 2 – Preparing The Water Bath Canner

- To prepare for the canning process, fill a large stockpot with enough water to cover the jars by 1.5 to 2 inches.
- Bring it to a boil on high heat, then lower the heat and let it simmer while preparing the jam.

### Step 3 – Preparing The jam

- Start by removing the rind, seeding, and roughly chopping the cantaloupes.
- Transfer the chopped cantaloup into a large bowl, then use a potato masher to crush it.
- Transfer 3 cups of crushed cantaloup into a stockpot with butter, sugar, and lemon juice then mix them well.
- Cook the cantaloup mixture over low heat while stirring the whole time until the sugar dissolves.
- After the sugar dissolves, bring the mixture to a rolling boil over medium-high heat while stirring constantly.
- Add the pectin to the mixture and stir them well, then bring to a boil one more time, and keep it boiling for 1 to 2 minutes until the mixture gels while stirring it constantly.
- Once the time is up, turn off the heat and let the jam sit for 5 minutes, while skimming the foam on top, and stirring it as well.

### Step 4 - Packing

- Quickly spoon the jam while it's hot into the sterilized jars, and make sure to leave 1/8 to ¼-inch of the space empty at the top of each jar.
- Wipe the sides of the jars with a clean and slightly wet rag, then put on the lids and secure them tightly. Press the center of the lids to ensure they are sealed properly.

### Step 5 - Canning

- Place the jars in a rack and lower them to the boiling water in the water bath canner.
- If you don't have a rack to use with your stockpot, you can make one using aluminum foil. Get 7 pieces of aluminum that are 6 inches tall, and roll them into stripes.
- Shape 3 stripes into circles by cramping their ends together, then use the remaining 4 pieces to make a net inside of the circle in a zig-zag pattern by cramping the ends of each stripe into the circle.

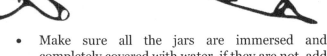

- Make sure all the jars are immersed and completely covered with water, if they are not, add more water until they are covered.
- Bring the water to a boil one more on medium to high heat, then put on the lid and let them process for 15 minutes at an altitude that is less than 1000. If you have a higher altitude, adjust your processing time according to your altitude, check the dedicated section. .

### Step 6 – Letting the Jars Rest

- Once the time is up, turn off the heat and remove the lid gently, then let the jars sit in the pot for 5 to 6 minutes to test.
- Once the time is up, drain the jars and place them on a large towel, then let them cool down completely for 24 hours until they cool down.

### Step 7 - Storing

- Double check the jars to make sure they are sealed then you can store them in a dark and cool place for up to 12 months.
- If you find some jars that are not sealed properly, you won't be able to store them in the pantry.
- You can still store them though in the fridge for up to 2 weeks and enjoy!

## Spring Dandelion Jelly

|Intro|: Dandelions are pretty little yellow flowers that greet spring every year with beautiful colors and petals, but they also make for a very tasty meal. You can eat them on their own, or even better, make dandelion jelly. It tastes amazing, but the most important part is that this jelly is healthy and includes a lot of nutrients that the dandelions provide.

### Equipment:

- StockPot
- Rack
- Thongs
- Towel
- Saucepan
- 6 Pint Jars
- Large Bowl
- Funnel
- Whisk

#### Nutrition Facts per 1 tablespoon

| Calories | 18.54kcal |
|---|---|
| Carbs | 4.81g |
| Protein | 0g |
| Fats | 0g |

### Core Ingredients

- 4 cups of fresh or dry dandelion petals, unsprayed.
- 4 cups of boiling water
- 4 cups of white granulated sugar
- 1/3 cup of pectin powder
- 2 tablespoons of fresh lemon juice

### Step 1 – Preparing Dandelion Tea

- Make sure your dandelion petals are organic and not sprayed.
- Wash them nicely with some cold water, then strain them, transfer them to a large jug, and add to them the boiling water.
- Allow the petals to steep overnight.

### Step 2 – Sterilizing The Jars

- In the meantime, start sterilizing the jars where you will be storing the jelly, and make sure the rings are wiped clean.
- To sterilize the jars, bring a large pot of water to a boil, then turn off the heat, place the jars in it, and let them sit in it for 5 to 10 minutes.
- Use thongs to pull them out then place them with the lid down on a towel to dry.

### Step 3 – Preparing The Water Bath Canner

- To prepare for the canning process, fill a large stockpot with enough water to cover the jars by 1.5 to 2 inches.
- Bring it to a boil on high heat, then lower the heat and let it simmer while preparing the jelly.

### Step 4 – Preparing The Jelly

- Strain the dandelion petals from the tea and measure 3 ½ cups of it, then pour it into a large saucepan.
- Add in the lemon juice with pectin to it then bring them to a boil over medium-high heat while stirring them the whole time with a whisk.
- Stir the sugar into the jelly mixture and bring it to a rolling boil while stirring, then keep boiling it for 2 more minutes until the sugar dissolves completely.

- Once the time is up, turn off the heat.

## Step 5 - Packing

- Quickly spoon the jelly while it's hot into the sterilized jars, and make sure to leave 1/8 to ¼-inch of the space empty at the top of each jar.
- Wipe the sides of the jars with a clean and slightly wet rag, then put on the lids and secure them tightly. Press the center of the lids to ensure they are sealed properly.

## Step 6 - Canning

- Place the jars in a rack and lower them to the boiling water in the water bath canner.
- If you don't have a rack to use with your stockpot, you can make one using aluminum foil. Get 7 pieces of aluminum that are 6 inches tall, and roll them into stripes.
- Shape 3 stripes into circles by cramping their ends together, then use the remaining 4 pieces to make a net inside of the circle in a zig-zag pattern by cramping the ends of each stripe into the circle.
- Make sure all the jars are immersed and completely covered with water, if they are not, add more water until they are covered.
- Bring the water to a boil one more on medium to high heat, then put on the lid and let them process for 10 minutes at an altitude that is less than 1000. If you have a higher altitude, adjust your processing time according to your altitude, check the dedicated section. .

## Step 7 – Letting the Jars Rest

- Once the time is up, turn off the heat and remove the lid gently, then remove the jars from the pot.
- Place them on a large towel, then let them cool down completely for at least 24 hours until they cool down.

## Step 8 - Storing

- Double check the jars to make sure they are sealed then you can store them in a dark and cool place for up to 14 months.
- If you find some jars that are not sealed properly, you won't be able to store them in the pantry.
- You can still store them though in the fridge for up to 2 weeks and enjoy!

## Summer Corn Jelly

|Intro|: Corn is a very popular veggie that kids and grown-ups love alike. You can grill, or steam it and serve it with some butter. However, you know what's even better? The fact that you don't have to throw away your leftover corn cobs anymore, you can use them instead to make delicious jelly that goes very well on top of bread, baked good, grilled meats...

## Equipment:

- 2 StockPots
- Rack
- Thongs
- Towel
- Saucepan
- 2 Pint Jars
- Large Bowl
- Funnel
- Whisk

### Nutrition Facts per 1 Pint Jar

| Calories | 942kcal |
|----------|---------|
| Carbs | 232g |
| Protein | 11g |
| Fats | 5g |

## Core Ingredients

- 12 medium  fresh corn cobs, kernels removed
- 2 quarts of water
- 3 cups of white granulated sugar
- 1.75 ounces package of pectin powder

## Step 1 – Preparation

- Chuck the corn cobs completely and wash them. You can use the kernels for other recipes.
- Place the cobs in a large stockpot then cover them with water and bring them to a boil.
- Once the pot starts boiling, lower the heat and cover it, then let them simmer for 45 minutes.

## Step 2 – Sterilizing The Jars

- In the meantime, start sterilizing the jars where you will be storing the jelly, and make sure the rings are wiped clean.
- To sterilize the jars, bring a large pot of water to a boil, then turn off the heat, place the jars in it, and let them sit in it for 5 to 10 minutes.

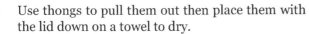

- Use thongs to pull them out then place them with the lid down on a towel to dry.

### Step 3 – Preparing The Water Bath Canner

- To prepare for the canning process, fill a large stockpot with enough water to cover the jars by 1.5 to 2 inches.
- Bring it to a boil on high heat, then lower the heat and let it simmer while preparing the jelly.

### Step 4 – Preparing The Jelly

- Once the time is up, use a double layer of cheesecloth to strain the corn juice then measure 3 cups and pour them into a large saucepan.
- Add the pectin powder to it, then whisk them over medium heat until the mixture starts boiling, and the pectin dissolves.
- Add the sugar to the jelly mixture then bring them to a boil again while stirring the whole time.
- Allow the jelly to keep boiling for 5 to 6 minutes until the sugar dissolves.
- Turn off the heat and discard the foam on top.

### Step 5 - Packing

- Quickly spoon the jelly while it's hot into the sterilized jars, and make sure to leave 1/8 to ¼-inch of the space empty at the top of each jar.
- Wipe the sides of the jars with a clean and slightly wet rag, then put on the lids and secure them tightly. Press the center of the lids to ensure they are sealed properly.

### Step 6 - Canning

- Place the jars in a rack and lower them to the boiling water in the water bath canner.
- If you don't have a rack to use with your stockpot, you can make one using aluminum foil. Get 7 pieces of aluminum that are 6 inches tall, and roll them into stripes.
- Shape 3 stripes into circles by cramping their ends together, then use the remaining 4 pieces to make a net inside of the circle in a zig-zag pattern by cramping the ends of each stripe into the circle.
- Make sure all the jars are immersed and completely covered with water, if they are not, add more water until they are covered.
- Bring the water to a boil one more on medium to high heat, then put on the lid and let them process for 5 minutes at an altitude that is less than 1000. If you have a higher altitude, adjust your

processing time according to your altitude, check the dedicated section. .

### Step 7 – Letting the Jars Rest

- Once the time is up, turn off the heat and remove the lid gently, then remove the jars from the pot.
- Place them on a large towel, then let them cool down completely for at least 24 hours until they cool down.

### Step 8 - Storing

- Double check the jars to make sure they are sealed then you can store them in a dark and cool place for up to 14 months.
- If you find some jars that are not sealed properly, you won't be able to store them in the pantry.
- You can still store them though in the fridge for up to 2 weeks and enjoy!

## Pomegranate Jelly

|Intro|: Pomegranates are one of the most underrated fruits. They are amazing all around, they look super beautiful with their ruby seeds, they taste fantastic and sweet, but most importantly, they are super healthy. The only way to enjoy them though is by eating them while they are fresh since they can't be preserved. However, Jelly is the best way to preserve its taste and enjoy it for up to 12 months!

### Equipment:

StockPot

Rack

Thongs

Towel

Saucepan/Pot

14 Pint Jars

Large Bowl

Funnel

Whisk

Cheese Cloth

### Nutrition Facts per 1 Pint Jar

| Calories | 566.24 kcal |
|----------|-------------|
| Carbs    | 145.68g     |
| Protein  | 0.27g       |

| Fats | 0.46g |
|------|-------|

### Core Ingredients

- 8 cups of fresh pomegranate juice
- 10 cups of granulated white sugar
- ½ cup of fresh lemon juice
- 3.5 ounces of pectin powder

### Step 1 - Preparation

- Start by juicing your pomegranates, and straining the juice with a cheesecloth.

### Step 2 – Sterilizing The Jars

- In the meantime, start sterilizing the jars where you will be storing the jam, and make sure the rings are wiped clean.
- To sterilize the jars, bring a large pot of water to a boil, then turn off the heat, place the jars in it, and let them sit in it for 5 to 10 minutes.
- Use thongs to pull them out then place them with the lid down on a towel to dry.

### Step 3 – Preparing The Water Bath Canner

- To prepare for the canning process, fill a large stockpot with enough water to cover the jars by 1.5 to 2 inches.
- Bring it to a boil on high heat, then lower the heat and let it simmer while preparing the jelly.

### Step 4 – Preparing The Jelly

- Combine the lemon juice with pomegranate juice and pectin in a large saucepan then bring them to a rolling boil over high heat while stirring them all the time.
- Add the sugar to the jelly mixture then bring to a rolling boil over high heat while stirring all the time for 60 seconds.
- Once the time is up, turn off the heat and discard the foam on top.

### Step 5 - Packing

- Quickly spoon the jelly while it's hot into the sterilized jars, and make sure to leave 1/8 to ¼ inch of the space empty at the top of each jar.
- Wipe the sides of the jars with a clean and slightly wet rag, then put on the lids and secure them tightly. Press the center of the lids to ensure they are sealed properly.

### Step 6 - Canning

- Place the jars in a rack and lower them to the boiling water in the water bath canner.
- If you don't have a rack to use with your stockpot, you can make one using aluminum foil. Get 7 pieces of aluminum that are 6 inches tall, and roll them into stripes.
- Shape 3 stripes into circles by cramping their ends together, then use the remaining 4 pieces to make a net inside of the circle in a zig-zag pattern by cramping the ends of each stripe into the circle.
- Make sure all the jars are immersed and completely covered with water, if they are not, add more water until they are covered.
- Bring the water to a boil one more on medium to high heat, then put on the lid and let them process for 5 minutes at an altitude that is less than 1000. If you have a higher altitude, adjust your processing time according to your altitude, check the dedicated section. .

### Step 7 – Letting the Jars Rest

- Once the time is up, turn off the heat and remove the lid gently, then remove the jars from the pot.
- Place them on a large towel, then let them cool down completely for at least 24 hours until they cool down.

### Step 8 - Storing

- Double check the jars to make sure they are sealed then you can store them in a dark and cool place for up to 12 months.
- If you find some jars that are not sealed properly, you won't be able to store them in the pantry.
- You can still store them though in the fridge for up to 3 weeks and enjoy!

## Section 3: Canned Vegetables

### Homemade Canned Diced Tomatoes

|Intro|: Tomato made itself a staple vegetable in our pantry, whether it's fresh, sauce, sundried...It's just a vegetable that we can't live without. So it only makes sense that water bath canning diced tomato is gonna be one of those few chores that you will love doing and it can last up to 18 months, and still taste amazing on its own, you can use it for a pasta sauce or with some baked, or grilled chicken.

## Equipment:

- 9 a 1 Pint Jars
- StockPot
- Rack
- Thongs
- Knife
- Cutting Board
- Towel
- Funnel

### Nutrition Facts per 1 Pint Jar

| Calories | 227kcal |
|----------|---------|
| Carbs | 49g |
| Protein | 11g |
| Fats | 3g |

## Core Ingredients

- 25 pounds of fresh tomatoes of your choice
- 3 tablespoons of fresh lemon juice

## Step 1 - Preparation

- Start by filling half of a large stockpot with water then bring it to a boil.
- Fill half of a big bowl with water and ice cubes to make a cold water bath then place it aside.
- Place a few tomatoes in the boiling water and cook them for 1 minute.
- Once the time is up, drain the tomatoes and transfer them to the ice bath then let them sit in it for a few minutes until they become cool to the touch.
- Drain the tomatoes and peel them gently, then cut them in half, squeeze the juice and seeds into a large bowl, then place them aside.

## Step 2 – Sterilizing The Pint Jars

- To sterilize the jars, bring a large pot of water to a boil, then turn off the heat, place the jars in it, and let them sit in it for 5 to 10 minutes.
- Use thongs to pull them out then place them with the lid down on a towel to dry.

## Step 3 – Preparing The Water Bath Canner

- To prepare the water bath canner, fill a large stockpot with enough water to cover the jars by 1.5 to 2 inches.

- Bring it to a boil on high heat, then lower the heat and let it simmer while preparing the tomatoes.

## Step 4 – Cooking The Tomatoes

- Dice the tomato into small or medium pieces depending on what you prefer.
- Transfer 1/6 of the diced tomato to a stockpot then bring them to a boil over high heat.
- Once the tomatoes soften, use a wooden spoon to crush them while stirring them at the same time to prevent the tomato from sticking to the pot.
- Add the remaining diced tomato to it, stir them well then bring them to a boil once again.
- Let the tomatoes cook for 5 minutes then turn off the heat and use a spoon or a ladle to transfer them to the jars.
- Drizzle 1 teaspoon of lemon juice on top of each jar then seal them tightly.
- Wipe the sides of the jars with a clean and slightly wet rag, then put on the lids and secure them tightly. Press the center of the lids to ensure they are sealed properly.

## Step 5 – Canning

- Place the jars in a rack in a rack and slowly lower them into the water bath canner you prepared.
- If you don't have a rack to use with your stockpot, you can make one using aluminum foil. Get 7 pieces of aluminum that are 6 inches tall, and roll them into stripes.
- Shape 3 stripes into circles by cramping their ends together, then use the remaining 4 pieces to make a net inside of the circle in a zig-zag pattern by cramping the ends of each stripe into the circle.
- Lower the aluminum rack into the pot, then use thongs to place the jar on top of it.
- Make sure that the jars are covered by 1.5 to 2 inches of water, if they are not, add enough water to cover them.
- Bring the water bath canner back to a boil on high heat.
- Process the tomatoes for 35 minutes at an altitude that is less than 1000. If you have a higher altitude, adjust your processing time according to your altitude, check the dedicated section. .

## Step 6 – Letting The Jars Rest

- Once the time is up, turn off the heat and place the pot on a large wet towel, then let it sit there for 24 hours.

- Once the time is up, remove the jars from the water and wipe them clean with a rug.

## Step 7 – Storing
- Store your sealed jars for up to 1 year in a dark cool place.
- If one of the jars is not sealed, you can serve it right away or store it in the fridge for up to 2 weeks.

## Homemade Canned Pickled Banana Peppers

|Intro|: These pickled hot banana peppers will make you fall in love with them even if you don't have an accommodating palate for hot foods for they taste incredible, soft yet crispy, simple yet bursting with flavor. You can serve them with sandwiches, roast, and most important of all, Pizza, and they will never fail you.

## Equipment:
6 Pint Jars

Stock Pot

Rack

Thongs

Knife

Cutting Board

Funnel

**Nutrition Facts** per 1 Pint Jar

| Calories | 44.42kcal |
|----------|-----------|
| Carbs | 4.94g |
| Protein | 1.12g |
| Fats | 0.29g |

## Core Ingredients
- 1 pound of fresh sweet banana peppers

## Water Solution
- 3 cups of cider vinegar
- 2 cups of water
- 3 teaspoons of pickling salt

## Pickling Spices
- 3 tablespoons of mustard seeds
- 1 ½ tablespoon of celery seeds
- 3 cloves of garlic, peeled

## Step 1 – Sterilizing The Pint Jars
- To sterilize the jars, bring a large pot of water to a boil, then turn off the heat, place the jars in it, and let them sit in it for 5 to 10 minutes.
- Use thongs to pull them out then place them with the lid down on a towel to dry.

## Step 2 – Water Bath Canner
- To prepare for the water bath canner, fill a large stockpot with enough water to cover the jars by 1.5 to 2 inches.
- Bring it to a boil on high heat, then lower the heat and let it simmer while preparing the banana peppers.

## Step 3 – Canning the Peppers
- Combine the pickling salt with water and vinegar in a medium saucepan then bring them to a boil.
- Slice the banana peppers into rings then distribute them between the pint jars and leave ½ inch of space empty in each jar.
- Place a half clove of garlic with ¾ teaspoon of celery seeds and 1 ½ teaspoon of mustard in each jar then fill them with the water and salt solution.

## Step 4 - Canning
- Wipe the sides of the jars with a clean and slightly wet rag, then put on the lids and secure them tightly. Press the center of the lids to ensure they are sealed properly.
- Place the jars in a rack and slowly lower them into the water bath canner you prepared.
- If you don't have a rack to use with your stockpot, you can make one using aluminum foil. Get 7 pieces of aluminum that are 6 inches tall, and roll them into stripes.
- Shape 3 stripes into circles by cramping their ends together, then use the remaining 4 pieces to make a net inside of the circle in a zig-zag pattern by cramping the ends of each stripe into the circle.
- Lower the aluminum rack into the pot, then use thongs to place the jar on top of it.
- Make sure that the jars are covered by 1.5 to 2 inches of water, if they are not, add enough water to cover them.
- Bring the water bath canner back to a boil on high heat.
- Process the banana peppers jars for 10 minutes at an altitude that is less than 1000. If you have a higher altitude, adjust your processing time

according to your altitude, check the dedicated section. .

### Step 5 - Letting The Jars Rest

- Once the time is up, turn off the heat and place the pot on a large wet towel, then let it sit there for 24 hours.
- Once the time is up, remove the jars from the water and wipe them clean with a rug.

### Step 6 - Storing

- Store your sealed banana peppers jars for up to 18 months in a dark cool place.
- If one of the jars is not sealed, you can serve it right away or store it in the fridge for up to 3 weeks.

## Homemade Canned Dill Pickles

|Intro|: Homemade water bath canned Dill pickles are so crunchy and flavorful with the perfect balance of tanginess and sweetness everyone craves. You can serve it on its own, use it as a topping, or with a salad. It will spice up your meals and you can enjoy them for a whole year since they can be stored for that long.

### Equipment:

6 Pint Jars

Stock Pot

Rack

Thongs

Knife

Cutting Board

Funnel

#### Nutrition Facts per 1 Cucumber

| Calories | 42kcal |
|----------|--------|
| Carbs | 9g |
| Protein | 0.68g |
| Fats | 0.12g |

### Core Ingredients

- 6 pounds of small cucumbers, trimmed
- 2 inches of horseradish root, peeled and finely chopped
- 12 cloves of garlic, peeled and slice in half
- 6 bay leaves

- 6 dill stems

### Ingredients for Pickling Solution

- 8 cups of water
- 6 cups of distilled white vinegar
- 1/3 cup of pickling salt
- 1/3 cup of granulated white sugar

### Step 1 - Preparation

- Start by sterilizing the jars where you will be storing dill pickles, and make sure the rings are wiped clean.
- To sterilize the jars, bring a large pot of water to a boil, then turn off the heat, place the jars in it, and let them sit in it for 5 to 10 minutes.
- Use thongs to pull them out then place them with the lid down on a towel to dry.

### Step 2 – Preparing The Cucumbers

- Trim and pack the cucumbers tightly into the jars leaving about 1/3 inch of space on top.
- Place 1 dill stem, bay leaf, and 2 cloves of garlic in each jar, then sprinkle the horseradish on top.

### Step 3 – Pickling Solution

- Place a large saucepan over high heat then combine in it all the pickling solution ingredients then bring them to a boil.
- Pour the pickling juice over the cucumbers and leave about ¼-inch of space empty.
- Add the lids and seal the jars tightly, then wipe them clean with a wet rag.

### Step 4 – Water Bath Canning

- To prepare for the water bath canner, fill a large stockpot with enough water to cover the jars by 1.5 to 2 inches.
- Place the jars in a rack and slowly lower them into the water bath canner you prepared.
- If you don't have a rack to use with your stockpot, you can make one using aluminum foil. Get 7 pieces of aluminum that are 6 inches tall, and roll them into stripes.
- Shape 3 stripes into circles by cramping their ends together, then use the remaining 4 pieces to make a net inside of the circle in a zig-zag pattern by cramping the ends of each stripe into the circle.
- Lower the aluminum rack into the pot, then use thongs to place the jar on top of it.

- Make sure that the jars are covered by 1.5 to 2 inches of water, if they are not, add enough water to cover them.
- Bring the water bath canner back to a boil on high heat.
- Process the jars for 15 minutes at an altitude that is less than 1000. If you have a higher altitude, adjust your processing time according to your altitude, check the dedicated section. .

### Step 5 – Letting The Jars Rest
- Once the time is up, turn off the heat and place the pot on a large wet towel, then let it sit there for 14 to 24 hours.
- Once the time is up, remove the jars from the water and wipe them clean with a rug.

### Step 6 - Storing
- Store your dill pickles jars for up to 18 months in a dark cool place, and do not open them until at least 3 months for the best results.
- If one of the jars is not sealed, you can serve it right away or store it in the fridge for up to 3 weeks.

## Homemade Canned Pickled Jalapeno Peppers

|Intro|: Jalapenos is another staple and versatile ingredient that you are bound to find in every home. Pickled jalapeno peppers add even more flavor to them and will please even the most difficult palates that don't like hot foods. Water bath canning them will allow you to store them and enjoy them for up to 18 months.

### Equipment:

5 Pint Jars

Stock Pot

Rack

Thongs

Knife

Cutting Board

Funnel

**Nutrition Facts** per ¼ cup of jalapenos

| Calories | 10kcal |
|----------|--------|
| Carbs | 1.8g |
| Protein | 0.4g |
| Fats | 0.2g |

### Core Ingredients
- 1 ½ pound of fresh Jalapeno peppers
- 3 cups of white distilled vinegar
- 1 cup of water
- 2 cloves of garlic, peeled and crushed

### Step 1 - Preparation
- Wash and trim the peppers, then slice them into rings.

### Step 2 – Sterilizing The Pint Jars
- Start by sterilizing the jars where you will be storing the jalapenos, and make sure the rings are wiped clean.
- To sterilize the jars, bring a large pot of water to a boil, then turn off the heat, place the jars in it, and let them sit in it for 5 to 10 minutes.
- Use thongs to pull them out then place them with the lid down on a towel to dry.

### Step 3 – Pickling Solution
- Place a large saucepan over high heat. Combine in it the water with vinegar, and garlic then bring them to a boil.
- Pack the jalapeno slices into the sterilized jars, then pour the pickling juice over the peppers and leave about ¼-inch of space empty.
- Add the lids and seal the jars tightly, then wipe them clean with a wet rag.

### Step 4 – Water Bath Canning
- To prepare for the water bath canner, fill a large stockpot with enough water to cover the jars by 1.5 to 2 inches.
- Place the jars in a rack and slowly lower them into the water bath canner you prepared.
- If you don't have a rack to use with your stockpot, you can make one using aluminum foil. Get 7 pieces of aluminum that are 6 inches tall, and roll them into stripes.
- Shape 3 stripes into circles by cramping their ends together, then use the remaining 4 pieces to make a net inside of the circle in a zig-zag pattern by cramping the ends of each stripe into the circle.
- Lower the aluminum rack into the pot, then use thongs to place the jar on top of it.

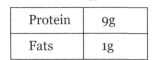

- Make sure that the jars are covered by 1.5 to 2 inches of water, if they are not, add enough water to cover them.
- Bring the water bath canner back to a boil on high heat.
- Process the jars for 10 minutes at an altitude that is less than 1000. If you have a higher altitude, adjust your processing time according to your altitude, check the dedicated section. .

### Step 5 – Letting The Jars Rest

- Once the time is up, turn off the heat and place the pot on a large wet towel, then let it sit there for 14 to 24 hours.
- Once the time is up, remove the jars from the water and wipe them clean with a rug.

### Step 6 - Storing

- Store your dill pickles jars from 14 to 18 months in a dark cool place, and do not open them until at least 5 weeks for the best results.
- If one of the jars is not sealed, you can serve it right away or store it in the fridge for up to 3 weeks.

## Homemade Canned Mushrooms

|Intro|: Canning mushrooms at home has been and still is a very common practice in so many households in different countries like France. The simple process of water bath canning it, and the unique taste the mushrooms acquire when preserved in a salty brine make it a fan favorite. You can use any type of mushrooms for this recipe, and preserve it for up to 2 years.

### Equipment:

8 Pint Jars

Stock Pot

Rack

Thongs

Knife

Cutting Board

Colander

Funnel

**Nutrition Facts** per 1-pint jar

| Calories | 68kcal |
|----------|--------|
| Carbs | 10g |
| Protein | 9g |
| Fats | 1g |

### Core Ingredients

- 6.6 pounds of fresh mushrooms of your preference
- 6 Tablespoons of distilled white vinegar
- Water

### Ingredients for the Water Solution

- 8 cups of water
- 2 tablespoons of pickling salt

### Step 1 - Preparation

- Start by cleaning the mushrooms nicely and removing the stalks.
- If the mushrooms you chose are small, keep them as they are. If the mushrooms are big, cut them into four pieces.

### Step 2 – Sterilizing the Mushrooms

- Bring a large pot of enough water to cover the mushrooms to a rolling boil.
- Add to it the mushrooms then boil them for 6 minutes to blanch them.
- Once the time is up, drain the mushrooms and place them aside.

### Step 3 – Sterilizing the Jars

- Start by sterilizing the jars where you will be storing the mushrooms, and make sure the rings are wiped clean.
- To sterilize the jars, bring a large pot of water to a boil, then turn off the heat, place the jars in it, and let them sit in it for 5 to 10 minutes.
- Use thongs to pull them out then place them with the lid down on a towel to dry.

### Step 4 – Preparing the Water Bath Canner

- To prepare for the water bath canner, fill a large stockpot with enough water to cover the jars by 1.5 to 2 inches.
- When done, lower the heat and let it simmer while preparing the jars.

### Step 5 – Water Bath Canning

- Pour 8 cups of water into a stock pot and stir into it the pickling salt then bring it to a boil over high heat.

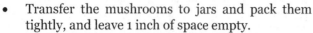

- Transfer the mushrooms to jars and pack them tightly, and leave 1 inch of space empty.
- Pour the hot water and salt solution over the mushrooms then seal the jars tightly.
- Place the jars in a rack and slowly lower them into the water bath canner you prepared.
- If you don't have a rack to use with your stockpot, you can make one using aluminum foil. Get 7 pieces of aluminum that are 6 inches tall, and roll them into stripes.
- Shape 3 stripes into circles by cramping their ends together, then use the remaining 4 pieces to make a net inside of the circle in a zig-zag pattern by cramping the ends of each stripe into the circle.
- Lower the aluminum rack into the pot, then use thongs to place the jar on top of it.
- Make sure that the jars are covered by 1.5 to 2 inches of water, if they are not, add enough water to cover them.
- Bring the water bath canner back to a boil on high heat.
- Process the jars for 1 hour at an altitude that is less than 1000. If you have a higher altitude, adjust your processing time according to your altitude, check the dedicated section. .

## Step 6 – Letting The Jars Rest

- Once the time is up, turn off the heat and remove the jars from the pot then let them cool down on the kitchen counter completely.
- Once they are cool, double-check the jars to make sure they are all sealed, then clean them with a rug.

## Step 7- Storing

- Store your mushroom jars for up to 2 years in a dark cool place, and do not open them until at least 2 months for the best results.
- If one of the jars is not sealed, you can serve it right away or store it in the fridge for up to 2 weeks.

## Homemade Canned Cabbage

|Intro|: This recipe is perfect for all cabbage lovers and even people that don't like cabbage. Even though cabbage is a low acid vegetable and it is preferred that is canned in a pressure cooker, the vinegar in this recipe increases its acidity and protects it when you water bath can it. You can store it for up to 2 years, or serve it the next day.

## Equipment:

6 Pint Jars

Stock Pot

Rack

Thongs

Knife

Cutting Board

Funnel

### Nutrition Facts per 1-pint jar

| Calories | 53.5kcal |
|----------|----------|
| Carbs | 12.88g |
| Protein | 1.88g |
| Fats | 0.15g |

## Core Ingredients

- 1 medium or large head of cabbage

## Ingredients The Brine

- 6 teaspoons of pickling salt
- 6 teaspoons of sugar
- 6 teaspoons of vinegar
- Water

## Step 1 - Preparation

- Start by trimming the cabbage and washing it nicely with water.
- Finely chop the cabbage then place it in a colander while preparing the jars and canner.

## Step 2 – Sterilizing the Jars

- Start by sterilizing the jars where you will be storing the cabbage, and make sure the rings are wiped clean.
- To sterilize the jars, bring a large pot of water to a boil, then turn off the heat, place the jars in it, and let them sit in it for 5 to 10 minutes.
- Use thongs to pull them out then place them with the lid down on a towel to dry.

## Step 3 – Preparing the Cabbage Jars

- Pack the shredded cabbage tightly into the jars and press it down.
- Add 1 teaspoon of sugar, and 1 teaspoon of vinegar to each jar then cover them with water.

- Put on the lids and seal them tightly, then use a wet rag to wipe them clean.

### Step 4 – Preparing the Water Bath Canner

- To prepare for the water bath canner, fill a large stockpot with enough water to cover the jars by 1.5 to 2 inches.
- Place the jars in a rack and slowly lower them into the water bath canner you prepared.
- If you don't have a rack to use with your stockpot, you can make one using aluminum foil. Get 7 pieces of aluminum that are 6 inches tall, and roll them into stripes.
- Shape 3 stripes into circles by cramping their ends together, then use the remaining 4 pieces to make a net inside of the circle in a zig-zag pattern by cramping the ends of each stripe into the circle.
- Lower the aluminum rack into the pot, then use thongs to place the jar on top of it.
- Make sure that the jars are covered by 1.5 to 2 inches of water, if they are not, add enough water to cover them.
- Bring the water bath canner back to a boil on high heat.
- Process the jars for 20 minutes at an altitude that is less than 1000. If you have a higher altitude, adjust your processing time according to your altitude, check the dedicated section. .

### Step 5 - Storing

- Remove the jars from the water and allow them to cool down completely.
- Double-check the jars to make sure all of them are sealed tightly. If one of the jars is not sealed, wash the cabbage nicely and use it for a salad.
- Store your cabbage jars for up to 1 year in a dark cool place, and do not open them until at least 3 weeks old.

## Homemade Canned Onions

|Intro|: Onions are the most important ingredient in every house. It's in a way the salt of vegetable, a staple veggie in every dish, which makes this recipe a perfect addition to your canning shelf. Water bath canning onion is a very simple task that will result in a very tasty condiment that you can add to your burgers, salads, and sauce, and that you store for up to 2 years.

### Equipment:

12 Pint Jars

Stock Pot

Rack

Thongs

Knife

Cutting Board

Colander

Funnel

### Nutrition Facts per 1-pint jar

| Calories | 68.01kcal |
|----------|-----------|
| Carbs | 10.99g |
| Protein | 3.04g |
| Fats | 0.23g |

### Core Ingredients

- 6 pounds of red onions
- 6 teaspoons of salt
- Water

### Step 1 - Preparation

- Start by washing the onions nicely and peeling them.
- If you are using small onions, leave them as they are. If you are using big onions, cut them into four.

### Step 2 – Sterilizing the Jars

- Start by sterilizing the jars where you will be storing the onions, and make sure the rings are wiped clean.
- To sterilize the jars, bring a large pot of water to a boil, then turn off the heat, place the jars in it, and let them sit in it for 5 to 10 minutes.
- Use thongs to pull them out then place them with the lid down on a towel to dry.

### Step 3 – Preparing The Onions

- Bring a large pot of water to a boil, then add to it the onions.
- Blanch them for 5 minutes then drain them and let them sit in a colander to drain for a few minutes.
- Pack the onions tightly into the jars then add ½ teaspoon of salt into each jar and cover them with water.
- Put on the lids and seal the jars tightly then wipe them with a wet rag.

### Step 4 - Canning

- To prepare for the water bath canner, fill a large stockpot with enough water to cover the jars by 1.5 to 2 inches.
- Place the jars in a rack and slowly lower them into the water bath canner you prepared.
- If you don't have a rack to use with your stockpot, you can make one using aluminum foil. Get 7 pieces of aluminum that are 6 inches tall, and roll them into stripes.
- Shape 3 stripes into circles by cramping their ends together, then use the remaining 4 pieces to make a net inside of the circle in a zig-zag pattern by cramping the ends of each stripe into the circle.
- Lower the aluminum rack into the pot, then use thongs to place the jar on top of it.
- Make sure that the jars are covered by 1.5 to 2 inches of water, if they are not, add enough water to cover them.
- Bring the water bath canner back to a boil on high heat.
- Process the jars for 10 minutes at an altitude that is less than 1000. If you have a higher altitude, adjust your processing time according to your altitude, check the dedicated section. .

### Step 5 – Letting the Jars Rest

- Once the time is up, turn off the heat and remove the jars from the pot, then place them on a towel.
- Let the onion jars sit until they cool down completely.

### Step 6 – Storing

- Double-check the jars to make sure all of them are sealed tightly. If one of the jars is not sealed, you can store them in the fridge instead for up to 4 days or you can freeze them for up to 2 months.
- Store your cabbage jars for up to 2 years in a dark cool place, and do not open them until at least 4 weeks old.

---

## Homemade Canned Eggplants

|Intro|: Eggplant might not be the most popular vegetable, but when cooked right, it makes a great addition to your meal. Also, it's a veggie that spoils quickly, so water bath canning is the best best way to preserve all year round and use it for your salads, sauces, salsas...

### Equipment:

7 Pint Jars

Stock Pot

Large Sauce Pan

Rack

Thongs

Knife

Cutting Board

Colander

Funnel

### Nutrition Facts per 1-pint jar

| Calories | 107.92 kcal |
|----------|-------------|
| Carbs | 25.23g |
| Protein | 4.03g |
| Fats | 0.85g |

### Core Ingredients

- 5 pounds of fresh and firm eggplants
- 7 bay leaves
- 7 cloves of garlic
- 7 dill heads
- 3 ½ cup of water
- 3 ½ cup of white vinegar
- 1/3 cup of kosher salt

### Step 1 - Preparation

- Start by washing the eggplants, remove their tops, then cut them into ¼-inch stripes or cubes.

### Step 2 – Sterilizing the Jars

- Start by sterilizing the jars where you will be storing the onions, and make sure the rings are wiped clean.
- You can sterilize them by placing them in a boiling pot of water and letting them sit in it for 5 to 10 minutes with the heat turned off.
- Use thongs to pull them out then place them with the lid down on a towel to dry.

### Step 3 – Preparing The Brine

- Combine the water and vinegar in a large saucepan then bring them to a boil over high heat.

### Step 4 – Packing the Jars

- Divide the garlic, bay leaves and dill stems between the jars, then add to them the eggplant pieces pressing them down.
- Pour the hot brine on top of the eggplant pieces gently leaving ¼-inch of space in the jar empty.
- Put on the lids and seal the jars tightly then wipe them with a wet rag.

### Step 5 – Preparing The Water Bath Canner

- To prepare for the water bath canner, fill a large stockpot with enough water to cover the jars by 1.5 to 2 inches then bring it to a boil.
- Place the jars in a rack and slowly lower them into the water bath canner you prepared.
- If you don't have a rack to use with your stockpot, you can make one using aluminum foil. Get 7 pieces of aluminum that are 6 inches tall, and roll them into stripes.
- Shape 3 stripes into circles by cramping their ends together, then use the remaining 4 pieces to make a net inside of the circle in a zig-zag pattern by cramping the ends of each stripe into the circle.
- Lower the aluminum rack into the pot, then use thongs to place the jar on top of it.

### Step 6 - Canning

- Make sure all the jars are immersed and completely covered with water, if they are not, add more water until they are covered.
- Bring the water to a boil one more on medium to high heat, then put on the lid and let them process for 15 minutes at an altitude that is less than 1000. If you have a higher altitude, adjust your processing time according to your altitude, check the dedicated section. .

### Step 7 – Letting the Jars Rest

- Once the time is up, gently remove the jars and place them on a large towel, then let them cool down completely for at least 24 hours.

### Step 8 - Storing

- Double check the jars to make sure they are sealed then you can store them in a dark and cool place for 12 months.
- If you find some jars that are not sealed properly, you won't be able to store them. You can let them sit in the fridge instead and serve them in 1 week by adding them to a sauce, salsa, meal... and enjoy!

## Section 4: Sauces and Condiments

### BBQ Sauce

|Intro|: This tomato-based BBQ sauce holds the perfect combination of acidity from the tomatoes, combined with the tanginess of the vinegar and the sweetness from the brown sugar and honey. The pineapple juice adds a very nice and tropical taste to it which makes it perfect for both grilled meats and baked ones as well.

### Equipment:

- StockPot
- Rack
- Thongs
- Towel
- Large Saucepan
- 3 Pint Jars
- Large Bowl
- Funnel

#### Nutrition Facts per 1 Pint Jar

| Calories | 649kcal |
|----------|---------|
| Carbs | 167g |
| Protein | 1g |
| Fats | 1g |

### Core Ingredients

- 84 ounces of tomato sauce
- 1 ½ cup of honey
- 1 ½ cup of brown sugar
- 1 ¼ cup of onion, diced
- 1 1/3 cup of red wine vinegar
- ¾ cup of molasses
- ¼ cup of pineapple juice
- ¼ cup of Worcestershire sauce
- ¼ cup of garlic, peeled and minced

### Step 1 - Preparation

- Place a large saucepan over medium heat, and heat in it the olive oil.
- Add the onion and cook it for 2 minutes while stirring.

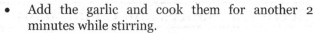

- Add the garlic and cook them for another 2 minutes while stirring.
- Add the remaining ingredients and mix them well then bring them to a simmer.
- Lower the heat and put on the lid, then allow the sauce to cook for 2 hours to 2.50 hours until reaches the consistency and thickness that you prefer.

## Step 2 – Sterilizing The Jars

- In the meantime, start sterilizing the jars where you will be storing the sauce, and make sure the rings are wiped clean.
- To sterilize the jars, bring a large pot of water to a boil, then turn off the heat, place the jars in it, and let them sit in it for 5 to 10 minutes.
- Use thongs to pull them out then place them with the lid down on a towel to dry.

## Step 3 – Preparing The Water Bath Canner

- To prepare for the canning process, fill a large stockpot with enough water to cover the jars by 1.5 to 2 inches.
- Bring it to a boil on high heat, then lower the heat and let it simmer while preparing the sauce.

## Step 5 - Packing

- Once the sauce is done, turn off the heat and allow it to cool down for a few minutes, then spoon it into the sterilized jars, and make sure to leave 1/8 to ¼-inch of the space empty at the top of each jar.
- Wipe the sides of the jars with a clean and slightly wet rag, then put on the lids and secure them tightly. Press the center of the lids to ensure they are sealed properly.

## Step 5 - Canning

- Place the jars in a rack and lower them to the boiling water in the water bath canner.
- If you don't have a rack to use with your stockpot, you can make one using aluminum foil. Get 7 pieces of aluminum that are 6 inches tall, and roll them into stripes.
- Shape 3 stripes into circles by cramping their ends together, then use the remaining 4 pieces to make a net inside of the circle in a zig-zag pattern by cramping the ends of each stripe into the circle.
- Make sure all the jars are immersed and completely covered with water, if they are not, add more water until they are covered.

- Bring the water to a boil one more on medium to high heat, then put on the lid and let them process for 15 minutes at an altitude that is less than 1000. If you have a higher altitude, adjust your processing time according to your altitude, check the dedicated section. .

## Step 6 – Letting the Jars Rest

- Once the time is up, turn off the heat and remove the lid gently, then remove the jars from the pot.
- Place them on a large towel, then let them cool down completely for at least 24 hours until they cool down.

## Step 7 - Storing

- Double check the jars to make sure they are sealed then you can store them for up to 5 months
- If you find some jars that are not sealed properly, you can still store them in the fridge for up to 3 days and enjoy!

## Marinara Sauce

|Intro|: Marinara sauce is a staple sauce in almost all homes. This Marinara sauce recipe is sweet thanks to the brown sugar, and the herbs add a lot of flavor to the sauce. You can store it for up to 2 years, and enjoy it with pasta, baked chicken...

### Equipment:

- 2 StockPots
- Rack
- Thongs
- Towel
- 7 Pint Jars
- Large Bowl
- Funnel

### Nutrition Facts per 1 Pint Jar

| Calories | 702kcal |
|----------|---------|
| Carbs | 141g |
| Protein | 9g |
| Fats | 17g |

### Core Ingredients

- 36 ounces of tomato paste
- 12 cups of fresh tomato puree

- 2 Large yellow or white onions, finely chopped
- 6 cups of water
- 3 cups of brown sugar
- ¼ cup of olive oil
- 10 cloves of garlic, peeled and minced
- 1 tablespoon of fennel, ground
- 1 tablespoon of dry oregano, ground
- 1 tablespoon of salt
- 2 teaspoons of black pepper

## Step 1 - Preparation

- Place a stockpot over medium heat, and heat in it the olive oil.
- Add the onion and cook it for 2 minutes, then add the garlic and cook them for another 2 minutes.
- Add the remaining ingredients and mix them until well combined.
- Lower the heat, and allow the sauce to simmer for 20 to 25 minutes while stirring it occasionally until reaches the consistency that you prefer.

## Step 2 – Sterilizing The Jars

- In the meantime, start sterilizing the jars where you will be storing the sauce, and make sure the rings are wiped clean.
- To sterilize the jars, bring a large pot of water to a boil, then turn off the heat, place the jars in it, and let them sit in it for 5 to 10 minutes.
- Use thongs to pull them out then place them with the lid down on a towel to dry.

## Step 3 – Preparing The Water Bath Canner

- To prepare for the canning process, fill a large stockpot with enough water to cover the jars by 1.5 to 2 inches.
- Bring it to a boil on high heat, then lower the heat and let it simmer while preparing the sauce.

## Step 4 - Packing

- Once the sauce is simmered to your liking, turn off the heat and allow it to cool down for 10 to 15 minutes, and becomes easy to handle.
- Spoon the sauce into the jars while making sure to leave 1/8 to ¼-inch of the jar empty, then put on the lids and seal them.
- Wipe the sides of the jars with a clean and slightly wet rag, then put on the lids and secure them tightly. Press the center of the lids to ensure they are sealed properly.

## Step 5 - Canning

- Place the jars in a rack and lower them to the boiling water in the water bath canner.
- If you don't have a rack to use with your stockpot, you can make one using aluminum foil. Get 7 pieces of aluminum that are 6 inches tall, and roll them into stripes.
- Shape 3 stripes into circles by cramping their ends together, then use the remaining 4 pieces to make a net inside of the circle in a zig-zag pattern by cramping the ends of each stripe into the circle.
- Make sure all the jars are immersed and completely covered with water, if they are not, add more water until they are covered.
- Bring the water to a boil one more on medium to high heat, then put on the lid and let them process for 20 minutes at an altitude that is less than 1000. If you have a higher altitude, adjust your processing time according to your altitude, check the dedicated section. .

## Step 6 – Letting the Jars Rest

- Once the time is up, turn off the heat and remove the lid gently, then remove the jars from the pot.
- Place them on a large towel, then let them cool down completely for at least 24 hours until they cool down.

## Step 7 - Storing

- Double check the jars to make sure they are sealed then you can store them for up to 18 months
- If you find some jars that are not sealed properly, you can still store them in the fridge for up to 5 days or 1 month in the freezer and enjoy!

## Ketchup

|Intro|: Ketchup is a very popular sauce that is almost in every home, which makes it perfect for canning. This ketchup comes out tangy, sweet, and tart at the same time which makes it very similar to Heinz ketchup. This recipe will save you a lot of money, and you can keep enjoying it for up to 1 year.

### Equipment:

- 2 StockPots
- Rack
- Thongs
- Towel
- 16 Pint Jars
- Large Bowl

- Funnel
- Whisk

**Nutrition Facts** per 1 Quart

| Calories | 676kcal |
|----------|---------|
| Carbs    | 156g    |
| Protein  | 18g     |
| Fats     | 3g      |

## Core Ingredients

- 22 pounds of fresh tomatoes
- 46 ounces of tomato paste
- 4 cups of white distilled vinegar
- 3 cups of white granulated sugar
- 1/3 cup of ThermFlo Canning Thickener
- 5 tablespoons of salt
- 1 tablespoon of onion powder
- ½ teaspoon of cloves, ground
- ½ teaspoon of cinnamon powder
- ½ teaspoon of all-spice, ground
- ½ teaspoon of cayenne pepper

## Step 1 – Preparation

- Start by peeling the tomatoes, and cut them into 4 pieces each.
- Transfer them to a large stockpot and bring them to a boil over medium-high heat while stirring them occasionally until they become soft.
- Once the time tomatoes are done, use an immersion blender to blend them smooth, or blend them in a food processor in batches.
- Measure 1 cup of tomato sauce and place it aside.
- Pour the remaining tomato sauce into the stockpot then cook it over low heat with half a lid on until it reduces by half, it should take from 2 hours to 2.5 hours.

## Step 2 – Sterilizing The Jars

- In the meantime, start sterilizing the jars where you will be storing the ketchup, and make sure the rings are wiped clean.
- To sterilize the jars, bring a large pot of water to a boil, then turn off the heat, place the jars in it, and let them sit in it for 5 to 10 minutes.

- Use thongs to pull them out then place them with the lid down on a towel to dry.

## Step 3 – Preparing The Water Bath Canner

- To prepare for the canning process, fill a large stockpot with enough water to cover the jars by 1.5 to 2 inches.
- Bring it to a boil on high heat, then lower the heat and let it simmer while preparing the ketchup.

## Step 4 – Preparing The Ketchup

- Once the tomato sauce is done, add to it the tomato paste with spices, and vinegar then mix them well with a whisk until well combined.
- Pour the ThermFlo into a medium bowl, then add to it the reserved cup of tomato sauce slowly while whisking the whole time until no lumps are found.
- Add the mixture gradually to the pot while stirring the whole time with a whisk until they are well combined.
- Spoon the ketchup into the jars while it's hot, and make sure to leave 1/8 to ¼-inch of the jar empty, then put on the lids and seal them.
- Wipe the sides of the jars with a clean and slightly wet rag, then put on the lids and secure them tightly. Press the center of the lids to ensure they are sealed properly.

## Step 5 - Canning

- Place the jars in a rack and lower them to the boiling water in the water bath canner.
- If you don't have a rack to use with your stockpot, you can make one using aluminum foil. Get 7 pieces of aluminum that are 6 inches tall, and roll them into stripes.
- Shape 3 stripes into circles by cramping their ends together, then use the remaining 4 pieces to make a net inside of the circle in a zig-zag pattern by cramping the ends of each stripe into the circle.
- Make sure all the jars are immersed and completely covered with water, if they are not, add more water until they are covered.
- Bring the water to a boil one more on medium to high heat, then put on the lid and let them process for 10 minutes at an altitude that is less than 1000. If you have a higher altitude, adjust your processing time according to your altitude, check the dedicated section. .

### Step 6 – Letting the Jars Rest

- Once the time is up, turn off the heat and remove the lid gently, then remove the jars from the pot.
- Place them on a large towel, then let them cool down completely for at least 24 hours until they cool down.

### Step 7 - Storing

- Double check the jars to make sure they are sealed then you can store them for up to 6 months
- If you find some jars that are not sealed properly, you can still store them in the fridge for up to 3 weeks or 6 months in the freezer and enjoy!

## Roasted Garlic Mustard

|Intro|: If you are a fan of roasted garlic, then this recipe is perfect for you. This recipe is straightforward to prepare. The garlic is baked to perfection, then combine with the remaining ingredients to make a delicious thick sauce that you spread on chicken, grilled meat, ham...You can store it and enjoy it for up to 1 year.

### Equipment:

- 2 StockPots
- Rack
- Thongs
- Towel
- 4 Pint Jars
- Large Bowl
- Funnel

### Nutrition Facts per ½ Pint

| Calories | 398.9kcal |
|----------|-----------|
| Carbs | 60.98g |
| Protein | 10.48g |
| Fats | 14.29g |

### Core Ingredients

- 2 pounds of garlic
- 1 pound of granny smith apples
- 1 pound of anaheim peppers
- 3 Serrano peppers
- 2 cups of apple juice
- 1 ½ cup of white vinegar
- 1/3 cup of olive oil
- ¼ cup of mustard powder
- 2 tablespoons of yellow mustard seeds
- 1 tablespoon of coriander seeds

### Step 1 – Preparation

- Roast the peppers on the stove until they become black on all sides, then transfer them into a Ziploc, seal it and allow them to cool down for 15 minutes.
- Once the time is up, peel the peppers by removing the black skin, discard the seeds, then finely chop them, and place them aside.
- Peel and core the apples, then dice them.
- Transfer the diced apples to the stockpot, then add to them 1 cup of apple juice and bring them to a simmer over medium heat.
- Lower the heat and let the apples cook for 5 more minutes, then turn off the heat and place the pot aside.

### Step 2 – Sterilizing The Jars

- Start by sterilizing the jars where you will be storing the roasted garlic mustard, and make sure the rings are wiped clean.
- To sterilize the jars, bring a large pot of water to a boil, then turn off the heat, place the jars in it, and let them sit in it for 5 to 10 minutes.
- Use thongs to pull them out then place them with the lid down on a towel to dry.

### Step 3 – Preparing The Water Bath Canner

- To prepare for the canning process, fill a large stockpot with enough water to cover the jars by 1.5 to 2 inches.
- Bring it to a boil on high heat, then lower the heat and let it simmer while preparing the remaining ingredients.

### Step 4 – Roasting The Garlic

- Preheat the oven to 400 F.
- Cover a baking sheet with a piece of foil, then place the bulbs of garlic in it.
- Drizzle some olive oil on top, then bake it for 30 to 40 minutes until it becomes soft and tender.
- Once the garlic is done, place it aside to cool down.

### Step 5 – Preparing The Roasted Garlic Mustard

- Peel the garlic and transfer the roasted cloves to a food processor with the cooked apples, and chopped peppers then process them until they become smooth.

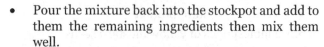

- Pour the mixture back into the stockpot and add to them the remaining ingredients then mix them well.
- Place the pot over high heat and bring it to a boil while stirring it occasionally, then keep it boiling for 12 minutes while stirring the whole time.

## Step 6 – Packing

- Spoon the mustard mixture into the jars while it's hot, and make sure to leave 1/8 to ¼-inch of the jar empty, then put on the lids and seal them.
- Wipe the sides of the jars with a clean and slightly wet rag, then put on the lids and secure them tightly. Press the center of the lids to ensure they are sealed properly.

## Step 7 - Canning

- Place the jars in a rack and lower them to the boiling water in the water bath canner.
- If you don't have a rack to use with your stockpot, you can make one using aluminum foil. Get 7 pieces of aluminum that are 6 inches tall, and roll them into stripes.
- Shape 3 stripes into circles by cramping their ends together, then use the remaining 4 pieces to make a net inside of the circle in a zig-zag pattern by cramping the ends of each stripe into the circle.
- Make sure all the jars are immersed and completely covered with water, if they are not, add more water until they are covered.
- Bring the water to a boil one more on medium to high heat, then put on the lid and let them process for 10 minutes at an altitude that is less than 1000. If you have a higher altitude, adjust your processing time according to your altitude, check the dedicated section. .

## Step 8 – Letting the Jars Rest

- Once the time is up, turn off the heat and remove the lid gently, then remove the jars from the pot.
- Place them on a large towel, then let them cool down completely for at least 24 hours until they cool down.

## Step 9 - Storing

- Double check the jars to make sure they are sealed then you can store them for up to 6 months
- If you find some jars that are not sealed properly, you can still store them in the fridge for up to 3 weeks and enjoy!

## Chili Tomato Salsa

|Intro|: This chili tomato salsa is the perfect way to preserve your tomatoes, and add even more flavor to them. It makes a great addition to your soups, and stew, and is a great and cheap alternative for store-bought tomato sauce. You can also serve it on its own as a dipping sauce with some breadsticks or chips and enjoy it for 12 months.

## Equipment:

- 2 StockPots
- Rack
- Thongs
- Towel
- 9 Pint Jars
- Large Bowl
- Funnel

### Nutrition Facts per ¼ cup

| Calories | 50kcal |
|----------|--------|
| Carbs | 12g |
| Protein | 1g |
| Fats | 0g |

## Core Ingredients

- 9 pounds of fresh tomatoes
- 12 ounces of tomato paste
- 3 large yellow or white onions, peeled and diced
- 2 cups of fresh or bottled lemon juice
- 1 cup of mild chilies, seeded and diced
- 4 cloves of garlic, peeled and finely chopped
- 1 tablespoon of sea salt
- 1 tablespoon of granulated cane sugar
- 1 teaspoon of black pepper

## Step 1 - Preparation

- Start by peeling the tomatoes, and dicing them, then transfer them to a large stock pot.
- Add to the remaining ingredients and mix them well until well combined.
- Place the pot over high heat and bring them to a boil, then lower the heat, put on the lid, and let the salsa cooking for 25 to 30 minutes until it becomes thick.

### Step 2 – Sterilizing The Jars

- Start by sterilizing the jars where you will be storing the salsa, and make sure the rings are wiped clean.
- To sterilize the jars, bring a large pot of water to a boil, then turn off the heat, place the jars in it, and let them sit in it for 5 to 10 minutes.
- Use thongs to pull them out then place them with the lid down on a towel to dry.

### Step 3 – Preparing The Water Bath Canner

- To prepare for the canning process, fill a large stockpot with enough water to cover the jars by 1.5 to 2 inches.
- Bring it to a boil on high heat, then lower the heat and let it simmer while preparing the salsa.

### Step 4 – Packing

- Once the salsa is done, spoon it while it's hot into the jars, and make sure to leave 1/8 to ¼-inch of the jar empty, then put on the lids and seal them.
- Wipe the sides of the jars with a clean and slightly wet rag, then put on the lids and secure them tightly. Press the center of the lids to ensure they are sealed properly.

### Step 5 - Canning

- Place the jars in a rack and lower them to the boiling water in the water bath canner.
- If you don't have a rack to use with your stockpot, you can make one using aluminum foil. Get 7 pieces of aluminum that are 6 inches tall, and roll them into stripes.
- Shape 3 stripes into circles by cramping their ends together, then use the remaining 4 pieces to make a net inside of the circle in a zig-zag pattern by cramping the ends of each stripe into the circle.
- Make sure all the jars are immersed and completely covered with water, if they are not, add more water until they are covered.
- Bring the water to a boil one more on medium to high heat, then put on the lid and let them process for 15 minutes at an altitude that is less than 1000. If you have a higher altitude, adjust your processing time according to your altitude, check the dedicated section. .

### Step 6 – Letting the Jars Rest

- Once the time is up, turn off the heat and remove the lid gently, then remove the jars from the pot.

- Place them on a large towel, then let them cool down completely for at least 24 hours until they cool down.

### Step 7 - Storing

- Double check the jars to make sure they are sealed then you can store them for up to 18 months
- If you find some jars that are not sealed properly, you can still store them in the fridge for up to 2 weeks or 1 month in the freezer and enjoy!

## Chocolate Syrup

|Intro|: Yes, you read it right, you and actually water ban can chocolate syrup, and it's completely safe because this recipe doesn't use any dairy ingredients. It's super delicious, you can add some of it to your morning coffee, pancakes, waffles...It's fantastic!

### Equipment:

- StockPot
- Rack
- Thongs
- Towel
- Saucepan
- 3 Pint Jars
- Large Bowl
- Funnel
- Whisk

#### Nutrition Facts per 1 tablespoon

| Calories | 55.17kcal |
|----------|-----------|
| Carbs | 14.17g |
| Protein | 0.47g |
| Fats | 0.34g |

### Core Ingredients

- 3 cups of granulated white sugar
- 1 ½ cups of water
- 1 ½ cup of dutch-processed cocoa powder
- 2 tablespoons of light corn syrup
- 1 tablespoon of vanilla extract
- ¼ teaspoon of kosher salt

### Step 1 - Preparation

- Combine the sugar with water in a large saucepan and bring them to a boil.
- Add the remaining ingredients and whisk them until no lumps are found.
- Lower the heat, and let the sauce cook for 10 to 15 minutes until it becomes slightly thick while stirring it occasionally.

### Step 2 – Sterilizing The Jars

- Start by sterilizing the jars where you will be storing the sauce, and make sure the rings are wiped clean.
- To sterilize the jars, bring a large pot of water to a boil, then turn off the heat, place the jars in it, and let them sit in it for 5 to 10 minutes.
- Use thongs to pull them out then place them with the lid down on a towel to dry.

### Step 3 – Preparing The Water Bath Canner

- To prepare for the canning process, fill a large stockpot with enough water to cover the jars by 1.5 to 2 inches.
- Bring it to a boil on high heat, then lower the heat and let it simmer while preparing the sauce.

### Step 4 – Packing

- Once the chocolate sauce is done, spoon it while it's hot into the jars, and make sure to leave 1/8 to ¼-inch of the jar empty, then put on the lids and seal them.
- Wipe the sides of the jars with a clean and slightly wet rag, then put on the lids and secure them tightly. Press the center of the lids to ensure they are sealed properly.

### Step 5 - Canning

- Place the jars in a rack and lower them to the boiling water in the water bath canner.
- If you don't have a rack to use with your stockpot, you can make one using aluminum foil.  Get 7 pieces of aluminum that are 6 inches tall, and roll them into stripes.
- Shape 3 stripes into circles by cramping their ends together, then use the remaining 4 pieces to make a net inside of the circle in a zig-zag pattern by cramping the ends of each stripe into the circle.
- Make sure all the jars are immersed and completely covered with water, if they are not, add more water until they are covered.

- Bring the water to a boil one more on medium to high heat, then put on the lid and let them process for 15 minutes at an altitude that is less than 1000. If you have a higher altitude, adjust your processing time according to your altitude, check the dedicated section.

### Step 6 – Letting the Jars Rest

- Once the time is up, turn off the heat and remove the lid gently, then remove the jars from the pot.
- Place them on a large towel, then let them cool down completely for at least 24 hours until they cool down.

### Step 7 - Storing

- Double check the jars to make sure they are sealed then you can store them for up to 6 months
- If you find some jars that are not sealed properly, you can still store them in the fridge for up to 2 weeks or 1 month in the freezer and enjoy!

## Cilantro Lime Enchilada Sauce

|Intro|: Enchiladas are a very comforting and soul-healing dish that can be prepared and enjoyed by everyone in no time, so having this homemade enchilada sauce stored in your pantry comes very handy. On your busiest days, you just have to throw in all the ingredients together and bake them to perfection. You can store it and enjoy it for up to 12 months.

### Equipment:

- StockPot
- Rack
- Thongs
- Towel
- Saucepan
- 3 Pint Jars or 6 Half Pint Jars
- Large Bowl
- Funnel

### Nutrition Facts per ¼ Pint Jar

| Calories | 29kcal |
|----------|--------|
| Carbs    | 6g     |
| Protein  | 1g     |
| Fats     | 1g     |

## Core Ingredients

- 6 cups of tomatillos, peeled and quartered
- 3 tbsp of finely cut cilantro
- ¾ cup of water
- ½ cup of yellow or white onion, finely chopped
- ¼ cup + 6 tablespoons of fresh or bottled lime juice
- 1 Anaheim pepper, seeded and finely chopped
- 1 jalapeno, seeded and finely chopped
- 3 cloves of garlic, peeled and sliced
- 1 ½ teaspoon of salt
- ½ teaspoon of cumin
- Olive oil

## Step 1 – Sterilizing The Jars

- Start by sterilizing the jars where you will be storing the sauce, and make sure the rings are wiped clean.
- To sterilize the jars, bring a large pot of water to a boil, then turn off the heat, place the jars in it, and let them sit in it for 5 to 10 minutes.
- Use thongs to pull them out then place them with the lid down on a towel to dry.

## Step 2 – Preparing The Water Bath Canner

- To prepare for the canning process, fill a large stockpot with enough water to cover the jars by 1.5 to 2 inches.
- Bring it to a boil on high heat, then lower the heat and let it simmer while preparing the sauce.

## Step 3 – Preparing The Enchilada Sauce

- Place a large saucepan over medium heat, and heat in it a drizzle of olive oil.
- Add to it the tomatillos, with garlic, peppers, and onion then cook them for 5 minutes while stirring until they become soft.
- Add the cumin with salt, water, and cilantro to the saucepan and mix them well.
- Lower the heat, and put on the lid, then let the salsa cook for 10 to 12 minutes until the veggies become tender.
- Once the salsa is done, turn off the heat, then transfer it into a big food processor, or use an immersion blender to blend it until smooth.
- Add to it ¼ cup of lime juice then mix them until well combined.

## Step 4 - Packing

- Quickly spoon the salsa while it's warm into the sterilized jars, and make sure to leave 1/8 to ¼-inch of the space empty at the top of each jar.
- Pour 2 tablespoons of lime juice on top of the salsa in each 1-pint jar. This process will enable you to store the salsa for a long time.
- Wipe the sides of the jars with a clean and slightly wet rag, then put on the lids and secure them tightly. Press the center of the lids to ensure they are sealed properly.

## Step 5 - Canning

- Place the jars in a rack and lower them to the boiling water in the water bath canner.
- If you don't have a rack to use with your stockpot, you can make one using aluminum foil. Get 7 pieces of aluminum that are 6 inches tall, and roll them into stripes.
- Shape 3 stripes into circles by cramping their ends together, then use the remaining 4 pieces to make a net inside of the circle in a zig-zag pattern by cramping the ends of each stripe into the circle.
- Make sure all the jars are immersed and completely covered with water, if they are not, add more water until they are covered.
- Bring the water to a boil one more on medium to high heat, then put on the lid and let them process for 40 minutes at an altitude that is less than 1000. If you have a higher altitude, adjust your processing time according to your altitude, check the dedicated section.

## Step 6 – Letting the Jars Rest

- Once the time is up, turn off the heat and remove the lid gently, then let the jars sit in the pot for 5 to 6 minutes to test.
- Once the time is up, drain the jars and place them on a large towel, then let them cool down completely for 24 hours until they cool down.

## Step 7 - Storing

- Double check the jars to make sure they are sealed then you can store them in a dark and cool place for up to 12 months.
- If you find some jars that are not sealed properly, you won't be able to store them in the pantry.
- You can still store them though in the fridge for up to 1 week, or in the freezer for 3 months and enjoy!

## Yummy Sloppy-Joe Sauce

|**Intro**|: Who doesn't like sloppy joes? That beef burger that is bursting with flavor and dripping with a delicious sauce. This water bath canning recipe makes preparing sloppy joe super easy, you just have to cook the beef, add the sauce to it, then serve it hot. So every time you crave it or don't have time to make a nice meal from scratch, you just have to open a jar, heat it, then serve some bread and cheese.

### Equipment:

- StockPot
- Rack
- Thongs
- Towel
- Saucepan
- 10 Pint Jars
- Large Bowl
- Funnel

**Nutrition Facts** per 1 Pint Jar

| Calories | 140kcal |
|---|---|
| Carbs | 3.6g |
| Protein | 19g |
| Fats | 5g |

### Core Ingredients

- 3 cups of tomato sauce
- 3 cups of celery, finely chopped
- 2 cups of yellow or white onion, diced
- 1 ½ cup of green bell pepper, diced
- 1 cup of brown sugar
- 7 tablespoons of tomato paste
- ½ cup of vinegar
- ¼ cup of honey
- 2 tablespoons of salt
- 1 tablespoon of dry mustard
- 1 tablespoon of smoked paprika
- 1 tablespoon of yellow mustard
- 1 clove of garlic, finely chopped
- ¾ teaspoon of black pepper

### Step 1 – Sterilizing The Jars

- Start by sterilizing the jars where you will be storing the sauce, and make sure the rings are wiped clean.
- To sterilize the jars, bring a large pot of water to a boil, then turn off the heat, place the jars in it, and let them sit in it for 5 to 10 minutes.
- Use thongs to pull them out then place them with the lid down on a towel to dry.

### Step 2 – Preparing The Sloppy-Joe Sauce

- Combine all the ingredients in a large saucepan and mix until well combined.
- Bring the sauce to a boil over high heat, then lower the heat, put on the lid, and let the sauce cook for 30 to 40 minutes until the veggies are cooked, and the sauce is thick to your liking.

### Step 3 – Preparing The Water Bath Canner

- To prepare for the canning process, fill a large stockpot with enough water to cover the jars by 1.5 to 2 inches.
- Bring it to a boil on high heat, then lower the heat and let it simmer while preparing the sauce.

### Step 4 - Packing

- Once the sauce is done, quickly spoon it while it's warm into the sterilized jars, and make sure to leave 1/8 to ¼-inch of the space empty at the top of each jar.
- Wipe the sides of the jars with a clean and slightly wet rag, then put on the lids and secure them tightly. Press the center of the lids to ensure they are sealed properly.

### Step 5 - Canning

- Place the jars in a rack and lower them to the boiling water in the water bath canner.
- If you don't have a rack to use with your stockpot, you can make one using aluminum foil. Get 7 pieces of aluminum that are 6 inches tall, and roll them into stripes.
- Shape 3 stripes into circles by cramping their ends together, then use the remaining 4 pieces to make a net inside of the circle in a zig-zag pattern by cramping the ends of each stripe into the circle.
- Make sure all the jars are immersed and completely covered with water, if they are not, add more water until they are covered.
- Bring the water to a boil one more on medium to high heat, then put on the lid and let them process

for 20 minutes at an altitude that is less than 1000. If you have a higher altitude, adjust your processing time according to your altitude, check the dedicated section.

### Step 6 – Letting the Jars Rest

- Once the time is up, turn off the heat and remove the lid gently, then let the jars sit in the pot for 5 to 6 minutes to test.
- Once the time is up, drain the jars and place them on a large towel, then let them cool down completely for 24 hours until they cool down.

### Step 7 - Storing

- Double check the jars to make sure they are sealed then you can store them in a dark and cool place for up to 12 months.
- If you find some jars that are not sealed properly, you won't be able to store them in the pantry.
- You can still store them though in the fridge for up to 3 days, or in the freezer for 2 weeks and enjoy!

## Sweet Thai Chili Sauce

|Intro|: Who doesn't like chili sauce? If you are a fan of it or not, you have to admit that some dishes can't be eaten without at least a small dash of hot sauce. This sweet chili sauce balances the sweet and hot perfectly in this sauce which makes it perfect to add to your baked beans, grilled meat, and stir fry.

### Equipment:

- StockPot
- Rack
- Thongs
- Towel
- Saucepan
- 5 Pint Jars
- Large Bowl
- Funnel

#### Nutrition Facts per 1 cup

| Calories | 526.9kcal |
|----------|-----------|
| Carbs | 128.36g |
| Protein | 1.27g |
| Fats | 0.31g |

### Core Ingredients

- 28 ounces of fresh red chilies, seeded and finely chopped
- 6 cups of white granulated sugar
- 6 cups of apple cider vinegar
- ¼ cup of fresh ginger, peeled and grated
- ¼ cup of garlic, peeled and minced
- 2 teaspoons of salt

### Step 1 – Sterilizing The Jars

- Start by sterilizing the jars where you will be storing the sauce, and make sure the rings are wiped clean.
- To sterilize the jars, bring a large pot of water to a boil, then turn off the heat, place the jars in it, and let them sit in it for 5 to 10 minutes.
- Use thongs to pull them out then place them with the lid down on a towel to dry.

### Step 2 – Preparing The Sweet Thai Chili Sauce

- Combine all the ingredients in a large saucepan and mix until well combined.
- Bring the sauce to a boil over high heat, then lower the heat, put on the lid, and let the sauce cook for 20 to 30 minutes until the peppers become soft and tender.
- You can leave the sauce as it is, or you can blend it smooth using a food processor or blender.

### Step 3 – Preparing The Water Bath Canner

- To prepare for the canning process, fill a large stockpot with enough water to cover the jars by 1.5 to 2 inches.
- Bring it to a boil on high heat, then lower the heat and let it simmer while preparing the sauce.

### Step 4 - Packing

- Once the sauce is done, quickly spoon it while it's warm into the sterilized jars, and make sure to leave 1/8 to ¼-inch of the space empty at the top of each jar.
- Wipe the sides of the jars with a clean and slightly wet rag, then put on the lids and secure them tightly. Press the center of the lids to ensure they are sealed properly.

### Step 5 - Canning

- Place the jars in a rack and lower them to the boiling water in the water bath canner.

- If you don't have a rack to use with your stockpot, you can make one using aluminum foil. Get 7 pieces of aluminum that are 6 inches tall, and roll them into stripes.
- Shape 3 stripes into circles by cramping their ends together, then use the remaining 4 pieces to make a net inside of the circle in a zig-zag pattern by cramping the ends of each stripe into the circle.
- Make sure all the jars are immersed and completely covered with water, if they are not, add more water until they are covered.
- Bring the water to a boil one more on medium to high heat, then put on the lid and let them process for 15 minutes at an altitude that is less than 1000. If you have a higher altitude, adjust your processing time according to your altitude, check the dedicated section. .

### Step 6 – Letting the Jars Rest
- Once the time is up, turn off the heat and remove the lid gently, then let the jars sit in the pot for 5 to 6 minutes to test.
- Once the time is up, drain the jars and place them on a large towel, then let them cool down completely for 24 hours until they cool down.

### Step 7 - Storing
- Double check the jars to make sure they are sealed then you can store them in a dark and cool place for up to 12 months.
- If you find some jars that are not sealed properly, you won't be able to store them in the pantry.
- You can still store them though in the fridge for up to 5 days, or in the freezer for 1 month and enjoy!

## Apple Sauce

|Intro|: Do you love apples and wish to be able to eat them all year? Your wish is granted. If you have harvesting apples, or you simply bought too many apples than you can eat, this canning recipe is perfect to preserve them all year long, so you can enjoy eating them with a spoon, or serve them with some baked goods and enjoy!

### Equipment:
- 2 StockPots
- Rack
- Thongs
- Towel
- 9 Pint Jars
- Large Bowl
- Funnel

### Nutrition Facts per 1-Pint Jar

| Calories | 296.8kcal |
|----------|-----------|
| Carbs | 79.23g |
| Protein | 1.68g |
| Fats | 0.81g |

### Core Ingredients
- 14 pounds of fresh apples
- ½ cup of warm water
- ¼ cup of fresh or bottled lemon juice
- Granulated white sugar, to taste
- Cinnamon, to taste

### Step 1 – Preparing The Apple Sauce
- Start by peeling, coring, and roughly chopping the apples.
- Transfer them into a large stock pot with warm water, then cook them with the lid on for 12 to 16 minutes while stirring them occasionally until the apples become soft.
- Once the apples are cooked, turn off the heat, and place them aside to cool down while you prepare the jars.

### Step 2 – Sterilizing The Jars
- Start by sterilizing the jars where you will be storing the sauce, and make sure the rings are wiped clean.
- To sterilize the jars, bring a large pot of water to a boil, then turn off the heat, place the jars in it, and let them sit in it for 5 to 10 minutes.
- Use thongs to pull them out then place them with the lid down on a towel to dry.

### Step 3 – Preparing The Water Bath Canner
- To prepare for the canning process, fill a large stockpot with enough water to cover the jars by 1.5 to 2 inches.
- Bring it to a boil on high heat, then lower the heat and let it simmer while preparing the sauce.

## Step 5 – Packing

- Once the jars and the water bath canner are ready, place the apples back on medium-high heat, and add to them the remaining ingredients.
- Mix them until well combined, then bring the mixture to a boil.
- Turn off the heat, and spoon the sauce while it's hot into the jars while making sure to leave 1/8 to ¼-inch of the jar empty, then put on the lids and seal them.
- Wipe the sides of the jars with a clean and slightly wet rag, then put on the lids and secure them tightly. Press the center of the lids to ensure they are sealed properly.

## Step 5 - Canning

- Place the jars in a rack and lower them to the boiling water in the water bath canner.
- If you don't have a rack to use with your stockpot, you can make one using aluminum foil. Get 7 pieces of aluminum that are 6 inches tall, and roll them into stripes.
- Shape 3 stripes into circles by cramping their ends together, then use the remaining 4 pieces to make a net inside of the circle in a zig-zag pattern by cramping the ends of each stripe into the circle.
- Make sure all the jars are immersed and completely covered with water, if they are not, add more water until they are covered.
- Bring the water to a boil one more on medium to high heat, then put on the lid and let them process for 15 minutes at an altitude that is less than 1000. If you have a higher altitude, adjust your processing time according to your altitude, check the dedicated section. .

## Step 6 – Letting the Jars Rest

- Once the time is up, turn off the heat and remove the lid gently, and allow the jars to rest in the pot for 5 minutes without moving them.
- Once the time is up, you can remove the jars from the pot.
- Place them on a large towel, then let them cool down completely for at least 24 hours until they cool down.

## Step 7 - Storing

- Double check the jars to make sure they are sealed then you can store them for up to 18 months.

- If you find some jars that are not sealed properly, you can still store them in the fridge for up to 1 week and enjoy!

## Peach Salsa

**|Intro|:** This peach salsa or as it used to be called fruit relish is very simple and easy to prepare. It tastes fantastic over some bread slices, or you can serve it with some grilled meat, fish, or chicken for the combination of sweet and hot flavors turns out amazing. This salsa recipe is very mild, so it's perfect for everyone, but you if your family are fans of jalapenos, you can feel free to add more.

### Equipment:

- StockPot
- Rack
- Thongs
- Towel
- Saucepan
- 4 Pint Jars
- Large Bowl
- Funnel

### Nutrition Facts per ½ Pint Jar

| Calories | 77.48kcal |
|----------|-----------|
| Carbs | 19g |
| Protein | 1.7g |
| Fats | 0.49g |

### Core Ingredients

- 6 cups of fresh peaches, peeled, pitted, and diced
- ½ cup of white vinegar
- 1 ¼ cup of yellow or white onion, peeled and finely chopped
- 4 jalapenos, seeded and finely chopped
- 2/3 cup of red bell pepper, seeded and finely chopped
- ½ cup of coriander leaves, finely chopped
- 2 tablespoons of fresh or bottled lime juice
- 2 tablespoons of honey
- 1 ½ teaspoon of cumin
- ½ teaspoon of cayenne pepper
- 1 clove of garlic, peeled and minced

### Step 1 – Sterilizing The Jars

- Start by sterilizing the jars where you will be storing the sauce, and make sure the rings are wiped clean.
- To sterilize the jars, bring a large pot of water to a boil, then turn off the heat, place the jars in it, and let them sit in it for 5 to 10 minutes.
- Use thongs to pull them out then place them with the lid down on a towel to dry.

### Step 2 – Preparing The Water Bath Canner

- To prepare for the canning process, fill a large stockpot with enough water to cover the jars by 1.5 to 2 inches.
- Bring it to a boil on high heat, then lower the heat and let it simmer while preparing the sauce.

### Step 3 – Preparing The Peach Salsa

- Combine the peaches with vinegar in a large saucepan, and bring them to a boil.
- Lower the heat, and cook the peaches for 6 to 8 minutes stirring them constantly until they become soft.
- Add the remaining ingredients, and mix them until well combined.
- Lower the heat, and cook the salsa uncovered for 6 to 10 minutes while stirring occasionally until the veggies and peaches become soft, and the sauce becomes thick.

### Step 4 - Packing

- Once the sauce is done, quickly spoon it while it's hot into the sterilized jars, and make sure to leave 1/8 to ¼-inch of the space empty at the top of each jar.
- Wipe the sides of the jars with a clean and slightly wet rag, then put on the lids and secure them tightly. Press the center of the lids to ensure they are sealed properly.

### Step 5 - Canning

- Place the jars in a rack and lower them to the boiling water in the water bath canner.
- If you don't have a rack to use with your stockpot, you can make one using aluminum foil. Get 7 pieces of aluminum that are 6 inches tall, and roll them into stripes.
- Shape 3 stripes into circles by cramping their ends together, then use the remaining 4 pieces to make a net inside of the circle in a zig-zag pattern by cramping the ends of each stripe into the circle.

- Make sure all the jars are immersed and completely covered with water, if they are not, add more water until they are covered.
- Bring the water to a boil one more on medium to high heat, then put on the lid and let them process for 15 minutes at an altitude that is less than 1000. If you have a higher altitude, adjust your processing time according to your altitude, check the dedicated section. .

### Step 6 – Letting the Jars Rest

- Once the time is up, turn off the heat and remove the lid gently, then let the jars sit in the pot for 5 to 6 minutes to test.
- Once the time is up, drain the jars and place them on a large towel, then let them cool down completely for 24 hours until they cool down.

### Step 7 - Storing

- Double check the jars to make sure they are sealed then you can store them in a dark and cool place for up to 12 months.
- If you find some jars that are not sealed properly, you won't be able to store them in the pantry.
- You can still store them though in the fridge for up to 5 days, or in the freezer for 1 month and enjoy!

## Pickle Relish

|Intro|: Hot dogs, burgers, sandwiches, grilled meats, and chickens...you name it, this pickle relish tastes amazing as a topping with all these dishes. The veggies in this relish go together very well, combined with salt and honey, it's a party of flavors waiting to burst n your mouth.

### Equipment:

- StockPot
- Rack
- Thongs
- Towel
- Saucepan
- 6 Pint Jars
- Large Bowl
- Funnel
- Colander

**Nutrition Facts** per 1 tablespoon

| Calories | 7 kcal |
|----------|--------|
| Carbs    | 1.4g   |

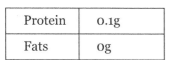

| | |
|---|---|
| Protein | 0.1g |
| Fats | 0g |

## Core Ingredients

- 8 cups of cucumbers, seeded and finely chopped
- 6 cups of yellow or white onion, finely chopped
- 3 cups of fresh green cabbage, finely chopped
- 1 cup of green bell pepper, seeded and finely chopped
- 1 cup of red bell pepper, seeded and finely chopped
- ½ cup of canning salt
- 5 cups of vinegar
- 1 cup of water
- ½ cup of honey
- 2 ½ teaspoons of mustard seeds
- 2 ½ teaspoons of celery seeds
- 2 teaspoons of turmeric

## Step 1 - Preparation

- Toss the cucumbers with onion, cabbage, bell peppers, and salt in a large bowl.
- Transfer the veggies mixture into a large colander, then let it sit for 6 hours to overnight to drain.

## Step 2 – Sterilizing The Jars

- Start by sterilizing the jars where you will be storing the relish, and make sure the rings are wiped clean.
- To sterilize the jars, bring a large pot of water to a boil, then turn off the heat, place the jars in it, and let them sit in it for 5 to 10 minutes.
- Use thongs to pull them out then place them with the lid down on a towel to dry.

## Step 3 – Preparing The Water Bath Canner

- To prepare for the canning process, fill a large stockpot with enough water to cover the jars by 1.5 to 2 inches.
- Bring it to a boil on high heat, then lower the heat and let it simmer while preparing the relish.

## Step 4 – Preparing The Relish

- Discard the liquid that accumulated from the veggies, rinse them well then drain well.

- Transfer the veggies into a large stockpot and add to them the remaining ingredients, then mix them until well combined.
- Bring the mixture to a boil over medium heat, then keep it boiling for 10 to 12 minutes while stirring it occasionally until the veggies become soft and tender, and the mixture thickens.

## Step 5 – Packing

- Turn off the heat, and spoon the relish while it's hot into the jars while making sure to leave 1/8 to ¼-inch of the jar empty, then put on the lids and seal them.
- Wipe the sides of the jars with a clean and slightly wet rag, then put on the lids and secure them tightly. Press the center of the lids to ensure they are sealed properly.

## Step 6 - Canning

- Place the jars in a rack and lower them to the boiling water in the water bath canner.
- If you don't have a rack to use with your stockpot, you can make one using aluminum foil. Get 7 pieces of aluminum that are 6 inches tall, and roll them into stripes.
- Shape 3 stripes into circles by cramping their ends together, then use the remaining 4 pieces to make a net inside of the circle in a zig-zag pattern by cramping the ends of each stripe into the circle.
- Make sure all the jars are immersed and completely covered with water, if they are not, add more water until they are covered.
- Bring the water to a boil one more on medium to high heat, then put on the lid and let them process for 10 minutes at an altitude that is less than 1000. If you have a higher altitude, adjust your processing time according to your altitude, check the dedicated section. .

## Step 7 – Letting the Jars Rest

- Once the time is up, turn off the heat and remove the lid gently, and allow the jars to rest in the pot for 5 minutes without moving them.
- Once the time is up, you can remove the jars from the pot.
- Place them on a large towel, then let them cool down completely for at least 24 hours until they cool down.

## Step 8 - Storing

- Double check the jars to make sure they are sealed then you can store them in a dark and cool place for up to 12 months.
- If you find some jars that are not sealed properly, you can still store them in the fridge for up to 4 weeks and enjoy!

# |Part 3| Pressure Canning Recipes

## Section 1: Pressure Canning Vegetables

### Asparagus

**|Intro|:** Pressure canning asparagus is a very easy process to enjoy asparagus all year round. The texture of the asparagus is softer than the frozen one, but the biggest advantage is that you can store it for a long time at room temperature without having to worry about it going bad if the power goes out.

#### Equipment:
- Pressure Canner
- Pot
- Rack/Trivet
- Thongs
- Towel
- 8 Pint Jars
- Funnel

**Nutrition Facts** per 1 cup

| Calories | 87 kcal |
|----------|---------|
| Carbs | 16g |
| Protein | 10g |
| Fats | 1g |

#### Core Ingredients
- 14 pounds of fresh asparagus, washed and trimmed
- 4 quarts of hot water
- 4 teaspoons of salt

#### Step 1 - Preparation
- Start by washing the asparagus, then trim off the tough ends enough to make the spears fit into the jars.

#### Step 2 – Sterilizing The Pint Jars
- To sterilize the jars, bring a large pot of water to a boil, then turn off the heat, place the jars in it, and let them sit in it for 5 to 10 minutes.
- Use thongs to pull them out then place them with the lid down on a towel to dry.

#### Step 3 – Preparing the pressure cooker
- Start by placing a trivet at the bottom of your pressure canner.
- Fill the pressure canner with enough water to cover the jars completely, and bring it to a simmer.

#### Step 4 - Packing
- Pack the asparagus tightly into the jars, then add to each jar ½ teaspoon of salt.
- Cover the asparagus with hot water while making sure to leave 1 inch at the top empty, then put on the lids and seal the jars tightly.
- Wipe the sides of the jars with a clean and slightly wet rag, then put on the lids and secure them tightly. Press the center of the lids to ensure they are sealed properly.

#### Step 5 – Pressure canning the asparagus
- Slowly lower the jars into the pressure canner to sit on the trivet.
- Put on the lid and seal it, then bring the pressure canner to pressure.
- Once the pressure canner comes up to pressure, allow the steam to continue to vent for 10 minutes to make sure there are no air pockets left in the canner.
- Process the asparagus for 30 minutes at 10 pounds of pressure for a weight gauge pressure canner, and at 11 pounds for 10 minutes if you are using a dial gauge pressure canner at an altitude of 1000 ft and less.
- Remember to adjust the processing time and pressure according to your altitude

#### Step 6 – Releasing the pressure
- Once the processing time is up, turn off the heat and allow the pressure canner to sit undisturbed until the pressure reaches 0.
- Do not move or attempt to open the pressure canner at all until all the pressure is released.

76

### Step 7 – Letting the jars rest

Once the pressure is released, open the pressure canner, and use thongs to gently remove the jars from the pot.

- Place them on a large towel, and let them cool down completely. They might take 12 to 24 hours.

### Step 8 – Storing

Double check the jars to make sure they are sealed then you can store them in a cool and dark place for up to 12 months.

If you find some jars that are not sealed properly, you can still store them in the fridge for up to 1 week and enjoy!

## Collard Greens – Pick Your Own

|Intro|: Collard greens might not be the first thing you think of canning because a lot of people think that their color might fade, however, that's not true. This recipe yields amazing canned greens that retain their color for a long time, and make for a great side dish, or an addition to your salads.

### Equipment:

- Pressure Canner
- Pot
- Rack/Trivet
- Thongs
- Towel
- 9 Pint Jars
- Funnel

#### Nutrition Facts per 1 Pint of Kale

| Calories | 328.94 kcal |
|----------|-------------|
| Carbs    | 58.74g      |
| Protein  | 28.73g      |
| Fats     | 6.24g       |

### Core Ingredients

- 18 pounds of fresh collard greens of your choice (kale, chard, spinach...)
- Salt (Optional)

### Step 1 - Preparation

- Start by washing and picking your greens to make sure they are all fresh and green.
- Remove any leaves that are damaged, wilted, or discolored, then place them in a colander to drain while preparing the jars.

Remove the tough stems and midribs because they become tough and bitter when canned.

### Step 2 – Sterilizing The Pint Jars

- To sterilize the jars, bring a large pot of water to a boil, then turn off the heat, place the jars in it, and let them sit in it for 5 to 10 minutes.
- Use thongs to pull them out then place them with the lid down on a towel to dry.

### Step 3 – Preparing the pressure cooker

- Start by placing a trivet at the bottom of your pressure canner.
- Fill the pressure canner with enough water to cover the jars completely, and bring it to a simmer.

### Step 4 - Packing

- Steam the greens in batches of 1 pound each for 4 minutes until they wilt.
- After you team each pound of greens pack it loosely into the jars, then add to each jar ½ teaspoon of salt.
- Cover the collard greens with hot water while making sure to leave 1 inch at the top empty, then put on the lids and seal the jars tightly.
- Wipe the sides of the jars with a clean and slightly wet rag, then put on the lids and secure them tightly. Press the center of the lids to ensure they are sealed properly.

### Step 6 – Pressure canning the collard greens

- Slowly lower the jars into the pressure canner to sit on the trivet.
- Put on the lid and seal it, then bring the pressure canner to pressure.
- Once the pressure canner comes up to pressure, allow the steam to continue to vent for 10 minutes to make sure there are no air pockets left in the canner.
- Process the collard greens for 70 minutes at 10 pounds of pressure for a weight gauge pressure canner, and at 11 pounds for 70 minutes if you are using a dial gauge pressure canner at an altitude of 1000 ft and less.

- Remember to adjust the processing time and pressure according to your altitude

### Step 7 – Releasing the pressure

- Once the processing time is up, turn off the heat and allow the pressure canner to sit undisturbed until the pressure reaches 0.
- Do not move or attempt to open the pressure canner at all until all the pressure is released.

### Step 8 – Letting the jars rest

Once the pressure is released, open the pressure canner, and use thongs to gently remove the jars from the pot.

- Place them on a large towel, and let them cool down completely. They might take 12 to 24 hours.

### Step 9 – Storing

Double check the jars to make sure they are sealed then you can store them in a cool and dark place for up to 12 months.

If you find some jars that are not sealed properly, you can still store them in the fridge for up to 2 weeks and enjoy!

## Corn

|Intro|: Corn is a great vegetable to have all year long and use in salads in the summer, in soups, and in stews in the winter. This makes it perfect to can and store so you can have it on hand whenever you wish without having to go all the way to the store, and it also saves you a lot of money so you don't even have to think about purchasing canned corn anymore. Also, you can use the corn cobs to make corn jelly when done. Two in one!

### Equipment:

- Pressure Canner
- Pot
- Bowl
- Rack/Trivet
- Thongs
- Towel
- 9 Pint Jars
- Funnel

### Nutrition Facts per ½ cup

| Calories | 70 kcal |
|----------|---------|
| Carbs | 13g |
| Protein | 1g |
| Fats | 0g |

### Core Ingredients

- 20 pounds of fresh ears of corn
- 8 cups of water
- 1/3 cup of white vinegar
- Salt (optional)

### Step 1 - Preparation

- Remove the corn husks and silk then wash them nicely.

Bring a large pot of water to a boil, then add to it the ears of corn, and cook them for 3 minutes on high heat.

In the meantime, fill a large bowl with cold water and some ice cubes.

Drain the ears of corn and add them to the cold water, then let them sit for a few minutes until they become cool down to the touch.

### Step 2 – Sterilizing The Pint Jars

- To sterilize the jars, bring a large pot of water to a boil, then turn off the heat, place the jars in it, and let them sit in it for 5 to 10 minutes.
- Use thongs to pull them out then place them with the lid down on a towel to dry.

### Step 3 – Preparing the pressure cooker

- Start by placing a trivet at the bottom of your pressure canner.
- Fill the pressure canner with enough water to cover the jars completely, and bring it to a simmer.

### Step 4 – Hot Packing

- Cut the corn from cobs but make sure to cut about 3/4th of depth only.
- Transfer the kernels to a large pot, then add to them 1 cup of water and bring them to a boil, and salt to taste if you wish to season them.
- Lower the heat, and simmer them for 5 minutes then ladle them into the jars while it's hot.
- Put on the lids and seal the jars tightly.
- Wipe the sides of the jars with a clean and slightly wet rag, then put on the lids and secure them tightly. Press the center of the lids to ensure they are sealed properly.

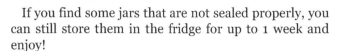

### Step 5 – Raw Packing

If you prefer to raw pack, cut the corn from cobs but make sure to cut about 3/4th of depth only.

- Transfer the kernels to the jars, add ½ teaspoon of salt to each jar if you wish, then cover them with boiling water while leaving 1 inch of space in the jars.
- Put on the lids and seal the jars tightly.
- Wipe the sides of the jars with a clean and slightly wet rag, then put on the lids and secure them tightly. Press the center of the lids to ensure they are sealed properly.

### Step 6 – Pressure canning the corn

- Slowly lower the jars into the pressure canner to sit on the trivet.
- Put on the lid and seal it, then bring the pressure canner to pressure.
- Once the pressure canner comes up to pressure, allow the steam to continue to vent for 10 minutes to make sure there are no air pockets left in the canner.
- Process the corn jars for 55 minutes at 10 pounds of pressure for a weight gauge pressure canner, and at 11 pounds for 55 minutes if you are using a dial gauge pressure canner at an altitude of 1000 ft and less.
- Remember to adjust the processing time and pressure according to your altitude

### Step 7 – Releasing the pressure

- Once the processing time is up, turn off the heat and allow the pressure canner to sit undisturbed until the pressure reaches 0.
- Do not move or attempt to open the pressure canner at all until all the pressure is released.

### Step 8 – Letting the jars rest

Once the pressure is released, open the pressure canner, and use thongs to gently remove the jars from the pot.

- Place them on a large towel, and let them cool down completely. They might take 12 to 24 hours.

### Step 9 – Storing

Double check the jars to make sure they are sealed then you can store them in a cool and dark place for up to 9 months.

If you find some jars that are not sealed properly, you can still store them in the fridge for up to 1 week and enjoy!

## Festive Pumpkins

|Intro|: Pumpkin is a super versatile vegetable that goes amazing with salads, soups, stews, and chili, and at the same time it makes a great pie filling, butter, cake...This recipe requires 2 ingredients only, pumpkin and water which makes canning easy, and will enable you to use it for both your savory and sweet meals.

### Equipment:

- Pressure Canner
- Rack/Trivet
- Thongs
- Towel
- 9 Pint Jars
- Funnel
- Plate
- Pot

### Nutrition Facts per ½ cup

| Calories | 50 kcal |
|----------|---------|
| Carbs | 10g |
| Protein | 1g |
| Fats | 0.5g |

### Core Ingredients

- 3 small sugar pie pumpkins (3 to 4 pounds each)
- 30 cups of water

### Step 1 – Sterilizing The Pint Jars

- Start by sterilizing the jars. Bring a large pot of water to a boil, then turn off the heat, place the jars in it, and let them sit in it for 5 to 10 minutes.
- Use thongs to pull them out then place them with the lid down on a towel to dry.

### Step 2 - Preparation

- Start by washing the pumpkins and pat them dry.
- Slice the pumpkins in half then, discard the stem and innards.
- Place the pumpkin half with the cut-up side facing down, then slice it into thick halves.

- Transfer some of the pumpkin slices to a plate, then working in batches, microwave them for 1 minute.
- Next, remove the rind from the slices, and slightly cut off the soft side in the middle as well to make sure to no strings are still stuck there.
- Cut the pumpkin slices into big pieces and place them aside.

## Step 3 – Preparing the pressure cooker
- Start by placing a trivet at the bottom of your pressure canner.
- Fill the pressure canner with enough water to cover the jars completely, and bring it to a simmer.

## Step 4 - Packing
- Bring a large pot of water to a boil, then cook in it the pumpkin pieces in batches for 2 minutes.
- Once the time is up, drain them, transfer them to the jars and pack them loosely.
- Cover them with clean hot water while making sure to leave 1 inch at the top empty, then put on the lids and seal the jars tightly.
- Wipe the sides of the jars with a clean and slightly wet rag, then put on the lids and secure them tightly. Press the center of the lids to ensure they are sealed properly.

## Step 5 – Pressure canning the pumpkins
- Slowly lower the jars into the pressure canner to sit on the trivet.
- Put on the lid and seal it, then bring the pressure canner to pressure.
- Once the pressure canner comes up to pressure, allow the steam to continue to vent for 10 minutes to make sure there are no air pockets left in the canner.
- Process the pumpkin jars for 55 minutes at 10 pounds of pressure for a weight gauge pressure canner, and at 11 pounds for 55 minutes if you are using a dial gauge pressure canner at an altitude of 1000 ft and less.
- Remember to adjust the processing time and pressure according to your altitude

## Step 6 – Releasing the pressure
- Once the processing time is up, turn off the heat and allow the pressure canner to sit undisturbed until the pressure reaches 0.
- Do not move or attempt to open the pressure canner at all until all the pressure is released.

## Step 7 – Letting the jars rest
Once the pressure is released, open the pressure canner, and use thongs to gently remove the jars from the pot.

- Place them on a large towel, and let them cool down completely. They might take 12 to 24 hours.

## Step 8 – Storing
Double check the jars to make sure they are sealed then you can store them in a cool and dark place for up to 12 months.

If you find some jars that are not sealed properly, you can still store them in the fridge for up to 2 weeks and enjoy!

## Life-Saving Tomatoes
|Intro|: Canned quartered or whole tomatoes are a pantry staple ingredient that is required for a lot of recipes, they add an amazing flavor to your meals that you can't get with fresh tomatoes, they are healthy, and will save you a lot of money.

### Equipment:
- Pressure Canner
- Rack/Trivet
- Thongs
- Towel
- 8 Pint Jars
- Funnel

### Nutrition Facts per ½ cup

| Calories | 21 kcal |
|----------|---------|
| Carbs | 5g |
| Protein | 1g |
| Fats | 0g |

### Core Ingredients
- 8 pounds of ripe tomatoes
- 8 tablespoons of bottled lemon juice
- 4 teaspoons of sea salt (optional)

## Step 1 - Preparation
- Start by washing and peeling the tomatoes, then depending on what you prefer, leave them whole and cut them in half if they are too big.

### Step 2 – Sterilizing The Pint Jars

- To sterilize the jars, bring a large pot of water to a boil, then turn off the heat, place the jars in it, and let them sit in it for 5 to 10 minutes.
- Use thongs to pull them out then place them with the lid down on a towel to dry.

### Step 3 – Preparing the pressure cooker

- Start by placing a trivet at the bottom of your pressure canner.
- Fill the pressure canner with enough water to cover the jars completely, and bring it to a simmer.

### Step 4 – Packing

If you wish to season your tomatoes, put ½ teaspoon of salt into each jar, if not you can omit it.

Pack the tomatoes tightly into the jars by pressing them to make sure there is no space left at the bottom.

If you have any tomato liquid from peeling the tomatoes, pour it into the jars if not use water until there is ½ inch of space left.

- Put on the lids and seal the jars tightly.
- Wipe the sides of the jars with a clean and slightly wet rag, then put on the lids and secure them tightly. Press the center of the lids to ensure they are sealed properly.

### Step 5 – Pressure canning the tomatoes

- Slowly lower the jars into the pressure canner to sit on the trivet.
- Put on the lid and seal it, then bring the pressure canner to pressure.
- Once the pressure canner comes up to pressure, allow the steam to continue to vent for 10 minutes to make sure there are no air pockets left in the canner.
- Process the tomato jars for 25 minutes at 10 pounds of pressure for a weight gauge pressure canner, and at 11 pounds for 25 minutes if you are using a dial gauge pressure canner at an altitude of 1000 ft and less.
- Remember to adjust the processing time and pressure according to your altitude

### Step 6 – Releasing the pressure

- Once the processing time is up, turn off the heat and allow the pressure canner to sit undisturbed until the pressure reaches 0.
- Do not move or attempt to open the pressure canner at all until all the pressure is released.

### Step 7 – Letting the jars rest

Once the pressure is released, open the pressure canner, and use thongs to gently remove the jars from the pot.

- Place them on a large towel, and let them cool down completely. They might take 12 to 24 hours.

### Step 8 – Storing

Double check the jars to make sure they are sealed then you can store them in a cool and dark place for up to 18 months.

If you find some jars that are not sealed properly, you can still store them in the fridge for up to 1 week and enjoy!

## Okra

**|Intro|:** Okra is the queen of vegetables, it's super delicious but most important of all, it is super healthy. Canning is so easy and will enable you to enjoy it all year long without having to wait for it to be in season. It tastes amazing in soups, stew, and fried.

### Equipment:

- Pressure Canner
- Rack/Trivet
- Thongs
- Towel
- 4 Pint Jars
- Funnel
- Saucepan

**Nutrition Facts** per 1 cup

| Calories | 84.59 kcal |
|----------|-----------|
| Carbs | 17.97g |
| Protein | 4.58g |
| Fats | 0.45g |

### Core Ingredients

- 3 quarts of Okra
- 7 cups of water
- 8 tablespoons of apple cider vinegar
- 1 ½ tablespoon of sea salt

### Step 1 - Preparation

- Start by brushing the okra and cleaning it properly then wash it and place it in a colander to drain.

### Step 2 – Sterilizing The Pint Jars

- In the meantime sterilize the jars, bring a large pot of water to a boil, then turn off the heat, place the jars in it, and let them sit in it for 5 to 10 minutes.
- Use thongs to pull them out then place them with the lid down on a towel to dry.

### Step 3 – Preparing the pressure cooker

- Start by placing a trivet at the bottom of your pressure canner.
- Fill the pressure canner with enough water to cover the jars completely, and bring it to a simmer.

### Step 4 – Packing

Cut the okra into bite-size pieces.

Pour the water into a large saucepan, then add to it the vinegar with salt and bring them to a boil.

Stir in the okra, then lower the heat and let it simmer for 6 minutes.

Once the time is up, pack the okra mixture into the jars while it's hot, then cover it with its cooking liquid while leaving ½ inch of the space empty in the jars.

- Put on the lids and seal the jars tightly.
- Wipe the sides of the jars with a clean and slightly wet rag, then put on the lids and secure them tightly. Press the center of the lids to ensure they are sealed properly.

### Step 5 – Pressure canning the okra

- Slowly lower the jars into the pressure canner to sit on the trivet.
- Put on the lid and seal it, then bring the pressure canner to pressure.
- Once the pressure canner comes up to pressure, allow the steam to continue to vent for 10 minutes to make sure there are no air pockets left in the canner.
- Process the okra jars for 40 minutes at 10 pounds of pressure for a weight gauge pressure canner, and at 11 pounds for 40 minutes if you are using a dial gauge pressure canner at an altitude of 1000 ft and less.
- Remember to adjust the processing time and pressure according to your altitude

### Step 6 – Releasing the pressure

- Once the processing time is up, turn off the heat and allow the pressure canner to sit undisturbed until the pressure reaches 0.
- Do not move or attempt to open the pressure canner at all until all the pressure is released.

### Step 7 – Letting the jars rest

Once the pressure is released, open the pressure canner, and use thongs to gently remove the jars from the pot.

- Place them on a large towel, and let them cool down completely. They might take 12 to 24 hours.

### Step 8 – Storing

Double check the jars to make sure they are sealed then you can store them in a cool and dark place for up to 18 months.

If you find some jars that are not sealed properly, you can still store them in the fridge for up to 1 week and enjoy!

## Sweet Peas

|Intro|: Who doesn't like peas? Just like corn and pumpkin, they make for great food to can and have all year round to use with your salads, soups, chilies, and stews. They also make for a great side dish when heated with a stick of butter.

### Equipment:

- Pressure Canner
- Rack/Trivet
- Thongs
- Towel
- 9 Pint Jars
- Funnel
- Pot

### Nutrition Facts per 1 cup

| Calories | 408.23 kcal |
|----------|-------------|
| Carbs    | 72.83g      |
| Protein  | 27.32g      |
| Fats     | 2.02g       |

### Core Ingredients

- 20 pounds of fresh green peas, peeled

- 9 teaspoons of canning salt (optional)
- Water

## Step 1 - Preparation

- Start by washing the peas nicely, then place them in a colander and let them drain.

## Step 2 – Sterilizing The Pint Jars

- To sterilize the jars, bring a large pot of water to a boil, then turn off the heat, place the jars in it, and let them sit in it for 5 to 10 minutes.
- Use thongs to pull them out then place them with the lid down on a towel to dry.

## Step 3 – Preparing the pressure cooker

- Start by placing a trivet at the bottom of your pressure canner.
- Fill the pressure canner with enough water to cover the jars completely, and bring it to a simmer.

## Step 4 – Hot Packing

- Bring a large pot of water to a boil, then cook in it the peas for 2 minutes.
- Once the time is up, drain the, and transfer them to the jars while they are hot.
- If you wish to season the peas, add 1 teaspoon of salt to each jar, if not you can leave it out.
- Cover the peas with fresh boiling water while making sure to leave ½ inch of space empty then put on the lids and seal them tightly.
- Wipe the sides of the jars with a clean and slightly wet rag, then put on the lids and secure them tightly. Press the center of the lids to ensure they are sealed properly.

## Step 4 – Raw Packing

If you prefer to use the raw packing method instead, add the peas after washing them to the jars.

If you wish to season them, add 1 teaspoon of salt to each jar, if not you can leave it out.

Cover the peas with boiling water while leaving ½ inch of space empty at the top, then put on the lids and seal them tightly.

- Wipe the sides of the jars with a clean and slightly wet rag, then put on the lids and secure them tightly. Press the center of the lids to ensure they are sealed properly.

## Step 6 – Pressure canning the peas

- Slowly lower the jars into the pressure canner to sit on the trivet.
- Put on the lid and seal it, then bring the pressure canner to pressure.
- Once the pressure canner comes up to pressure, allow the steam to continue to vent for 10 minutes to make sure there are no air pockets left in the canner.
- Process the peas jars for 40 minutes at 10 pounds of pressure for a weight gauge pressure canner, and at 11 pounds for 40 minutes if you are using a dial gauge pressure canner at an altitude of 1000 ft and less.
- Remember to adjust the processing time and pressure according to your altitude

## Step 7 – Releasing the pressure

- Once the processing time is up, turn off the heat and allow the pressure canner to sit undisturbed until the pressure reaches 0.
- Do not move or attempt to open the pressure canner at all until all the pressure is released.

## Step 8 – Letting the jars rest

Once the pressure is released, open the pressure canner, and use thongs to gently remove the jars from the pot.

- Place them on a large towel, and let them cool down completely. They might take 12 to 24 hours.

## Step 9 – Storing

Double check the jars to make sure they are sealed then you can store them in a cool and dark place for up to 12 months.

If you find some jars that are not sealed properly, you can still store them in the fridge for up to 2 weeks and enjoy!

## Green Beans

|Intro|: Green beans is a very easy vegetable to grow and care for, so if you have a big harvest that you don't know what to do with, or you simply bought too much, this recipe is a great way to preserve your beans and use them all year. You can add it to your stew and salads, or toss it with some butter and enjoy it warm!

## Equipment:

- Pressure Canner

- Rack/Trivet
- Thongs
- Towel
- 9 Pint Jars
- Funnel
- Pot

### Nutrition Facts per 1 tablespoon

| Calories | 78 kcal |
|----------|---------|
| Carbs | 18g |
| Protein | 4.6g |
| Fats | 0.3g |

## Core Ingredients

- 10 pounds of fresh green beans, trimmed
- Canning salt

## Step 1 - Preparation

- Wash the beans, trim them, and cut them into 1-inch pieces.

## Step 2 – Sterilizing The Pint Jars

- To sterilize the jars, bring a large pot of water to a boil, then turn off the heat, place the jars in it, and let them sit in it for 5 to 10 minutes.
- Use thongs to pull them out then place them with the lid down on a towel to dry.

## Step 3 – Preparing the pressure cooker

- Start by placing a trivet at the bottom of your pressure canner.
- Fill the pressure canner with enough water to cover the jars completely, and bring it to a simmer.

## Step 4 – Hot Packing

- Bring a large pot of water to a boil, then cook in it the green beans for 5 minutes.
- Once the time is up, drain the, and transfer them to the jars while they are hot.
- If you wish to season the beans, add 1 teaspoon of salt to each jar, if not you can leave it out.
- Cover the beans with fresh boiling water while making sure to leave ½ inch of space empty then put on the lids and seal them tightly.
- Wipe the sides of the jars with a clean and slightly wet rag, then put on the lids and secure them tightly. Press the center of the lids to ensure they are sealed properly.

## Step 5 – Raw Packing

If you prefer to use the raw packing method instead, add the beans after washing them to the jars.

If you wish to season them, add 1 teaspoon of salt to each jar, if not you can leave it out.

Cover the beans with boiling water while leaving ½ inch of space empty at the top, then put on the lids and seal them tightly.

- Wipe the sides of the jars with a clean and slightly wet rag, then put on the lids and secure them tightly. Press the center of the lids to ensure they are sealed properly.

## Step 6 – Pressure canning the peas

- Slowly lower the jars into the pressure canner to sit on the trivet.
- Put on the lid and seal it, then bring the pressure canner to pressure.
- Once the pressure canner comes up to pressure, allow the steam to continue to vent for 10 minutes to make sure there are no air pockets left in the canner.
- Process the green beans jars for 20 minutes at 10 pounds of pressure for a weight gauge pressure canner, and at 11 pounds for 20 minutes if you are using a dial gauge pressure canner at an altitude of 1000 ft and less.
- Remember to adjust the processing time and pressure according to your altitude

## Step 7 – Releasing the pressure

- Once the processing time is up, turn off the heat and allow the pressure canner to sit undisturbed until the pressure reaches 0.
- Do not move or attempt to open the pressure canner at all until all the pressure is released.

## Step 8 – Letting the jars rest

Once the pressure is released, open the pressure canner, and use thongs to gently remove the jars from the pot.

- Place them on a large towel, and let them cool down completely. They might take 12 to 24 hours.

### Step 9 – Storing

Double check the jars to make sure they are sealed then you can store them in a cool and dark place for up to 12 months.

If you find some jars that are not sealed properly, you can still store them in the fridge for up to 2 weeks and enjoy!

## Homemade Canned Butternut Squash

**Intro|:** Butternut squash is one of the easiest vegetables to can, and most popular especially in the winter when you require diced veggies. By canning it, you could easily pull out a jar and add it to your stews, chilies, or soup, and enjoy!

### Equipment:

Pressure Canner

Rack/Trivet

Thongs

Towel

9 Pint Jars

Funnel

Plate

Pot

**Nutrition Facts** per 1 pound (without salt)

| Calories | 134.72 kcal |
|----------|-------------|
| Carbs | 35g |
| Protein | 2.99g |
| Fats | 0.3g |

### Core Ingredients

- Fresh butternut squash
- Boiling Water
- Salt (Optional)

### Step 1 – Sterilizing The Pint Jars

- Start by sterilizing the jars. Bring a large pot of water to a boil, then turn off the heat, place the jars in it, and let them sit in it for 5 to 10 minutes.
- Use thongs to pull them out then place them with the lid down on a towel to dry.

### Step 2 - Preparation

- Start by washing the butternut squash, then peel it and cut it into cubes of the size you prefer.

### Step 3 – Preparing the pressure cooker

- Start by placing a trivet at the bottom of your pressure canner.
- Fill the pressure canner with enough water to cover the jars completely, and bring it to a simmer.

### Step 4 - Packing

- Bring a large pot of water to a boil, then cook in it the butternut squash cubes for 2 minutes.
- If you wish to salt them, then add a bit of salt to the water while cooking them.
- Once the time is up, drain them, transfer them to the jars and pack them loosely.
- Cover them with clean hot water while making sure to leave 1 inch at the top empty, then put on the lids and seal the jars tightly.
- Wipe the sides of the jars with a clean and slightly wet rag, then put on the lids and secure them tightly. Press the center of the lids to ensure they are sealed properly.

### Step 5 – Pressure canning the butternut squash

- Slowly lower the jars into the pressure canner to sit on the trivet.
- Put on the lid and seal it, then bring the pressure canner to pressure.
- Once the pressure canner comes up to pressure, allow the steam to continue to vent for 10 minutes to make sure there are no air pockets left in the canner.
- Process the pumpkin jars for 55 minutes at 10 pounds of pressure for a weight gauge pressure canner, and at 11 pounds for 55 minutes if you are using a dial gauge pressure canner at an altitude of 1000 ft and less.
- Make sure to adjust the processing weight according to your altitude, check the dedicated section.

### Step 6 – Releasing the pressure

- Once the processing time is up, turn off the heat and allow the pressure canner to sit undisturbed until the pressure reaches 0.
- Do not move or attempt to open the pressure canner at all until all the pressure is released.

### Step 7 – Letting the jars rest

- Once the pressure is released, open the pressure canner, and use thongs to gently remove the jars from the pot.
- Place them on a large towel, and let them cool down completely. They might take 12 to 24 hours.

### Step 8 – Storing

- Double check the jars to make sure they are sealed then you can store them in a cool and dark place for up to 12 months.
- If you find some jars that are not sealed properly, you can still store them in the fridge for up to 2 weeks and enjoy!

## Section 2: Pressure Canning Root Vegetables & Tubers

### Yummy Carrots

**|Intro|**: Canning carrots are the perfect way to preserve them and always have them on hand whenever you need them. What's best about canning them though, is that the canning and storing process seems to enhance their flavor, and make them taste even better. You may can them with salt or without it, either way, they taste fantastic.

### Equipment:

- Pressure Canner
- Rack/Trivet
- Thongs
- Towel
- 9 Pint Jars
- Funnel

**Nutrition Facts** per 1 tablespoon

| Calories | 202.3 kcal |
|----------|------------|
| Carbs    | 47.27g     |
| Protein  | 4.59g      |
| Fats     | 1.18g      |

### Core Ingredients

- 11 pounds of fresh and green carrots
- Salt

### Step 1 - Preparation

- Wash the carrots, trim their ends and remove the tops.
- Depending on what you like, cut the carrots into sticks or chunks.

### Step 2 – Sterilizing The Pint Jars

- To sterilize the jars, bring a large pot of water to a boil, then turn off the heat, place the jars in it, and let them sit in it for 5 to 10 minutes.
- Use thongs to pull them out then place them with the lid down on a towel to dry.

### Step 3 – Preparing the pressure cooker

- Start by placing a trivet at the bottom of your pressure canner.
- Fill the pressure canner with enough water to cover the jars completely, and bring it to a simmer.

### Step 4 – Hot Packing

- Bring a large pot of water to a boil, then cook in it the carrots for 5 minutes.
- Once the time is up, drain the, and transfer them to the jars while they are hot.
- If you wish to season your carrots, add 1 teaspoon of salt to each jar, if not you can leave it out.
- Cover the carrots with fresh boiling water while making sure to leave ½ inch of space empty then put on the lids and seal them tightly.
- Wipe the sides of the jars with a clean and slightly wet rag, then put on the lids and secure them tightly. Press the center of the lids to ensure they are sealed properly.

### Step 4 – Raw Packing

If you prefer to use the raw packing method instead, add the carrots after washing them to the jars.

If you wish to season them, add 1 teaspoon of salt to each jar, if not you can leave it out.

Cover the carrots with boiling water while leaving ½ inch of space empty at the top, then put on the lids and seal them tightly.

- Wipe the sides of the jars with a clean and slightly wet rag, then put on the lids and secure them tightly. Press the center of the lids to ensure they are sealed properly.

### Step 6 – Pressure canning the carrots

- Slowly lower the jars into the pressure canner to sit on the trivet.
- Put on the lid and seal it, then bring the pressure canner to pressure.
- Once the pressure canner comes up to pressure, allow the steam to continue to vent for 10 minutes to make sure there are no air pockets left in the canner.
- Process the carrot jars for 25 minutes at 10 pounds of pressure for a weight gauge pressure canner, and at 11 pounds for 25 minutes if you are using a dial gauge pressure canner at an altitude of 1000 ft and less.
- Remember to adjust the processing time and pressure according to your altitude

### Step 7 – Releasing the pressure

- Once the processing time is up, turn off the heat and allow the pressure canner to sit undisturbed until the pressure reaches 0.
- Do not move or attempt to open the pressure canner at all until all the pressure is released.

### Step 8 – Letting the jars rest

Once the pressure is released, open the pressure canner, and use thongs to gently remove the jars from the pot.

- Place them on a large towel, and let them cool down completely. They might take 12 to 24 hours.

### Step 9 – Storing

Double check the jars to make sure they are sealed then you can store them in a cool and dark place for up to 12 months.

If you find some jars that are not sealed properly, you can still store them in the fridge for up to 3 weeks and enjoy!

## Beets

|Intro|: Most people prefer pickled beets to plain beets, however, this recipe will change your mind for sure. It uses Chioggia beets, they are a sweet type of beets, so it's perfect for canning. Storing it for a long time causes the beet's lovely red color to fade, however, the taste intensifies, and turns out even more delicious.

### Equipment:

- Pressure Canner
- Rack/Trivet
- Thongs
- Towel
- 6 Pint Jars
- Funnel
- Pot
- Large Bowl

### Nutrition Facts per 1 Pint Jar

| Calories | 159.36 kcal |
|----------|-------------|
| Carbs | 35.41g |
| Protein | 5.96g |
| Fats | 0.63g |

### Core Ingredients

- 10 pounds of Chioggia beets
- Water

### Step 1 - Preparation

- Start by washing and scrubbing the beets until they become nicely cleaned.
- Trim their stems but leave their roots attached.
- Bring a large pot of water to a boil then add to it the beets gently, and simmer it over low heat with the lid on for 25 to 30 minutes until they become soft.

### Step 2 – Sterilizing The Pint Jars

- To sterilize the jars, bring a large pot of water to a boil, then turn off the heat, place the jars in it, and let them sit in it for 5 to 10 minutes.
- Use thongs to pull them out then place them with the lid down on a towel to dry.

### Step 3 – Preparing the pressure cooker

- Start by placing a trivet at the bottom of your pressure canner.
- Fill the pressure canner with enough water to cover the jars completely, and bring it to a simmer.

### Step 4 – Packing

- Once the beets are cooked, drain them and transfer them to a large bowl, then cover them with cold water.
- Allow the beets to sit in the water until they become cool to the touch enough to be able to handle them.

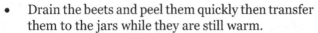

- Drain the beets and peel them quickly then transfer them to the jars while they are still warm.
- Cover the beets with fresh boiling water while making sure to leave ½ inch of space empty then put on the lids and seal them tightly.
- If you wish to season them, ½ teaspoon of salt to each jar, if not, you can leave it out then seal then put on the lids, and seal them.
- Wipe the sides of the jars with a clean and slightly wet rag, then put on the lids and secure them tightly. Press the center of the lids to ensure they are sealed properly.

## Step 5 – Pressure canning the beets

- Slowly lower the jars into the pressure canner to sit on the trivet.
- Put on the lid and seal it, then bring the pressure canner to pressure.
- Once the pressure canner comes up to pressure, allow the steam to continue to vent for 10 minutes to make sure there are no air pockets left in the canner.
- Process the beet jars for 30 minutes at 10 pounds of pressure for a weight gauge pressure canner, and at 11 pounds for 30 minutes if you are using a dial gauge pressure canner at an altitude of 1000 ft and less.
- Remember to adjust the processing time and pressure according to your altitude

## Step 6 – Releasing the pressure

- Once the processing time is up, turn off the heat and allow the pressure canner to sit undisturbed until the pressure reaches 0.
- Do not move or attempt to open the pressure canner at all until all the pressure is released.

## Step 7 – Letting the jars rest

Once the pressure is released, open the pressure canner, and use thongs to gently remove the jars from the pot.

- Place them on a large towel, and let them cool down completely. They might take 12 to 24 hours.

## Step 8 – Storing

Double check the jars to make sure they are sealed then you can store them in a cool and dark place for up to 12 months.

If you find some jars that are not sealed properly, you can still store them in the fridge for up to 3 weeks and enjoy!

## Onions

|Intro|: Onions are a staple vegetable that you just can't afford to not have stocked in your house. Canned onions make them soft and very flavorful, so they make the perfect condiment to add to stew, burgers, sandwiches, and sauces.

### Equipment:

- Pressure Canner
- Rack/Trivet
- Thongs
- Towel
- 10 Pint Jars
- Funnel
- Pot

**Nutrition Facts** per 1 Pint Jar

| Calories | 161.48 kcal |
|----------|-------------|
| Carbs | 37.71g |
| Protein | 4.44g |
| Fats | 0.4g |

### Core Ingredients

- 10 pounds of fresh red onions
- Water
- 5 teaspoons of canning salt

### Step 1 – Sterilizing The Pint Jars

- To sterilize the jars, bring a large pot of water to a boil, then turn off the heat, place the jars in it, and let them sit in it for 5 to 10 minutes.
- Use thongs to pull them out then place them with the lid down on a towel to dry.

### Step 2 – Preparing the pressure cooker

- Start by placing a trivet at the bottom of your pressure canner.
- Fill the pressure canner with enough water to cover the jars completely, and bring it to a simmer.

### Step 3 - Preparation

- Peel the onions and wash them.
- If you are using small onions you can keep them as they are, if you are using medium or large onions, slice them.
- Bring a large pot of water to a boil, then cook in it the onions for 5 minutes until they become soft.

### Step 4 – Packing

- Once the onions are cooked, drain them and transfer them while hot into the jars and pack them tightly.
- Cover the onions with fresh boiling water while making sure to leave 1 to ½ inch of space empty then put on the lids and seal them tightly.
- If you wish to season them, ½ teaspoon of salt to each jar, if not, you can leave it out.
- Wipe the sides of the jars with a clean and slightly wet rag, then put on the lids and secure them tightly. Press the center of the lids to ensure they are sealed properly.

### Step 5 – Pressure canning the onions

- Slowly lower the jars into the pressure canner to sit on the trivet.
- Put on the lid and seal it, then bring the pressure canner to pressure.
- Once the pressure canner comes up to pressure, allow the steam to continue to vent for 10 minutes to make sure there are no air pockets left in the canner.
- Process the onion jars for 40 minutes at 10 pounds of pressure for a weight gauge pressure canner, and at 11 pounds for 40 minutes if you are using a dial gauge pressure canner at an altitude of 1000 ft and less.
- Remember to adjust the processing time and pressure according to your altitude

### Step 6 – Releasing the pressure

- Once the processing time is up, turn off the heat and allow the pressure canner to sit undisturbed until the pressure reaches 0.
- Do not move or attempt to open the pressure canner at all until all the pressure is released.

### Step 7 – Letting the jars rest

Once the pressure is released, open the pressure canner, and use thongs to gently remove the jars from the pot.

- Place them on a large towel, and let them cool down completely. They might take 12 to 24 hours.

### Step 8 – Storing

Double check the jars to make sure they are sealed then you can store them in a cool and dark place for up to 12 months.

If you find some jars that are not sealed properly, you can still store them in the fridge for up to 3 weeks and enjoy!

## Rutabega

**|Intro|**: Rutabaga or swede is a root vegetable that resembles a turnip, but it's not a turnip. It has a nice orange color on the inside and tastes like a slightly sweet combination of turnips and cabbages. You can serve it as a side dish, add it to a salad, or turn it into a puree. It's better to consume it though in the first few months of storing because its tastes become too strong if left for a long.

### Equipment:

- Pressure Canner
- Rack/Trivet
- Thongs
- Towel
- 8 Pint Jars
- Funnel
- Pot

**Nutrition Facts** per 1 Pint Jar

| Calories | 77.56 kcal |
| --- | --- |
| Carbs | 18.07g |
| Protein | 2.26g |
| Fats | 0.34g |

### Core Ingredients

- 12 cups of rutabaga, peeled and diced
- Water

### Step 1 – Sterilizing The Pint Jars

- To sterilize the jars, bring a large pot of water to a boil, then turn off the heat, place the jars in it, and let them sit in it for 5 to 10 minutes.
- Use thongs to pull them out then place them with the lid down on a towel to dry.

### Step 2 – Preparing the pressure cooker

- Start by placing a trivet at the bottom of your pressure canner.
- Fill the pressure canner with enough water to cover the jars completely, and bring it to a simmer.

### Step 3 - Preparation

- Wash and scrub the rutabagas until clean, then peel them, and cut them into 1 ½ to 2 inches thick chunks.
- Bring a large pot of water to a boil, then cook in it the rutabaga chunks for 4 to 6 minutes until they become tender.

### Step 4 – Packing

- Once the rutabaga chunks are cooked, drain them and transfer them while hot in the jars and pack them gently to not crush them.
- Cover the rutabaga chunks with fresh boiling water while making sure to leave 1 to ½ inch of space empty then put on the lids and seal them tightly.
- If you wish to season them, ½ teaspoon of salt to each jar, if not, you can leave it out.
- Wipe the sides of the jars with a clean and slightly wet rag, then put on the lids and secure them tightly. Press the center of the lids to ensure they are sealed properly.

### Step 5 – Pressure canning the rutabaga

- Slowly lower the jars into the pressure canner to sit on the trivet.
- Put on the lid and seal it, then bring the pressure canner to pressure.
- Once the pressure canner comes up to pressure, allow the steam to continue to vent for 10 minutes to make sure there are no air pockets left in the canner.
- Process the rutabaga jars for 30 minutes at 10 pounds of pressure for a weight gauge pressure canner, and at 11 pounds for 30 minutes if you are using a dial gauge pressure canner at an altitude of 1000 ft and less.
- Remember to adjust the processing time and pressure according to your altitude

### Step 6 – Releasing the pressure

- Once the processing time is up, turn off the heat and allow the pressure canner to sit undisturbed until the pressure reaches 0.

- Do not move or attempt to open the pressure canner at all until all the pressure is released.

### Step 7 – Letting the jars rest

Once the pressure is released, open the pressure canner, and use thongs to gently remove the jars from the pot.

- Place them on a large towel, and let them cool down completely. They might take 12 to 24 hours.

### Step 8 – Storing

Double check the jars to make sure they are sealed then you can store them in a cool and dark place for up to 16 months.

If you find some jars that are not sealed properly, you can still store them in the fridge for up to 3 weeks and enjoy!

## Turnip

|**Intro**|: Pressure canning turnips in water is one of the simplest and easiest ways to preserve them for a whole year while keeping them versatile and ideal to use with a lot of recipes because their flavors don't change, it just gets better.

### Equipment:

- Pressure Canner
- Rack/Trivet
- Thongs
- Towel
- 8 Pint Jars
- Funnel
- Pot

**Nutrition Facts** per 1 Pint Jar

| Calories | 54.7 kcal |
|----------|-----------|
| Carbs | 12.56g |
| Protein | 17.6g |
| Fats | 0.2g |

### Core Ingredients

- 12 cups of turnip, peeled and diced
- Water

### Step 1 – Sterilizing The Pint Jars

- To sterilize the jars, bring a large pot of water to a boil, then turn off the heat, place the jars in it, and let them sit in it for 5 to 10 minutes.
- Use thongs to pull them out then place them with the lid down on a towel to dry.

### Step 2 – Preparing the pressure cooker

- Start by placing a trivet at the bottom of your pressure canner.
- Fill the pressure canner with enough water to cover the jars completely, and bring it to a simmer.

### Step 3 - Preparation

- Peel the turnips and peel them, then cut them into 1-inch thick cubes or sticks.

Bring a large pot of water to a boil, then cook in it the turnip cubes for 5 to 6 minutes until they become soft and tender.

### Step 4 – Packing

- Once the turnips are cooked, drain them and transfer them while hot in the jars and pack them gently to not crush them.
- Cover the turnips with fresh boiling water while making sure to leave 1 to ½ inch of space empty then put on the lids and seal them tightly.
- If you wish to season them, ½ teaspoon of salt to each jar, if not, you can leave it out.
- Wipe the sides of the jars with a clean and slightly wet rag, then put on the lids and secure them tightly. Press the center of the lids to ensure they are sealed properly.

### Step 5 – Pressure canning the turnips

- Slowly lower the jars into the pressure canner to sit on the trivet.
- Put on the lid and seal it, then bring the pressure canner to pressure.
- Once the pressure canner comes up to pressure, allow the steam to continue to vent for 10 minutes to make sure there are no air pockets left in the canner.
- Process the turnip jars for 30 minutes at 10 pounds of pressure for a weight gauge pressure canner, and at 11 pounds for 30 minutes if you are using a dial gauge pressure canner at an altitude of 1000 ft and less.
- Remember to adjust the processing time and pressure according to your altitude

### Step 6 – Releasing the pressure

- Once the processing time is up, turn off the heat and allow the pressure canner to sit undisturbed until the pressure reaches 0.
- Do not move or attempt to open the pressure canner at all until all the pressure is released.

### Step 7 – Letting the jars rest

Once the pressure is released, open the pressure canner, and use thongs to gently remove the jars from the pot.

- Place them on a large towel, and let them cool down completely. They might take 12 to 24 hours.

### Step 8 – Storing

Double check the jars to make sure they are sealed then you can store them in a cool and dark place for up to 18 months.

If you find some jars that are not sealed properly, you can still store them in the fridge for up to 3 weeks and enjoy!

## Sweet Potatoes

|Intro|: Sweet potatoes are an ideal food to have available at all time, in all seasons, for it is perfect for all occasions. Salads, side dishes, baked goods...whatever it is, you name it, sweet potatoes are perfect. Also the longer you store them, the better they taste.

### Equipment:

- Pressure Canner
- Rack/Trivet
- Thongs
- Towel
- 5 Pint Jars
- Funnel
- Pot

#### Nutrition Facts per 1 tablespoon

| Calories | 7 kcal |
|----------|--------|
| Carbs | 1.4g |
| Protein | 0.1g |
| Fats | 0g |

### Core Ingredients

- 6 pounds of sweet potatoes, peeled

- 5 ¼ cup of water
- 2 ¼ cup of white granulated sugar

## Step 1 – Sterilizing The Pint Jars

- To sterilize the jars, bring a large pot of water to a boil, then turn off the heat, place the jars in it, and let them sit in it for 5 to 10 minutes.
- Use thongs to pull them out then place them with the lid down on a towel to dry.

## Step 2 – Preparing the pressure cooker

- Start by placing a trivet at the bottom of your pressure canner.
- Fill the pressure canner with enough water to cover the jars completely, and bring it to a simmer.

## Step 3 - Preparation

- Start by washing and scrubbing the sweet potatoes until they become nicely cleaned.
- Peel them, and cut them into 1 ½ inch thick chunks.

## Step 4 – Packing

- Combine the water with sugar in a large saucepan, then bring them to a boil while stirring occasionally until the sugar dissolves.
- Pack the sweet potato chunks into the jars, then ladle the hot syrup to cover them while making sure to leave 1-inch of space empty.
- Put on the lids and seal them tightly.
- Wipe the sides of the jars with a clean and slightly wet rag, then put on the lids and secure them tightly. Press the center of the lids to ensure they are sealed properly.

## Step 5 – Pressure canning the sweet potatoes

- Slowly lower the jars into the pressure canner to sit on the trivet.
- Put on the lid and seal it, then bring the pressure canner to pressure.
- Once the pressure canner comes up to pressure, allow the steam to continue to vent for 10 minutes to make sure there are no air pockets left in the canner.
- Process the sweet potato jars for 1 hour 5 minutes at 10 pounds of pressure for a weight gauge pressure canner, and 11 pounds for 1 hour 5 minutes if you are using a dial gauge pressure canner at an altitude of 1000 ft and less.

- Remember to adjust the processing time and pressure according to your altitude

## Step 6 – Releasing the pressure

- Once the processing time is up, turn off the heat and allow the pressure canner to sit undisturbed until the pressure reaches 0.
- Do not move or attempt to open the pressure canner at all until all the pressure is released.

## Step 7 – Letting the jars rest

Once the pressure is released, open the pressure canner, and use thongs to gently remove the jars from the pot.

- Place them on a large towel, and let them cool down completely. They might take 12 to 24 hours.

## Step 8 – Storing

Double check the jars to make sure they are sealed then you can store them in a cool and dark place for up to 12 months.

If you find some jars that are not sealed properly, you can still store them in the fridge for up to 3 weeks and enjoy!

## Potatoes

|Intro|: Who doesn't love potatoes? However, you love them even more when you can them, because they are peeled, cut, and cooked then canned. So every time you wish to prepare a meal that requires potatoes, you can just pull out a jar, open it, strain it and add it to your salads, side dishes, or meals. It comes in very handy, especially on your busy days.

## Equipment:

- Pressure Canner
- Rack/Trivet
- Thongs
- Towel
- 9 Pint Jars
- Funnel

**Nutrition Facts** per ½ cup

| Calories | 60 kcal |
|----------|---------|
| Carbs | 14g |
| Protein | 1g |
| Fats | 0g |

### Core Ingredients

- 6 pounds of fresh potatoes
- Water
- 4 ½ teaspoons of canning salt (optional)

### Step 1 – Sterilizing The Pint Jars

- To sterilize the jars, bring a large pot of water to a boil, then turn off the heat, place the jars in it, and let them sit in it for 5 to 10 minutes.
- Use thongs to pull them out then place them with the lid down on a towel to dry.

### Step 2 – Preparing the pressure cooker

- Start by placing a trivet at the bottom of your pressure canner.
- Fill the pressure canner with enough water to cover the jars completely, and bring it to a simmer.

### Step 3 - Preparation

- Wash and scrub the potatoes until they become nicely cleaned.
- Peel them, and cut them into 1 ½ to 2 inches thick chunks, or if you are using small potatoes, you can leave them as they are.
- Bring a large pot of water to a boil, then cook in it the potatoes for 9 to 10 minutes until they become tender but not too soft so they don't turn into a mashed potatoes in the jars.

### Step 4 – Packing

- Pack potato chunks into the jars gently without pressing them so they don't get crushed, then cover them with fresh boiling water.
- If you wish to season them, ½ teaspoon of salt to each jar, if not, you can leave it out.
- Put on the lids and seal them tightly.

Wipe the sides of the jars with a clean and slightly wet rag, then put on the lids and secure them tightly. Press the center of the lids to ensure they are sealed properly.

### Step 5 – Pressure canning the sweet potatoes

- Slowly lower the jars into the pressure canner to sit on the trivet.
- Put on the lid and seal it, then bring the pressure canner to pressure.
- Once the pressure canner comes up to pressure, allow the steam to continue to vent for 10 minutes

to make sure there are no air pockets left in the canner.

- Process the potato jars for 35 minutes at 10 pounds of pressure for a weight gauge pressure canner, and at 11 pounds for 35 minutes if you are using a dial gauge pressure canner at an altitude of 1000 ft and less.
- Remember to adjust the processing time and pressure according to your altitude

### Step 6 – Releasing the pressure

- Once the processing time is up, turn off the heat and allow the pressure canner to sit undisturbed until the pressure reaches 0.
- Do not move or attempt to open the pressure canner at all until all the pressure is released.

### Step 7 – Letting the jars rest

Once the pressure is released, open the pressure canner, and use thongs to gently remove the jars from the pot.

- Place them on a large towel, and let them cool down completely. They might take 12 to 24 hours.

### Step 8 – Storing

Double check the jars to make sure they are sealed then you can store them in a cool and dark place for up to 12 months.

If you find some jars that are not sealed properly, you can still store them in the fridge for up to 3 weeks and enjoy!

## Section 3: Pressure Canning Soup Recipes

### Asparagus Soup

|Intro|: Hearty, creamy, and delicious! The perfect words to describe this recipe. You just have to prepare the soup, pressure can it, then store it. When you are ready to enjoy it, pop up a jar, heat, blend it smooth then serve it with some grated cheese and enjoy this delicacy. It's the perfect way to enjoy asparagus throughout all year, and also makes for an ideal 3 minutes meal or side dish to make on your busy days.

### Equipment:

- Pressure Canner

- Rack/Trivet
- Thongs
- Towel
- 8 Pint Jars
- Funnel
- Skillet
- Saucepan

### Nutrition Facts per 1 tablespoon

| Calories | 102.63 kcal |
|----------|-------------|
| Carbs | 17.17g |
| Protein | 9.7g |
| Fats | 1.36g |

## Core Ingredients

- 6 pounds of fresh asparagus, trimmed

16 cups of chicken broth

2 cups of shallots, peeled and minced

2 tablespoons of garlic, minced

1 teaspoon of salt

½ teaspoon of black pepper

Olive oil

## Step 1 – Sterilizing The Pint Jars

- To sterilize the jars, bring a large pot of water to a boil, then turn off the heat, place the jars in it, and let them sit in it for 5 to 10 minutes.
- Use thongs to pull them out then place them with the lid down on a towel to dry.

## Step 2 – Preparing the pressure cooker

- Start by placing a trivet at the bottom of your pressure canner.
- Fill the pressure canner with enough water to cover the jars completely, and bring it to a simmer.

## Step 3 - Preparation

Wash the asparagus spears and remove the hard part of the stems, then them into 1-inch pieces.

- Heat a small splash of olive oil in a large skillet, then cook in its shallot with garlic for 2 to 3 minutes until it becomes translucent then place them aside.

Pour the broth into a large saucepan and bring it to a boil, then turn off the heat.

## Step 4 – Packing

- Divide the asparagus between the jars evenly along with the shallots and garlic mix.
- Add ¼ teaspoon of salt, and 1/8 teaspoon of black pepper to each jar, then cover them with the hot broth.
- Put on the lids, and seal them tightly.

Wipe the sides of the jars with a clean and slightly wet rag, then put on the lids and secure them tightly. Press the center of the lids to ensure they are sealed properly.

## Step 5 – Pressure canning the asparagus soup

- Slowly lower the jars into the pressure canner to sit on the trivet.
- Put on the lid and seal it, then bring the pressure canner to pressure.
- Once the pressure canner comes up to pressure, allow the steam to continue to vent for 10 minutes to make sure there are no air pockets left in the canner.
- Process the asparagus soup jars for 1 hour 15 minutes at 10 pounds of pressure for a weight gauge pressure canner, and 11 pounds for 1 hour 15 minutes if you are using a dial gauge pressure canner at an altitude of 1000 ft and less.
- Remember to adjust the processing time and pressure according to your altitude

## Step 6 – Releasing the pressure

- Once the processing time is up, turn off the heat and allow the pressure canner to sit undisturbed until the pressure reaches 0.
- Do not move or attempt to open the pressure canner at all until all the pressure is released.

## Step 7 – Letting the jars rest

Once the pressure is released, open the pressure canner, and use thongs to gently remove the jars from the pot.

- Place them on a large towel, and let them cool down completely. They might take 12 to 24 hours.

## Step 8 – Storing

Double check the jars to make sure they are sealed then you can store them in a cool and dark place for up to 12 months.

If you find some jars that are not sealed properly, you can still store them in the fridge for up to 1 week.

### Step 9 – Preparing and serving the soup

When you wish to prepare some asparagus soup, pop a jar open and pour it into a large saucepan. Add to it ¼ cup of heavy cream and bring to a simmer over medium heat.

Transfer the soup to a food processor and blend it until smooth.

Adjust the seasoning of the soup, then heat it again and serve it hot.

## Fennel and Carrot Soup

|Intro|: This fennel and carrot soup is hearty, delicious, and creamy. All takes is several hours of your time for 1 day, then you can enjoy it for the rest of the year. It makes a great quick, and light dinner or a side dish that is both delicious and healthy.

### Equipment:

- Pressure Canner
- Rack/Trivet
- Thongs
- Towel
- 12 Pint Jars
- Funnel
- Pot

#### Nutrition Facts per 1 cup

| Calories | 48 kcal |
| --- | --- |
| Carbs | 10.1g |
| Protein | 1g |
| Fats | 0.7g |

### Core Ingredients

- 4 pounds of fresh carrots, peeled and sliced
- 1 pound of fennel bulbs
- 12 cups of vegetable stock
- 2 tablespoons of fresh or bottled lemon juice
- 2 tablespoons of salt
- 1 tablespoon of olive oil
- 2 teaspoons of onion powder
- 1 teaspoon of ground ginger
- 1 teaspoon of dry thyme
- 1 teaspoon of dry coriander
- 1 teaspoon of black pepper
- ½ teaspoon of cumin

### Step 1 - Preparation

- Start by washing the carrots, then peel and slice them.
- Next, wash and trim the fennel bulbs, then roughly chop them.

### Step 2 – Cooking the soup

- Heat the olive oil in a large pot then cook in it the fennel for 5 to 7 minutes until it becomes transparent.
- Add 4 cups of broth with the remaining ingredients and stir them until well combined, then bring them to a boil.
- Lower the heat and put on the lid, then let the soup cook for 30 to 35 minutes until the carrots and fennel become soft.

Once the soup is done, turn off the heat and allow it to sit until it becomes cool to handle.

Use an immersion blender or a food processor to blend the soup in batches until it becomes smooth.

Pour the soup back into the pot, and add to it the remaining broth, then bring to a simmer over low medium heat.

Lower the heat even further and put on the lid, then let the soup simmer for 25 minutes.

### Step 3 – Sterilizing The Pint Jars

- To sterilize the jars, bring a large pot of water to a boil, then turn off the heat, place the jars in it, and let them sit in it for 5 to 10 minutes.
- Use thongs to pull them out then place them with the lid down on a towel to dry.

### Step 4 – Preparing the pressure cooker

- Start by placing a trivet at the bottom of your pressure canner.
- Fill the pressure canner with enough water to cover the jars completely, and bring it to a simmer.

### Step 5 – Packing

- Once the soup is done, transfer it to the jars while it's hot gently, and leave ½ to 1 inch of space.
- Put on the lids, and seal them tightly.

Wipe the sides of the jars with a clean and slightly wet rag, then put on the lids and secure them tightly. Press the center of the lids to ensure they are sealed properly.

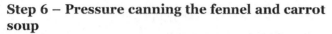

### Step 6 – Pressure canning the fennel and carrot soup

- Slowly lower the jars into the pressure canner to sit on the trivet.
- Put on the lid and seal it, then bring the pressure canner to pressure.
- Once the pressure canner comes up to pressure, allow the steam to continue to vent for 10 minutes to make sure there are no air pockets left in the canner.
- Process the soup jars for 40 minutes at 10 pounds of pressure for a weight gauge pressure canner, and at 11 pounds for 40 minutes if you are using a dial gauge pressure canner at an altitude of 1000 ft and less.
- Remember to adjust the processing time and pressure according to your altitude

### Step 7 – Releasing the pressure

- Once the processing time is up, turn off the heat and allow the pressure canner to sit undisturbed until the pressure reaches 0.
- Do not move or attempt to open the pressure canner at all until all the pressure is released.

### Step 8 – Letting the jars rest

Once the pressure is released, open the pressure canner, and use thongs to gently remove the jars from the pot.

- Place them on a large towel, and let them cool down completely. They might take 12 to 24 hours.

### Step 9 – Storing

Double check the jars to make sure they are sealed then you can store them in a cool and dark place for up to 12 months.

If you find some jars that are not sealed properly, you can still store them in the fridge for up to 1 week.

### Step 10 – Preparing and serving the soup

When you wish to serve the soup, you just have to add a splash of broth.

Bring to a simmer then serve it and enjoy!

## Tomato Soup

|Intro|: Nothing beats a hot tomato soup with some grated cheese and toasted bread, in the summer, fall, winter, and spring. The fact that this tomato soup is canned, and preserved for a long time, allows the flavors to combine well, and make it taste even better. It's very concentrated, so when you plan to serve it, heat it with some extra broth or milk and enjoy!

### Equipment:

Pressure Canner

Rack/Trivet

Thongs

Towel

8 Pint Jars

Funnel

Pot

### Nutrition Facts per 1 Pint Jar

| Calories | 138.94 kcal |
|----------|-------------|
| Carbs | 31.58g |
| Protein | 4.45g |
| Fats | 0.98g |

### Core Ingredients

- 16 pounds of ripe tomatoes, peeled and quartered
- 4 cups of yellow or white onion, peeled and roughly chopped
- 2 cups of celery, diced
- 2 cups of fresh parsley leaves, finely chopped
- 1 ½ cup of Clear Gel
- 12 bay leaves
- 4 tablespoons of salt
- 1 teaspoon of black pepper
- Olive oil

### Step 1 - Preparation

- Start by washing and peeling the tomatoes, then cut them into quarters.
- Peel and wash the onions, then roughly chop them.

### Step 2 – Cooking the soup

Heat a small splash of olive oil in a large pot, then cook in it the celery with onion for 3 to 5 minutes until they start to become soft.

Add in the tomato with parsley and bay leaves, then lower the heat and let them cook until they reduce by half or until the mixture starts to become thick about 20 to 30 minutes.

### Step 3 – Sterilizing The Pint Jars

- To sterilize the jars, bring a large pot of water to a boil, then turn off the heat, place the jars in it, and let them sit in it for 5 to 10 minutes.
- Use thongs to pull them out then place them with the lid down on a towel to dry.

### Step 4 – Preparing the pressure cooker

- Start by placing a trivet at the bottom of your pressure canner.
- Fill the pressure canner with enough water to cover the jars completely, and bring it to a simmer.

### Step 5 – Packing

- Once the soup is done, use a blender or a food processor to blend it smooth, then pour it back into the pot.
- Measure 2 cups of the soup and pour it into a bowl, then set aside until it cools down.

Add the Clear Jel to the reserved soup and whisk them until well combined.

Bring the soup to a boil, then add to it the Clear Jell mixture and boil it for 2 minutes while stirring it occasionally.

Season the soup with salt and pepper, then ladle it while it's hot to the jars, and make sure to leave ½ to 1 inch of empty space.

- Put on the lids, and seal them tightly.

Wipe the sides of the jars with a clean and slightly wet rag, then put on the lids and secure them tightly. Press the center of the lids to ensure they are sealed properly.

### Step 6 – Pressure canning the tomato soup

- Slowly lower the jars into the pressure canner to sit on the trivet.
- Put on the lid and seal it, then bring the pressure canner to pressure.
- Once the pressure canner comes up to pressure, allow the steam to continue to vent for 10 minutes to make sure there are no air pockets left in the canner.
- Process the soup jars for 25 minutes at 10 pounds of pressure for a weight gauge pressure canner, and at 11 pounds for 25 minutes if you are using a dial gauge pressure canner at an altitude of 1000 ft and less.
- Remember to adjust the processing time and pressure according to your altitude

### Step 7 – Releasing the pressure

- Once the processing time is up, turn off the heat and allow the pressure canner to sit undisturbed until the pressure reaches 0.
- Do not move or attempt to open the pressure canner at all until all the pressure is released.

### Step 8 – Letting the jars rest

Once the pressure is released, open the pressure canner, and use thongs to gently remove the jars from the pot.

- Place them on a large towel, and let them cool down completely. They might take 12 to 24 hours.

### Step 9 – Storing

Double check the jars to make sure they are sealed then you can store them in a cool and dark place for up to 12 months.

If you find some jars that are not sealed properly, you can still store them in the fridge for up to 1 week.

### Step 10 – Preparing and serving the soup

This soup is very concentrated. When you wish to serve it, add milk or both with the same amount of soup that you wish to use. For example, if you have 1 cup of soup, add to it 1 cup of milk or both.

You can also reduce the broth or milk depending on the consistency that you prefer for the soup.

Serve it hot, and enjoy!

## Vegetable Beef Soup

|Intro|: Nothing beats a hearty, and hot bowl of soup in the cold days of winter, especially if it's a vegetable beef soup that you can enjoy with some bread on the side. This recipe is relatively easy that makes for a great pantry cleaner, money saver, and a healthy delicious meal to warm your soul.

### Equipment:

- Pressure Canner
- Rack/Trivet
- Thongs
- Towel
- 7 Pint Jars
- Funnel
- Pot

**Nutrition Facts** per 1 Pint Jar

| Calories | 262.11 kcal |
|----------|-------------|
| Carbs | 29.67g |
| Protein | 26.81g |
| Fats | 5.16g |

## Core Ingredients

- 1 ½ pound of beef cubes
- 4 cups of beef broth
- 28 ounces of canned tomatoes (homemade or storebought)
- 3 large carrots, peeled and sliced
- 2 large potatoes, peeled and diced
- 1 cup of yellow or white onion, peeled and finely chopped
- 1 tablespoon of white granulated sugar
- 2 teaspoons of salt
- 1 ½ teaspoon of Italian seasoning
- ½ teaspoon of black pepper
- ½ teaspoon of dry rosemary, ground
- ½ teaspoon of dry marjoram, ground
- ½ teaspoon of dry thyme, ground
- Olive oil

## Step 1 - Preparation

- Start by peeling the carrots and potatoes then dice them.
- Peel the onions, wash them and finely chop them.

## Step 2 – Sterilizing The Pint Jars

- To sterilize the jars, bring a large pot of water to a boil, then turn off the heat, place the jars in it, and let them sit in it for 5 to 10 minutes.
- Use thongs to pull them out then place them with the lid down on a towel to dry.

## Step 3 – Preparing the pressure cooker

- Start by placing a trivet at the bottom of your pressure canner.
- Fill the pressure canner with enough water to cover the jars completely, and bring it to a simmer.

## Step 4 – Cooking the soup

- Heat a splash of oil in a large pot, then add to it the meat cubes, and cook them for 7 to 10 minutes until they start to become brown.
- Stir in the remaining ingredients and bring them to a boil.
- Lower the heat, and put on the lid, then let the soup cook for 12 minutes until the veggies become soft.

## Step 5 – Packing

- Once the soup is done, ladle it while it is hot to the jars, and make sure to leave ½ to 1 inch of empty space.
- Put on the lids, and seal them tightly.

Wipe the sides of the jars with a clean and slightly wet rag, then put on the lids and secure them tightly. Press the center of the lids to ensure they are sealed properly.

## Step 6 – Pressure canning the vegetable beef soup

- Slowly lower the jars into the pressure canner to sit on the trivet.
- Put on the lid and seal it, then bring the pressure canner to pressure.
- Once the pressure canner comes up to pressure, allow the steam to continue to vent for 10 minutes to make sure there are no air pockets left in the canner.
- Process the soup jars for 1 hour 15 minutes at 10 pounds of pressure for a weight gauge pressure canner, and 11 pounds for 1 hour 15 minutes if you are using a dial gauge pressure canner at an altitude of 1000 ft and less.
- Remember to adjust the processing time and pressure according to your altitude

## Step 7 – Releasing the pressure

- Once the processing time is up, turn off the heat and allow the pressure canner to sit undisturbed until the pressure reaches 0.
- Do not move or attempt to open the pressure canner at all until all the pressure is released.

## Step 8 – Letting the jars rest

Once the pressure is released, open the pressure canner, and use thongs to gently remove the jars from the pot.

- Place them on a large towel, and let them cool down completely. They might take 12 to 24 hours.

### Step 9 – Storing

Double check the jars to make sure they are sealed then you can store them in a cool and dark place for up to 12 months.

If you find some jars that are not sealed properly, you can still store them in the fridge for up to 1 week.

### Step 10 – Preparing and serving the soup

To prepare the soup, pour it into a saucepan and bring it to a boil.

Lower the heat and simmer it for 6 to 10 minutes until the veggies become soft and tender.

Serve it hot and enjoy!

## Section 4: Pressure Canning Broth Recipes

### Bone Broth

|Intro|: With canning, you really can't lose. Everything is good for something even bones. Every time you have chicken, fish, lamb, or beef, save up their bones in the freezer separately to make this delicious bone broth that will save you a lot of money, and add more flavor to your meals.

### Equipment:

- Pressure Canner
- Rack/Trivet
- Thongs
- Towel
- Pint Jars
- Funnel
- Stockpot
- Roasting Pan

#### Nutrition Facts per 1 Cup

| Calories | 45 kcal |
|----------|---------|
| Carbs | 0g |
| Protein | 11g |
| Fats | 0g |

### Core Ingredients

- 10 pounds of beef bones
- 6 stalks of celery, roughly chopped
- 4 carrots, roughly chopped
- 2 yellow onions, peeled and quartered
- 2 heads of garlic, cut in half
- ¼ cup of black peppercorns
- 2 tablespoons of apple cider vinegar
- 4 bay leaves
- 4-star anise
- 2 cinnamon sticks

### Step 1 – Roasting the bones

- Preheat the oven to 450 F.
- Spread the bones in a roasting pan then roast them in the oven for 1 hour while stirring and flipping them every 30 minutes.

### Step 2 – Cooking the bones and veggies

- Transfer the roasted bones with the remaining ingredients then cover them completely with water.
- If the pot you have is not big enough, you can split them between two pots.
- Bring them to a boil, then lower the heat and put on half a lid.
- Lower the heat and let them simmer for at least 8 to 24 while adding water when needed to make sure the bones and veggies are always covered with water.
- The cooking process doesn't have to be consecutive, you can start for example in the morning, let it all day, then turn off the heat at night, and resume the cooking process the next day.
- Throughout the cooking process, make sure to skim off and discard the fat on top.
- Once the time is up, strain your broth using a fine mesh sieve.

### Step 3 – Sterilizing The Pint Jars

- To sterilize the jars, bring a large pot of water to a boil, then turn off the heat, place the jars in it, and let them sit in it for 5 to 10 minutes.
- Use thongs to pull them out then place them with the lid down on a towel to dry.

### Step 4 – Preparing the pressure cooker

- Start by placing a trivet at the bottom of your pressure canner.

- Fill the pressure canner with enough water to cover the jars completely, and bring it to a simmer.

### Step 5 – Packing

Reheat the broth, then ladle it into the jars, and make sure to leave ½ to 1 inch of empty space.

- Put on the lids, and seal them tightly.

Wipe the sides of the jars with a clean and slightly wet rag, then put on the lids and secure them tightly. Press the center of the lids to ensure they are sealed properly.

### Step 6 – Pressure canning the bone broth

- Slowly lower the jars into the pressure canner to sit on the trivet.
- Put on the lid and seal it, then bring the pressure canner to pressure.
- Once the pressure canner comes up to pressure, allow the steam to continue to vent for 10 minutes to make sure there are no air pockets left in the canner.
- Process the stock jars for 25 minutes at 10 pounds of pressure for a weight gauge pressure canner, and at 11 pounds for 25 minutes if you are using a dial gauge pressure canner at an altitude of 1000 ft and less.
- Remember to adjust the processing time and pressure according to your altitude

### Step 7 – Releasing the pressure

- Once the processing time is up, turn off the heat and allow the pressure canner to sit undisturbed until the pressure reaches 0.
- Do not move or attempt to open the pressure canner at all until all the pressure is released.

### Step 8 – Letting the jars rest

Once the pressure is released, open the pressure canner, and use thongs to gently remove the jars from the pot.

- Place them on a large towel, and let them cool down completely. They might take 12 to 24 hours.

### Step 9 – Storing

Double check the jars to make sure they are sealed then you can store them in a cool and dark place for up to 2 years.

If you find some jars that are not sealed properly, you can still store them in the freezer for up to 6 months.

## Strong Fish Stock

|Intro|: This fish stock is a healthy and delicious stock that is great to to add more flavors to your dishes. All it takes is 1 day of hard work, then you can enjoy this stock for up to 18 months.

### Equipment:

- Pressure Canner
- Rack/Trivet
- Thongs
- Towel
- Pint Jars
- Funnel
- Pot

### Nutrition Facts per 1 Pint Ja

| Calories | 136.99 kcal |
|----------|-------------|
| Carbs | 17.83g |
| Protein | 2.25g |
| Fats | 5.94g |

### Core Ingredients

- 8 pounds of mixed fish bones
- 4 quarts of hot water
- 2 pounds of yellow or white onions, peeled and roughly chopped
- 8 carrots, peeled and roughly chopped
- 8 stalks of celery, roughly chopped
- ½ cup of dry white wine
- 12 sprigs of fresh thyme
- 4 tablespoons of butter, unsalted
- 2 tablespoons of black peppercorns
- 4 bay leaves
- Salt

### Step 1 – Preparation

- Start by peeling, washing, and cutting the veggies.

### Step 2 – Cooking the bones and veggies

- Place a large pot over medium heat and melt in it the butter.
- Add to it the veggies with thyme, peppercorns, bay leaves, and salt then cook them for 15 to 16 minutes until the veggies soften.

- Turn off the heat, and add the fish bones on top with white wine, then let them sit for 20 minutes.
- Once the time is up, turn on the heat to high and stir in the water, then bring them to a boil.
- Put on the lid, lower the heat, then let the stock simmer for 12 minutes.
- Allow the stock to cool down until it becomes easy to handle.
- Skim off the fat on top, then use a fine mesh cloth to strain the stock.

### Step 3 – Sterilizing The Pint Jars

- To sterilize the jars, bring a large pot of water to a boil, then turn off the heat, place the jars in it, and let them sit in it for 5 to 10 minutes.
- Use thongs to pull them out then place them with the lid down on a towel to dry.

### Step 4 – Preparing the pressure cooker

- Start by placing a trivet at the bottom of your pressure canner.
- Fill the pressure canner with enough water to cover the jars completely, and bring it to a simmer.

### Step 5 – Packing

After you strain the stock, discard the solids, and pour the stock into a clean pot.

Heat it, then ladle it into the jars, and make sure to leave ½ to 1 inch of empty space.

- Put on the lids, and seal them tightly.

Wipe the sides of the jars with a clean and slightly wet rag, then put on the lids and secure them tightly. Press the center of the lids to ensure they are sealed properly.

### Step 6 – Pressure canning the fish stock

- Slowly lower the jars into the pressure canner to sit on the trivet.
- Put on the lid and seal it, then bring the pressure canner to pressure.
- Once the pressure canner comes up to pressure, allow the steam to continue to vent for 10 minutes to make sure there are no air pockets left in the canner.
- Process the stock jars for 30 minutes at 10 pounds of pressure for a weight gauge pressure canner, and at 11 pounds for 30 minutes if you are using a dial gauge pressure canner at an altitude of 1000 ft and less.
- Remember to adjust the processing time and pressure according to your altitude

### Step 7 – Releasing the pressure

- Once the processing time is up, turn off the heat and allow the pressure canner to sit undisturbed until the pressure reaches 0.
- Do not move or attempt to open the pressure canner at all until all the pressure is released.

### Step 8 – Letting the jars rest

Once the pressure is released, open the pressure canner, and use thongs to gently remove the jars from the pot.

- Place them on a large towel, and let them cool down completely. They might take 12 to 24 hours.

### Step 9 – Storing

Double check the jars to make sure they are sealed then you can store them in a cool and dark place for up to 2 years.

If you find some jars that are not sealed properly, you can still store them in the freezer for up to 6 months.

## Organs Meat Stock

|Intro|: Organ meat stock means that the stock that you are used to making will turn out rich in flavor, complex, and has more depth. This recipe calls for organs, so if you have some that you don't know what to do with, this is the perfect recipe to use them up, and preserve their stock for up to 18 months.

### Equipment:

- Pressure Canner
- Rack/Trivet
- Thongs
- Towel
- Pint Jars
- Funnel
- Pot

#### Nutrition Facts per 1 cup

| Calories | 89 kcal |
|----------|---------|
| Carbs | 9g |
| Protein | 7g |
| Fats | 5g |

### Core Ingredients

- 8 pounds of beef organs

- 6 quarts of water
- 2 large yellow or white onions, roughly chopped
- 2 stalks of celery, roughly chopped
- 2 large carrots, roughly chopped
- 10 whole peppercorns
- 3 cloves of garlic, peeled and crushed
- 2 bay leaves
- 1 teaspoon of dry parsley
- ½ teaspoon of rosemary

### Step 1 – Cooking the stock
- Combine all the ingredients in a large pot then cover them completely with water.
- If the pot you have is not big enough, you can split the ingredients between two pots.
- Bring them to a boil, then lower the heat and put on half a lid.
- Lower the heat and let them simmer for at least 8 to 24 while adding water when needed to make sure the bones and veggies are always covered with water.
- The cooking process doesn't have to be consecutive, you can start for example in the morning, let it all day, then turn off the heat at night, and resume the cooking process the next day.
- Throughout the cooking process, make sure to skim off and discard the fat on top.
- Once the time is up, strain your broth using a fine mesh sieve.

### Step 2 – Sterilizing The Pint Jars
- To sterilize the jars, bring a large pot of water to a boil, then turn off the heat, place the jars in it, and let them sit in it for 5 to 10 minutes.
- Use thongs to pull them out then place them with the lid down on a towel to dry.

### Step 3 – Preparing the pressure cooker
- Start by placing a trivet at the bottom of your pressure canner.
- Fill the pressure canner with enough water to cover the jars completely, and bring it to a simmer.

### Step 4 – Packing
Reheat the stock, then ladle it into the jars, and make sure to leave ½ to 1 inch of empty space.

- Put on the lids, and seal them tightly.

Wipe the sides of the jars with a clean and slightly wet rag, then put on the lids and secure them tightly. Press the center of the lids to ensure they are sealed properly.

### Step 5 – Pressure canning the organs meat stock
- Slowly lower the jars into the pressure canner to sit on the trivet.
- Put on the lid and seal it, then bring the pressure canner to pressure.
- Once the pressure canner comes up to pressure, allow the steam to continue to vent for 10 minutes to make sure there are no air pockets left in the canner.
- Process the stock jars for 20 minutes at 10 pounds of pressure for a weight gauge pressure canner, and at 11 pounds for 20 minutes if you are using a dial gauge pressure canner at an altitude of 1000 ft and less.
- Make sure to adjust the processing weight depending on your altitude

### Step 6 – Releasing the pressure
- Once the processing time is up, turn off the heat and allow the pressure canner to sit undisturbed until the pressure reaches 0.
- Do not move or attempt to open the pressure canner at all until all the pressure is released.

### Step 7 – Letting the jars rest
Once the pressure is released, open the pressure canner, and use thongs to gently remove the jars from the pot.

- Place them on a large towel, and let them cool down completely. They might take 12 to 24 hours.

### Step 8 – Storing
Double check the jars to make sure they are sealed then you can store them in a cool and dark place for up to 2 years.

If you find some jars that are not sealed properly, you can still store them in the freezer for up to 6 months.

## Pheasant Stock

|Intro|: If you hunt or someone in your family hunt pheasants after you enjoy the delicious meat, this is the perfect way to use the bones. They make for a delicious and hearty stock that goes with all of your savory dishes.

**Equipment:**
• Pressure Canner

- Rack/Trivet
- Thongs
- Towel
- Pint Jars
- Funnel
- Stockpot

### Nutrition Facts per 1 Cup

| Calories | 36 kcal |
|----------|---------|
| Carbs    | 7g      |
| Protein  | 1g      |
| Fats     | 1g      |

## Core Ingredients

- 6 pheasant carcasses with organs
- 4 stalks of celery, roughly chopped
- 3 large carrots, peeled and roughly chopped
- 1 large yellow or white onion, peeled and roughly chopped
- 3 tablespoons of vegetable oil
- 4 cloves of garlic, peeled and roughly chopped
- 1 bunch of fresh parsley, roughly chopped
- 1 tablespoon of cracked peppercorns
- 1 tablespoon of juniper berries, crushed
- 4 bay leaves
- 2 teaspoons of dry thyme
- Water

## Step 1 – Roasting the bones

- Preheat the oven to 400 F.
- Spread the bones in a roasting pan then roast them in the oven for 1 hour while stirring and flipping them every 30 minutes.

## Step 2 – Letting the pheasant carcasses steep

- Transfer the roasted bones to a large stock pot then cover them completely with water.
- Add some boiling water to the roasting pan, and scrap the bottom to mix the remaining juices from the pan with water.
- Add the mixture to the stockpot then bring them to a boil.
- Turn off the heat and put on the lid, then let the stock sit overnight.

## Step 2 – Cooking the stock

- Add the remaining ingredients to the pot with enough water to cover everything, then stir them until well combined.
- If the pot you have is not big enough, you can split them between two pots.
- Bring them to a boil, then lower the heat and put on the lid.
- Lower the heat and let them simmer for at least 1 hour 30 minutes while adding water when needed to make sure the bones and veggies are always covered with water.
- Throughout the cooking process, make sure to skim off and discard the fat on top.
- Once the time is up, strain your broth using a fine mesh sieve, or fine mesh cloth.

## Step 3 – Sterilizing The Pint Jars

- To sterilize the jars, bring a large pot of water to a boil, then turn off the heat, place the jars in it, and let them sit in it for 5 to 10 minutes.
- Use thongs to pull them out then place them with the lid down on a towel to dry.

## Step 4 – Preparing the pressure cooker

- Start by placing a trivet at the bottom of your pressure canner.
- Fill the pressure canner with enough water to cover the jars completely, and bring it to a simmer.

## Step 5 – Packing

Adjust the seasoning of the stock, then reheat it, then into the jars, and make sure to leave ½ to 1 inch of space.

- Put on the lids, and seal them tightly.

Wipe the sides of the jars with a clean and slightly wet rag, then put on the lids and secure them tightly. Press the center of the lids to ensure they are sealed properly.

## Step 6 – Pressure canning the pheasant stock

- Slowly lower the jars into the pressure canner to sit on the trivet.
- Put on the lid and seal it, then bring the pressure canner to pressure.
- Once the pressure canner comes up to pressure, allow the steam to continue to vent for 10 minutes to make sure there are no air pockets left in the canner.
- Process the stock jars for 20 minutes at 10 pounds of pressure for a weight gauge pressure canner, and at 11 pounds for 20 minutes if you are using a dial

gauge pressure canner at an altitude of 1000 ft and less.
- Remember to adjust the processing time and pressure according to your altitude

## Step 7 – Releasing the pressure
- Once the processing time is up, turn off the heat and allow the pressure canner to sit undisturbed until the pressure reaches 0.
- Do not move or attempt to open the pressure canner at all until all the pressure is released.

## Step 8 – Letting the jars rest
Once the pressure is released, open the pressure canner, and use thongs to gently remove the jars from the pot.
- Place them on a large towel, and let them cool down completely. They might take 12 to 24 hours.

## Step 9 – Storing
Double check the jars to make sure they are sealed then you can store them in a cool and dark place for up to 2 years.

If you find some jars that are not sealed properly, you can still store them in the freezer for up to 6 months.

## Pork Stock

|Intro|: If you include a lot of pork meats in your meals, this recipe is perfect for you to use and get another use of the bones. The stock comes out delicious, and will for sure add a unique flavor to your dishes.

### Equipment:
- Pressure Canner
- Rack/Trivet
- Thongs
- Towel
- Pint Jars
- Funnel
- Stockpot

### Nutrition Facts per Pint Jar

| Calories | 13.5 kcal |
|----------|-----------|
| Carbs | 3g |
| Protein | 0.5g |
| Fats | 0.5g |

## Core Ingredients
- 3 pounds of pork bones
- 3 stalks of celery, roughly chopped
- 3 medium onions, peeled and quartered
- 1 bunch of fresh celery, washed
- 6 sprigs of fresh thyme
- 6 sprigs of fresh rosemary
- Water

## Step 1 – Cooking the stock
- Combine all the ingredients in a large pot then cover them completely with water.
- Bring them to a boil, then lower the heat and put on half a lid.
- Lower the heat and let them simmer for at least 8 to 12 hours while adding water when needed to make sure the bones and veggies are always covered with water.
- The cooking process doesn't have to be consecutive, you can start for example in the morning, let it all day, then turn off the heat at night, and resume the cooking process the next day.
- Throughout the cooking process, make sure to skim off and discard the fat on top.
- Once the time is up, strain your broth using a fine mesh sieve.

## Step 2 – Sterilizing The Pint Jars
- To sterilize the jars, bring a large pot of water to a boil, then turn off the heat, place the jars in it, and let them sit in it for 5 to 10 minutes.
- Use thongs to pull them out then place them with the lid down on a towel to dry.

## Step 3 – Preparing the pressure cooker
- Start by placing a trivet at the bottom of your pressure canner.
- Fill the pressure canner with enough water to cover the jars completely, and bring it to a simmer.

## Step 4 – Packing
Re-heat the stock, then ladle it into the jars, and make sure to leave ½ to 1 inch of empty space.
- Put on the lids, and seal them tightly.

Wipe the sides of the jars with a clean and slightly wet rag, then put on the lids and secure them tightly. Press the center of the lids to ensure they are sealed properly.

### Step 5 – Pressure canning the pork stock

- Slowly lower the jars into the pressure canner to sit on the trivet.
- Put on the lid and seal it, then bring the pressure canner to pressure.
- Once the pressure canner comes up to pressure, allow the steam to continue to vent for 10 minutes to make sure there are no air pockets left in the canner.
- Process the stock jars for 20 minutes at 10 pounds of pressure for a weight gauge pressure canner, and at 11 pounds for 20 minutes if you are using a dial gauge pressure canner at an altitude of 1000 ft and less.
- Remember to adjust the processing time and pressure according to your altitude

### Step 6 – Releasing the pressure

- Once the processing time is up, turn off the heat and allow the pressure canner to sit undisturbed until the pressure reaches 0.
- Do not move or attempt to open the pressure canner at all until all the pressure is released.

### Step 7 – Letting the jars rest

Once the pressure is released, open the pressure canner, and use thongs to gently remove the jars from the pot.

- Place them on a large towel, and let them cool down completely. They might take 12 to 24 hours.

### Step 8 – Storing

Double check the jars to make sure they are sealed then you can store them in a cool and dark place for up to 2 years.

If you find some jars that are not sealed properly, you can still store them in the freezer for up to 6 months.

---

### Shrimp Stock

|Intro|: Now that you have tried all these stocks and broths, it's time to take a chance on this shrimp stock. It's simply delicious and will elevate the taste of your dishes, as well as save you a lot of money.

### Equipment:
- Pressure Canner
- Rack/Trivet
- Thongs
- Towel
- Pint Jars
- Funnel

### Nutrition Facts per 1 Pint Jar

| Calories | 133.39 kcal |
|----------|-------------|
| Carbs | 5.93g |
| Protein | 21.6g |
| Fats | 1.82g |

### Core Ingredients

- 2 ½ pound of shrimp shells
- 2 ½ quarts of water
- 1 cup of cold water
- ½ cup of mushroom trimmings
- ½ cup of celery, roughly chopped
- ½ cup of carrot, roughly chopped
- 1 tablespoon of fresh garlic, roughly chopped
- 4 sprigs of parsley
- ¼ teaspoon of ground black peppercorns
- ¼ teaspoon of dry thyme
- 1 bay leaf

### Step 1 – Cooking the stock

- Combine all the ingredients in a large pot then cover them completely with water.
- Bring them to a boil, then lower the heat and put on the lid.
- Lower the heat and let them simmer for 60 minutes.

Once the time is up, allow the stock to cool down until it becomes safe to handle, then strain it.

### Step 2 – Sterilizing The Pint Jars

- To sterilize the jars, bring a large pot of water to a boil, then turn off the heat, place the jars in it, and let them sit in it for 5 to 10 minutes.
- Use thongs to pull them out then place them with the lid down on a towel to dry.

### Step 3 – Preparing the pressure cooker

- Start by placing a trivet at the bottom of your pressure canner.
- Fill the pressure canner with enough water to cover the jars completely, and bring it to a simmer.

## Step 4 – Packing

Re-heat the stock, then ladle it into the jars, and make sure to leave ½ to 1 inch of empty space.

- Put on the lids, and seal them tightly.

Wipe the sides of the jars with a clean and slightly wet rag, then put on the lids and secure them tightly. Press the center of the lids to ensure they are sealed properly.

## Step 5 – Pressure canning the shrimp stock

- Slowly lower the jars into the pressure canner to sit on the trivet.
- Put on the lid and seal it, then bring the pressure canner to pressure.
- Once the pressure canner comes up to pressure, allow the steam to continue to vent for 10 minutes to make sure there are no air pockets left in the canner.
- Process the stock jars for 25 minutes at 10 pounds of pressure for a weight gauge pressure canner, and at 11 pounds for 25 minutes if you are using a dial gauge pressure canner at an altitude of 1000 ft and less.
- Remember to adjust the processing time and pressure according to your altitude

## Step 6 – Releasing the pressure

- Once the processing time is up, turn off the heat and allow the pressure canner to sit undisturbed until the pressure reaches 0.
- Do not move or attempt to open the pressure canner at all until all the pressure is released.

## Step 7 – Letting the jars rest

Once the pressure is released, open the pressure canner, and use thongs to gently remove the jars from the pot.

- Place them on a large towel, and let them cool down completely. They might take 12 to 24 hours.

## Step 8 – Storing

Double check the jars to make sure they are sealed then you can store them in a cool and dark place for up to 2 years.

If you find some jars that are not sealed properly, you can still store them in the freezer for up to 6 months.

## Section 5: Pressure Canning Chili

## Chili Con Carne

|Intro|: Chili Con Carne is a delicious stew that tastes even better when canned, and makes for an amazing quick winter meal that you just have to heat with some toasted bread. You can enjoy it for a full year.

### Equipment:

- Pressure Canner
- Rack/Trivet
- Thongs
- Towel
- 22 Pint Jars
- Funnel
- Stockpot
- Bowl

### Nutrition Facts per 1 Pint Ja

| Calories | 402.89 kcal |
|----------|-------------|
| Carbs | 52.01g |
| Protein | 29.24g |
| Fats | 10.07g |

### Core Ingredients

- 22 pounds of pinto beans
- 87 ounces of canned tomatoes, diced (homemade canned or storebought)
- 87 ounces of canned tomato sauce (homemade canned storebought)
- 3 pounds of lean beef, ground
- 3 large yellow or white onions, peeled and finely chopped
- 6 cups of water
- 1/3 cup of chili powder
- 3 tablespoons of vegetable oil
- 6 cloves of garlic, peeled and finely chopped
- 3 tablespoons of beef bouillon granules
- 2 tablespoons of ground cumin
- 2 tablespoons of salt
- 1 tablespoon of onion powder
- 1 tablespoon of white granulated sugar
- 1 teaspoon of black pepper
- 1 teaspoon of garlic powder

### Step 1 – Soaking the beans

- Place the beans in a large pot and cover them with water.
- Allow them to sit overnight.
- The next day, drain the beans and discard the soaking liquid.

### Step 2 – Preparing the beans

- Place the pinto beans in a large pot and cover them with water.
- Bring the pot to a boil, then lower the heat, put on the lid, and let them cook for 30 to 40 minutes until the beans become soft.
- Once the beans are done, transfer them into a colander.

### Step 3 – Sterilizing The Pint Jars

- To sterilize the jars, bring a large pot of water to a boil, then turn off the heat, place the jars in it, and let them sit in it for 5 to 10 minutes.
- Use thongs to pull them out then place them with the lid down on a towel to dry.

### Step 4 – Preparing the pressure cooker

- Start by placing a trivet at the bottom of your pressure canner.
- Fill the pressure canner with enough water to cover the jars completely, and bring it to a simmer.

### Step 5 – Cooking the chili

Place a large pot over high heat and heat in it the oil.

Add the beef then cook it for 8 to 10 minutes until it becomes brown while stirring it constantly to break it down.

Once the beef is done, transfer it to a colander and press it down to drain it.

Transfer the beef back to the pot, then add to it the remaining ingredients and stir them until well combined.

Bring the chili to a boil over high heat, then lower the heat and let it cook for 6 minutes.

### Step 6 – Packing

Ladle the hot chili into the jars, and make sure to leave ½ to 1 inch of empty space.

- Put on the lids, and seal them tightly.

Wipe the sides of the jars with a clean and slightly wet rag, then put on the lids and secure them tightly. Press the center of the lids to ensure they are sealed properly.

### Step 7 – Pressure canning the chili

- Slowly lower the jars into the pressure canner to sit on the trivet.
- Put on the lid and seal it, then bring the pressure canner to pressure.
- Once the pressure canner comes up to pressure, allow the steam to continue to vent for 10 minutes to make sure there are no air pockets left in the canner.
- Process the chili jars for 1 hour 15 minutes at 10 pounds of pressure for a weight gauge pressure canner, and 11 pounds for 1 hour 15 minutes if you are using a dial gauge pressure canner at an altitude of 1000 ft and less.
- Remember to adjust the processing time and pressure according to your altitude

### Step 8 – Releasing the pressure

- Once the processing time is up, turn off the heat and allow the pressure canner to sit undisturbed until the pressure reaches 0.
- Do not move or attempt to open the pressure canner at all until all the pressure is released.

### Step 9 – Letting the jars rest

Once the pressure is released, open the pressure canner, and use thongs to gently remove the jars from the pot.

- Place them on a large towel, and let them cool down completely. They might take 12 to 24 hours.

### Step 10 – Storing

Double check the jars to make sure they are sealed then you can store them in a cool and dark place for up to 1 year.

If you find some jars that are not sealed properly, you can still store them in the freezer for up to 6 months.

## Hearty Chili

|Intro|: This hearty chili is exactly like its name, it's thick, hearty, wholesome, and simply delicious! It smells and tastes so cozy which is perfect for winter if you wish to whip up a nice dinner in a matter of minutes. Once you try it, it will quickly become a big hit and a family favorite.

### Equipment:

- Pressure Canner
- Rack/Trivet

- Thongs
- Towel
- 9 Pint Jars
- Funnel
- Bowl
- Stockpot

**Nutrition Facts** per 2 cups

| Calories | 556 kcal |
|----------|----------|
| Carbs | 52.1g |
| Protein | 60.2g |
| Fats | 12.7g |

## Core Ingredients

- 3 pounds of ground lean beef
- 64 ounces of crushed tomatoes
- 3 cups of kidney beans
- 1 ½ cup of yellow or white onion, peeled and finely chopped
- 1 cup of green bell pepper, seeded and finely chopped
- 2 tablespoons of cocoa powder
- 2 tablespoons of lime juice
- 2 tablespoons of salt
- 1 tablespoon of chili powder
- 1 tablespoon of garlic powder
- 1 tablespoon of black pepper
- 1 tablespoon of dry and ground oregano
- 1 tablespoon of cumin
- Olive oil

## Step 1 – Soaking the beans

- Place the beans in a large pot and cover them with water.
- Allow them to sit overnight.
- The next day, drain the beans and discard the soaking liquid.

## Step 2 – Preparing the beans

- Place the beans in a large pot and cover them with water.
- Bring the pot to a boil, then lower the heat, put on the lid, and let them cook for 30 to 40 minutes until the beans become soft.

- Once the beans are done, transfer them into a colander.

## Step 3 – Sterilizing The Pint Jars

- To sterilize the jars, bring a large pot of water to a boil, then turn off the heat, place the jars in it, and let them sit in it for 5 to 10 minutes.
- Use thongs to pull them out then place them with the lid down on a towel to dry.

## Step 4 – Preparing the pressure cooker

- Start by placing a trivet at the bottom of your pressure canner.
- Fill the pressure canner with enough water to cover the jars completely, and bring it to a simmer.

## Step 5 – Cooking the chili

Place a large pot over high heat and heat in it a small splash of oil.

Add to it the beef, with pepper onion then cook them for 10 to 12 minutes until it becomes brown while stirring it constantly to break down the beef.

Once the beef and veggie are done, transfer the mixture to a colander and press it down to drain it from the oil and fat.

Transfer the beef mixture back to the pot, then add to it the remaining ingredients with beans and bring them to a boil.

Lower the heat, and allow the chili to cook for 5 to 7 minutes while stirring it occasionally until it is heated.

## Step 6 – Packing

Ladle the hot chili into the jars, and make sure to leave ½ to 1 inch of empty space.

- Put on the lids, and seal them tightly.

Wipe the sides of the jars with a clean and slightly wet rag, then put on the lids and secure them tightly. Press the center of the lids to ensure they are sealed properly.

## Step 7 – Pressure canning the chili

- Slowly lower the jars into the pressure canner to sit on the trivet.
- Put on the lid and seal it, then bring the pressure canner to pressure.
- Once the pressure canner comes up to pressure, allow the steam to continue to vent for 10 minutes to make sure there are no air pockets left in the canner.

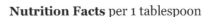

- Process the chili jars for 1 hour 15 minutes at 10 pounds of pressure for a weight gauge pressure canner, and 11 pounds for 1 hour 15 minutes if you are using a dial gauge pressure canner at an altitude of 1000 ft and less.
- Remember to adjust the processing time and pressure according to your altitude

### Step 8 – Releasing the pressure

- Once the processing time is up, turn off the heat and allow the pressure canner to sit undisturbed until the pressure reaches 0.
- Do not move or attempt to open the pressure canner at all until all the pressure is released.

### Step 9 – Letting the jars rest

Once the pressure is released, open the pressure canner, and use thongs to gently remove the jars from the pot.

- Place them on a large towel, and let them cool down completely. They might take 12 to 24 hours.

### Step 10 – Storing

Double check the jars to make sure they are sealed then you can store them in a cool and dark place for up to 1 year.

If you find some jars that are not sealed properly, you can still store them in the freezer for up to 6 months.

## Canning Dry Beans for Chili

|Intro|: Winter is when everyone is stocked up with ingredients for chilies, soups, and stews. Most of those recipes though require beans, and beans need to be soaked in water overnight to be used, which means every time you wish to make a stew or chili...you have to plan it ahead. Pressure canning beans relieve you from that burden so you can have ready-to-eat beans for 18 months. You can serve them as they are, or add them to your meals in a minute.

### Equipment:

- Pressure Canner
- Rack/Trivet
- Thongs
- Towel
- 10 Pint Jars
- Funnel
- Bowl
- Stockpot

**Nutrition Facts** per 1 tablespoon

| Calories | 487.16 kcal |
|----------|-------------|
| Carbs | 92.42g |
| Protein | 25.68g |
| Fats | 2.75g |

### Core Ingredients

- 3 pounds of dry pinto beans (or any other beans of your choice)
- Water
- Salt

### Step 1 – Soaking the beans

- Place the beans in a large bowl, then cover them with water and let them soak overnight.
- The next day, transfer the beans to a colander to drain them and discard the soaking liquid.

### Step 2 – Sterilizing The Pint Jars

- To sterilize the jars, bring a large pot of water to a boil, then turn off the heat, place the jars in it, and let them sit in it for 5 to 10 minutes.
- Use thongs to pull them out then place them with the lid down on a towel to dry.

### Step 3 – Preparing the pressure cooker

- Start by placing a trivet at the bottom of your pressure canner.
- Fill the pressure canner with enough water to cover the jars completely, and bring it to a simmer.

### Step 4 – Cooking the beans

- Place the beans in a large pot and cover them with water, then season them with some salt to taste.
- Bring the beans to a boil, then put on the lid, and cook them over low heat for 35 minutes until the beans become slightly tender, but not cooked completely.

### Step 5 – Packing

Ladle the beans with some of their cooking liquid while they are hot into the jars, and make sure to leave ½ to 1 inch of empty space.

- Put on the lids, and seal them tightly.

Wipe the sides of the jars with a clean and slightly wet rag, then put on the lids and secure them tightly. Press the center of the lids to ensure they are sealed properly.

### Step 6 – Pressure canning the chili

- Slowly lower the jars into the pressure canner to sit on the trivet.
- Put on the lid and seal it, then bring the pressure canner to pressure.
- Once the pressure canner comes up to pressure, allow the steam to continue to vent for 10 minutes to make sure there are no air pockets left in the canner.
- Process the beans jars for 1 hour 15 minutes at 10 pounds of pressure for a weight gauge pressure canner, and 11 pounds for 1 hour 15 minutes if you are using a dial gauge pressure canner at an altitude of 1000 ft and less.
- Remember to adjust the processing time and pressure according to your altitude

### Step 7 – Releasing the pressure

- Once the processing time is up, turn off the heat and allow the pressure canner to sit undisturbed until the pressure reaches 0.
- Do not move or attempt to open the pressure canner at all until all the pressure is released.

### Step 8 – Letting the jars rest

Once the pressure is released, open the pressure canner, and use thongs to gently remove the jars from the pot.

- Place them on a large towel, and let them cool down completely. They might take 12 to 24 hours.

### Step 9 – Storing

Double check the jars to make sure they are sealed then you can store them in a cool and dark place for up to 2 years.

If you find some jars that are not sealed properly, you can still store them in the freezer for up to 6 months.

## Section 6: Pressure Canning Meat

### Beef

|Intro|: Pressure canning is the best and safest method to can beef meat, as it is a simple and easy way to preserve it for up to 18 months without having to worry about freezing it in which case, it tends to lose its flavor with time, or about the power fails.

### Equipment:

- Pressure Canner
- Rack/Trivet
- Thongs
- Towel
- 6 Pint Jars
- Funnel
- Skillet

### Nutrition Facts per 1 Pint Jar

| Calories | 398.03 kcal |
|----------|-------------|
| Carbs | 0g |
| Protein | 78.48g |
| Fats | 9.15g |

### Core Ingredients

- 4 ½ pounds of lean beef, cubed or cut into strips
- Boiling water
- Salt
- Vegetable oil

### Step 1 – Browning the beef

Heat a splash of oil in a large skillet, then brown in it the beef cubes or stripes in batches.

When done, transfer the meat to a colander and let it for 4 to 5 minutes to drain as much fat and oil as possible.

### Step 2 – Sterilizing The Pint Jars

- To sterilize the jars, bring a large pot of water to a boil, then turn off the heat, place the jars in it, and let them sit in it for 5 to 10 minutes.
- Use thongs to pull them out then place them with the lid down on a towel to dry.

### Step 3 – Preparing the pressure cooker

- Start by placing a trivet at the bottom of your pressure canner.
- Fill the pressure canner with enough water to cover the jars completely, and bring it to a simmer.

### Step 5 – Packing

Pack the beef stripes or cubes into the jars loosely, then cover them with boiling water, and make sure to leave ½ to 1 inch of space.

- Put on the lids, and seal them tightly.

Wipe the sides of the jars with a clean and slightly wet rag, then put on the lids and secure them tightly. Press the center of the lids to ensure they are sealed properly.

### Step 6 – Pressure canning the beef

- Slowly lower the jars into the pressure canner to sit on the trivet.
- Put on the lid and seal it, then bring the pressure canner to pressure.
- Once the pressure canner comes up to pressure, allow the steam to continue to vent for 10 minutes to make sure there are no air pockets left in the canner.
- Process the beef jars for 1 hour 15 minutes at 10 pounds of pressure for a weight gauge pressure canner, and 11 pounds for 1 hour 15 minutes if you are using a dial gauge pressure canner at an altitude of 1000 ft and less.
- Remember to adjust the processing time and pressure according to your altitude

### Step 7 – Releasing the pressure

- Once the processing time is up, turn off the heat and allow the pressure canner to sit undisturbed until the pressure reaches 0.
- Do not move or attempt to open the pressure canner at all until all the pressure is released.

### Step 8 – Letting the jars rest

Once the pressure is released, open the pressure canner, and use thongs to gently remove the jars from the pot.

- Place them on a large towel, and let them cool down completely. They might take 12 to 24 hours.

### Step 9 – Storing

Double check the jars to make sure they are sealed then you can store them in a cool and dark place for up to 12 months.

If you find some jars that are not sealed properly, you can store them in the fridge or the freezer and use them in the next 2 days.

**|Intro|:** Whether you are pressure canning leftovers or fresh turkey, this recipe makes for a great way to have it always on hand, and makes for a quick meal to prepare since it's already cooked.

### Equipment:

- Pressure Canner
- Rack/Trivet
- Thongs
- Towel
- 8 Pint Jars
- Funnel

### Nutrition Facts per ½ cup

| Calories | 234 kcal |
|----------|----------|
| Carbs | 0g |
| Protein | 41g |
| Fats | 7g |

### Core Ingredients

- 18 pounds cooked turkey meat, boneless
- 4 quarts of turkey stock

### Step 1 – Preparing the Turkey

Fresh turkey meat doesn't store well, so you must cook it.

You can use turkey leftovers or roast it from scratch using your favorite recipe.

Cut the turkey meat into 1-inch cubes, and strips, or shred them into big pieces.

### Step 2 – Sterilizing The Pint Jars

- To sterilize the jars, bring a large pot of water to a boil, then turn off the heat, place the jars in it, and let them sit in it for 5 to 10 minutes.
- Use thongs to pull them out then place them with the lid down on a towel to dry.

### Step 3 – Preparing the pressure cooker

- Start by placing a trivet at the bottom of your pressure canner.
- Fill the pressure canner with enough water to cover the jars completely, and bring it to a simmer.

**Turkey**

### Step 4 – Packing

Use a spoon or thongs to pick up the turkey pieces and pack them into the jars.

Heat the turkey stock then pour it over the turkey meat, and make sure to leave ½ to 1 inch of empty space.

Wipe the sides of the jars with a clean and slightly wet rag, then put on the lids and secure them tightly. Press the center of the lids to ensure they are sealed properly.

### Step 5 – Pressure canning the turkey

- Slowly lower the jars into the pressure canner to sit on the trivet.
- Put on the lid and seal it, then bring the pressure canner to pressure.
- Once the pressure canner comes up to pressure, allow the steam to continue to vent for 10 minutes to make sure there are no air pockets left in the canner.
- Process the turkey jars for 1 hour 15 minutes at 10 pounds of pressure for a weight gauge pressure canner, and 11 pounds for 1 hour 15 minutes if you are using a dial gauge pressure canner at an altitude of 1000 ft and less.
- Remember to adjust the processing time and pressure according to your altitude

### Step 6 – Releasing the pressure

- Once the processing time is up, turn off the heat and allow the pressure canner to sit undisturbed until the pressure reaches 0.
- Do not move or attempt to open the pressure canner at all until all the pressure is released.

### Step 7 – Letting the jars rest

Once the pressure is released, open the pressure canner, and use thongs to gently remove the jars from the pot.

- Place them on a large towel, and let them cool down completely. They might take 12 to 24 hours.

### Step 8 – Storing

Double check the jars to make sure they are sealed then you can store them in a cool and dark place for up to 12 months.

If you find some jars that are not sealed properly, you can store them in the fridge or the freezer and use them in the next 2 days.

**Chicken**

|Intro|: Preserving chickens have never been easier with this recipe. It makes a perfect ready-to-eat meal for your busy days, or when you don't have time to cook. You can just toss it with a salad, add it to a sandwich or serve it with some sauce and noodles and enjoy!

### Equipment:

Pressure Canner

Rack/Trivet

Thongs

Towel

8 Pint Jars

Funnel

**Nutrition Facts** per ½ cup

| Calories | 86 kcal |
|----------|---------|
| Carbs    | 0g      |
| Protein  | 16g     |
| Fats     | 1g      |

### Core Ingredients

- 4 ½ pounds of chicken breasts, cubed
- 2 cups of hot water
- 4 teaspoons of salt

### Step 1 – Preparing the chicken

Rinse the chicken well then cut into cubes or strips.

If you have some pieces with bones in them, you can use them as well.

### Step 2 – Sterilizing The Pint Jars

- To sterilize the jars, bring a large pot of water to a boil, then turn off the heat, place the jars in it, and let them sit in it for 5 to 10 minutes.
- Use thongs to pull them out then place them with the lid down on a towel to dry.

### Step 3 – Preparing the pressure cooker

- Start by placing a trivet at the bottom of your pressure canner.
- Fill the pressure canner with enough water to cover the jars completely, and bring it to a simmer.

### Step 4 – Packing

Use a spoon or thongs to pick up the chicken pieces and pack them into the jars, then cover them with boiling water, and make sure to leave ½ to 1 inch of space.

- If you wish to season your chicken, add ¼ teaspoon of salt and other seasonings of your choice to the jars, then put on the lids, and seal them tightly. The salt gives them a nice flavor.

Wipe the sides of the jars with a clean and slightly wet rag, then put on the lids and secure them tightly. Press the center of the lids to ensure they are sealed properly.

### Step 5 – Pressure canning the chicken

- Slowly lower the jars into the pressure canner to sit on the trivet.
- Put on the lid and seal it, then bring the pressure canner to pressure.
- Once the pressure canner comes up to pressure, allow the steam to continue to vent for 10 minutes to make sure there are no air pockets left in the canner.
- Process the chicken jars for 1 hour 15 minutes at 10 pounds of pressure for a weight gauge pressure canner, and 11 pounds for 1 hour 15 minutes if you are using a dial gauge pressure canner at an altitude of 1000 ft and less.
- Remember to adjust the processing time and pressure according to your altitude

### Step 6 – Releasing the pressure

- Once the processing time is up, turn off the heat and allow the pressure canner to sit undisturbed until the pressure reaches 0.
- Do not move or attempt to open the pressure canner at all until all the pressure is released.

### Step 7 – Letting the jars rest

Once the pressure is released, open the pressure canner, and use thongs to gently remove the jars from the pot.

- Place them on a large towel, and let them cool down completely. They might take 12 to 24 hours.

### Step 8 – Storing

Double check the jars to make sure they are sealed then you can store them in a cool and dark place for up to 12 months.

If you find some jars that are not sealed properly, you can store them in the fridge or the freezer and use them in the next 2 days.

## Pork

**|Intro|:** Meats are one of the most expensive foods that are required for your daily meals, however, when you purchase them a bulk, you get a better deal. However, storing them is still difficult because their taste fades when stored in the freezer for so long. This is when this recipe comes in handy for pork, and makes for a perfectly quick, and delicious meal to prepare.

### Equipment:

- Pressure Canner
- Rack/Trivet
- Thongs
- Towel
- 16 Pint Jars
- Funnel

#### Nutrition Facts per 1 Pint Jar

| Calories | 509.58 kcal |
|----------|-------------|
| Carbs | 15.65g |
| Protein | 86.33g |
| Fats | 15.65g |

### Core Ingredients

- 16 pounds of pork loin
- Pork stock or boiling water
- 4 teaspoons of salt

### Step 1 – Preparing the pork

Trim the fat from the pork loin, then cut it into 1-inch cubes.

### Step 2 – Sterilizing The Pint Jars

- To sterilize the jars, bring a large pot of water to a boil, then turn off the heat, place the jars in it, and let them sit in it for 5 to 10 minutes.
- Use thongs to pull them out then place them with the lid down on a towel to dry.

### Step 3 – Preparing the pressure cooker

- Start by placing a trivet at the bottom of your pressure canner.

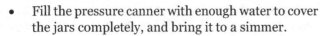

- Fill the pressure canner with enough water to cover the jars completely, and bring it to a simmer.

## Step 4 – Packing

Use a spoon or thongs to pick up the pork cubes and pack them loosely into the jars, then cover them with boiling water or the heated stock, and make sure to leave ½ to 1 inch of empty space.

- If you wish to season the port, you can add ¼ teaspoon of salt to each jar, along with other seasonings of your choice. The salt in particular adds a nice flavor to the meat.

Wipe the sides of the jars with a clean and slightly wet rag, then put on the lids and secure them tightly. Press the center of the lids to ensure they are sealed properly.

## Step 5 – Pressure canning the chicken

- Slowly lower the jars into the pressure canner to sit on the trivet.
- Put on the lid and seal it, then bring the pressure canner to pressure.
- Once the pressure canner comes up to pressure, allow the steam to continue to vent for 10 minutes to make sure there are no air pockets left in the canner.
- Process the pork jars for 1 hour 15 minutes at 10 pounds of pressure for a weight gauge pressure canner, and 11 pounds for 1 hour 15 minutes if you are using a dial gauge pressure canner at an altitude of 1000 ft and less.
- Remember to adjust the processing time and pressure according to your altitude

## Step 6 – Releasing the pressure

- Once the processing time is up, turn off the heat and allow the pressure canner to sit undisturbed until the pressure reaches 0.
- Do not move or attempt to open the pressure canner at all until all the pressure is released.

## Step 7 – Letting the jars rest

Once the pressure is released, open the pressure canner, and use thongs to gently remove the jars from the pot.

- Place them on a large towel, and let them cool down completely. They might take 12 to 24 hours.

## Step 8 – Storing

Double check the jars to make sure they are sealed then you can store them in a cool and dark place for up to 12 months.

If you find some jars that are not sealed properly, you can store them in the fridge or the freezer and use them in the next 2 days.

## Section 7: Pressure Canning Seafood

### Clams

|Intro|: Pressure canning clams make it the most convenient to preserve them and use them all year round without having to worry about preparing them every time you can crave them. You just have to pop open a jar, then use it for clam chowder, soup, or pasta sauce and enjoy!

### Equipment:

Pressure Canner

Rack/Trivet

Thongs

Towel

Pint Jars

Funnel

### Nutrition Facts per 1 tablespoon

| Calories | 35.01 kcal |
|----------|------------|
| Carbs | 1.59g |
| Protein | 6.54g |
| Fats | 0.52g |

### Core Ingredients

- Clams
- Boiling water
- Bottled lemon juice
- Salt

### Step 1 - Preparation

- The first thing to do is to make sure your clams are alive until you are ready to cook them.

- When ready to prepare the clams, scrub them clean, then rinse them thoroughly.

## Step 2 – Steaming the clams

- Prepare a steamer, and place in it the clams.
- Steam them for 4 to 5 minutes until the clams open.

Reserve the steaming liquid for later juice.

## Step 3 – Rinsing the clams meat

- Place the clams in a large bowl of water, then add 1 teaspoon of salt to each gallon of water that you used.
- Rinse the meat nicely in the water and solution then drain it, discard the water, and add the meat back to the bowl.
- Depending on how much meat you have, stir 2 tablespoons of bottled lemon juice with 1 gallon of boiling water, and double the amount until you get enough water to cover the clams' meat.

## Step 4 – Sterilizing The Pint Jars

- To sterilize the jars, bring a large pot of water to a boil, then turn off the heat, place the jars in it, and let them sit in it for 5 to 10 minutes.
- Use thongs to pull them out then place them with the lid down on a towel to dry.

## Step 5 – Preparing the pressure cooker

- Start by placing a trivet at the bottom of your pressure canner.
- Fill the pressure canner with enough water to cover the jars completely, and bring it to a simmer.

## Step 6 – Preparing the clams for canning

Transfer the clams meat, then cover it with the boiling water and lemon juice solution.

Bring them to a rolling boil for 2 minutes.

Once the time is up, drain the clams meat, and transfer it to a colander to drain for a minute or 2.

At this point, you can water bath can the clam meat as it is, or transfer it to a food processor, and pulse it several times until it is minced.

## Step 7 – Packing

Use a spoon to pack the clams meat into half-pint or pint jars.

Heat the reserved clam juice, then pour it on top of the clam meat. If it's not enough to fill all the jars, you can use boiling water.

Put on the lids and seal them tightly.

Wipe the sides of the jars with a clean and slightly wet rag, then put on the lids and secure them tightly. Press the center of the lids to ensure they are sealed properly.

## Step 8 – Pressure canning the clams

- Slowly lower the jars into the pressure canner to sit on the trivet.
- Put on the lid and seal it, then bring the pressure canner to pressure.
- Once the pressure canner comes up to pressure, allow the steam to continue to vent for 10 minutes to make sure there are no air pockets left in the canner.
- Process the clam jars for 70 minutes for pint jars, and 60 minutes for half pint jars at 10 pounds of pressure for a weight gauge pressure canner, and 11 pounds for 70 minutes for pint jars, and 60 minutes for half pint jars if you are using a dial gauge pressure canner at an altitude of 1000 ft and less.
- Remember to adjust the processing time and pressure according to your altitude

## Step 9 – Releasing the pressure

- Once the processing time is up, turn off the heat and allow the pressure canner to sit undisturbed until the pressure reaches 0.
- Do not move or attempt to open the pressure canner at all until all the pressure is released.

## Step 10 – Letting the jars rest

Once the pressure is released, open the pressure canner, and use thongs to gently remove the jars from the pot.

- Place them on a large towel, and let them cool down completely. They might take 12 to 24 hours.

## Step 11 – Storing

Double check the jars to make sure they are sealed then you can store them in a cool and dark place for up to 12 months.

If you find some jars that are not sealed properly, you can store them in the fridge or the freezer and use them in the next 3 days.

## Crab Meat

**|Intro|:** If you love crab, canning it is the best way to preserve it and enjoy it all year round while saving money. Just like all preserved meats heat, canned crab also makes for a quick meal that you can quickly prepare because it's already cooked. You just have to drain it, then toss it with a salad, add it to a soup, chowder, dipping sauce...and enjoy!

## Equipment:

- Pressure Canner
- Rack/Trivet
- Thongs
- Towel
- Pint Jars
- Funnel
- Stockpot
- Bowl

### Nutrition Facts per 1 Pint Jar

| Calories | 298.96 kcal |
|----------|-------------|
| Carbs | 4.14g |
| Protein | 62.43g |
| Fats | 2.19g |

## Core Ingredients

- Crabs
- Bottled lemon juice
- Salt
- Water

## Step 1 – Preparing the crabs

- Make sure the crabs are stored in ice until you plan to use them.
- Start by washing the crabs in water several times until the water comes out clean.

## Step 2 – Cooking the crabs

Bring a large pot of water to boil with the water depending on the number of crabs you have.

Add to it a ratio of 1/4 cup of lemon juice and 2 tablespoons of salt per gallon of water.

Add the crabs to the boiling water, then lower the heat and cook the, uncovered for 20 minutes.

## Step 3 – Sterilizing The Pint Jars

- To sterilize the jars, bring a large pot of water to a boil, then turn off the heat, place the jars in it, and let them sit in it for 5 to 10 minutes.
- Use thongs to pull them out then place them with the lid down on a towel to dry.

## Step 4 – Preparing the pressure cooker

- Start by placing a trivet at the bottom of your pressure canner.
- Fill the pressure canner with enough water to cover the jars completely, and bring it to a simmer.

## Step 5 – Preparing the crab meat

Once the time is up, drain the crabs and rinse them with cold water.

Fill a large bowl with water, and add to it a ratio of 2 cups of lemon juice and 2 tablespoons of salt.

Remove the crab shells, pull out the meat, then add it to the bowl with the water solution.

Allow the minutes to sit for 2 to 3 minutes in it.

## Step 6 – Packing

Once the time is up, drain the crab meat and squeeze it from the water solution, then use a spoon to pack it into half-pint or pint jars.

Add 4 tablespoons of bottled lemon juice to each pint jar, then cover the meat with boiling water, while leaving ½ to 1 inch of space at the top.

Put on the lids and seal them tightly.

Wipe the sides of the jars with a clean and slightly wet rag, then put on the lids and secure them tightly. Press the center of the lids to ensure they are sealed properly.

## Step 7 – Pressure canning the crab meat

- Slowly lower the jars into the pressure canner to sit on the trivet.
- Put on the lid and seal it, then bring the pressure canner to pressure.
- Once the pressure canner comes up to pressure, allow the steam to continue to vent for 10 minutes to make sure there are no air pockets left in the canner.
- Process the crab meat jars for 80 minutes for pint jars, and 70 minutes for half pint jars at 10 pounds of pressure for a weight gauge pressure canner, and 11 pounds for 80 minutes for pint jars, and 70 minutes for half pint jars if you are using a dial

gauge pressure canner at an altitude of 1000 ft and less.

- Remember to adjust the processing time and pressure according to your altitude

## Step 8 – Releasing the pressure

- Once the processing time is up, turn off the heat and allow the pressure canner to sit undisturbed until the pressure reaches 0.
- Do not move or attempt to open the pressure canner at all until all the pressure is released.

## Step 9 – Letting the jars rest

Once the pressure is released, open the pressure canner, and use thongs to gently remove the jars from the pot.

- Place them on a large towel, and let them cool down completely. They might take 12 to 24 hours.

## Step 10 – Storing

Double check the jars to make sure they are sealed then you can store them in a cool and dark place for up to 12 months.

If you find some jars that are not sealed properly, you can store them in the fridge or the freezer and use them in the next 3 days.

## Tuna

|Intro|: When in season, canning tuna is an ideal way to preserve it instead of freezing it. You can cold pack it or hot pack it, both methods yield amazing results, however, the hot packing method proves to be even better because it helps remove the oils and strong scent from the tuna, and makes it even more delicious.

## Equipment:

- Pressure Canner
- Rack/Trivet
- Thongs
- Towel
- Pint Jars
- Funnel
- Baking pan
- Oven

### Nutrition Facts per 1 Pint jar

| Calories | 544.31 kcal |
|---|---|
| Carbs | 0g |
| Protein | 88.19g |
| Fats | 18.52g |

## Core Ingredients

- Fresh Tuna
- Salt
- Water

## Step 1 – Preparing the tuna

- Start by cutting open the tuna stomach, then clean it, remove the viscera, and clean it thoroughly with water until no blood is left.

## Step 2 – Baking the tuna

Preheat the oven to 250 F.

Place the tuna on a lined-up cooking sheet, then bake it for 2 hours 30 minutes to 4 hours until it becomes tender.

Once the tuna is done, allow it to cool down completely, then transfer it to the fridge and allow it to sit overnight.

## Step 3 – Sterilizing The Pint Jars

- To sterilize the jars, bring a large pot of water to a boil, then turn off the heat, place the jars in it, and let them sit in it for 5 to 10 minutes.
- Use thongs to pull them out then place them with the lid down on a towel to dry.

## Step 4 – Preparing the pressure cooker

- Start by placing a trivet at the bottom of your pressure canner.
- Fill the pressure canner with enough water to cover the jars completely, and bring it to a simmer.

## Step 5 – Preparing the tuna meat

Cut the tuna meat into medium size chunks. Use white meat only, because dark meat doesn't taste good when canned.

Make sure to remove the bones, fins, and blood vessels...you can use them later to make fish stock.

## Step 6 – Packing

Pack the tuna chunks tightly into half-pint or pint jars, and be careful not to press it to mush and ruin the meat.

If you wish to season it, add 1 teaspoon of salt to each pint jar, it adds a nice flavor to the tuna, or you can leave it out.

Pour boiling water over the meat to cover it while leaving ½ to 1 inch of space on top.

Put on the lids and seal them tightly.

Wipe the sides of the jars with a clean and slightly wet rag, then put on the lids and secure them tightly. Press the center of the lids to ensure they are sealed properly.

## Step 7 – Pressure canning the tuna

- Slowly lower the jars into the pressure canner to sit on the trivet.
- Put on the lid and seal it, then bring the pressure canner to pressure.
- Once the pressure canner comes up to pressure, allow the steam to continue to vent for 10 minutes to make sure there are no air pockets left in the canner.
- Process the tuna jars for 100 minutes for pint jars and half pint jars at 10 pounds of pressure for a weight gauge pressure canner, and at 11 pounds for 100 minutes for pint jars and half pint jars if you are using a dial gauge pressure canner at an altitude of 1000 ft and less.
- Remember to adjust the processing time and pressure according to your altitude

## Step 8 – Releasing the pressure

- Once the processing time is up, turn off the heat and allow the pressure canner to sit undisturbed until the pressure reaches 0.
- Do not move or attempt to open the pressure canner at all until all the pressure is released.

## Step 9 – Letting the jars rest

Once the pressure is released, open the pressure canner, and use thongs to gently remove the jars from the pot.

- Place them on a large towel, and let them cool down completely. They might take 12 to 24 hours.

## Step 10 – Storing

Double check the jars to make sure they are sealed then you can store them in a cool and dark place for up to 12 months.

If you find some jars that are not sealed properly, you can store them in the fridge or the freezer and use them the next day.

## Salmon

|Intro|: If you caught a lot of salmon, or got a good deal on a big amount, there is no better way to preserve it and enjoy it all year round than pressure canning it. The process is very easy, and the end result is very versatile salty salmon that you can use with any recipe.

### Equipment:

- Pressure Canner
- Rack/Trivet
- Thongs
- Towel
- Pint Jars
- Funnel

### Nutrition Facts per 1 Pint

| Calories | 362 kcal |
|----------|----------|
| Carbs | 1g |
| Protein | 45g |
| Fats | 19g |

### Core Ingredients

- Salmon Fillets
- Canning Salt

### Step 1 – Preparing the salmon

- Start by cleaning the salmon fillets. Remove the blood vessels and any remaining bones.
- Use a sharp knife to remove the skin from the filling then cut them into medium size chunks.

### Step 2 – Sterilizing The Pint Jars

- To sterilize the jars, bring a large pot of water to a boil, then turn off the heat, place the jars in it, and let them sit in it for 5 to 10 minutes.
- Use thongs to pull them out then place them with the lid down on a towel to dry.

### Step 3 – Preparing the pressure cooker

- Start by placing a trivet at the bottom of your pressure canner.
- Fill the pressure canner with enough water to cover the jars completely, and bring it to a simmer.

### Step 4 – Packing

Pack the salmon chunks tightly into half-pint or pint jars. You don't need to add any liquid because the salmon will release its juices.

If you wish to season it, add 1 teaspoon of salt to each pint jar, it adds a nice flavor to the salmon, or you can leave it out.

Put on the lids and seal them tightly.

Wipe the sides of the jars with a clean and slightly wet rag, then put on the lids and secure them tightly. Press the center of the lids to ensure they are sealed properly.

### Step 5 – Pressure canning the salmon

- Slowly lower the jars into the pressure canner to sit on the trivet.
- Put on the lid and seal it, then bring the pressure canner to pressure.
- Once the pressure canner comes up to pressure, allow the steam to continue to vent for 10 minutes to make sure there are no air pockets left in the canner.
- Process the salmon jars for 1 hour 50 minutes for pint jars and half pint jars at 10 pounds of pressure for a weight gauge pressure canner, and at 11 pounds for 1 hour 50 minutes for pint jars and half pint jars if you are using a dial gauge pressure canner at an altitude of 1000 ft and less.
- Remember to adjust the processing time and pressure according to your altitude

### Step 6 – Releasing the pressure

- Once the processing time is up, turn off the heat and allow the pressure canner to sit undisturbed until the pressure reaches 0.
- Do not move or attempt to open the pressure canner at all until all the pressure is released.

### Step 7 – Letting the jars rest

Once the pressure is released, open the pressure canner, and use thongs to gently remove the jars from the pot.

- Place them on a large towel, and let them cool down completely. They might take 12 to 24 hours.

### Step 8 – Storing

Double check the jars to make sure they are sealed then you can store them in a cool and dark place for up to 12 months.

If you find some jars that are not sealed properly, you can store them in the fridge or the freezer and use them the next day.

---

## Shrimp

|Intro|: Shrimp is a very healthy food that is packed with nutrients and protein, so it will make a great addition to your canning project. At the same time, canning, and storing it makes it even more flavorful which makes a great addition to your meals.

### Equipment:

- Pressure Canner
- Rack/Trivet
- Thongs
- Towel
- Pint Jars
- Funnel
- Stockpot
- Bowl
- Jug

### Nutrition Facts per 1 Pint Jar

| Calories | 189.44 kcal |
|----------|-------------|
| Carbs | 4.58g |
| Protein | 33.42g |
| Fats | 2.72g |

### Core Ingredients

- Shrimp
- Water
- White vinegar
- Salt

### Step 1 – Preparing the Shrimp

- Make sure to keep the shrimp chilled until you are ready to use it.
- Next, wash the shrimp several times, and drain it.

### Step 2 – Cooking the shrimp

Bring a large pot of water to boil with the water depending on the number of crabs you have.

Add to it a ratio of 1/4 cup of salt and 1 cup of vinegar per gallon of water.

Add the shrimp to the boiling water, then lower the heat and cook, uncovered for 9 minutes.

### Step 3 – Sterilizing The Pint Jars

- To sterilize the jars, bring a large pot of water to a boil, then turn off the heat, place the jars in it, and let them sit in it for 5 to 10 minutes.
- Use thongs to pull them out then place them with the lid down on a towel to dry.

### Step 4 – Preparing the pressure cooker

- Start by placing a trivet at the bottom of your pressure canner.
- Fill the pressure canner with enough water to cover the jars completely, and bring it to a simmer.

### Step 5 – Preparing the shrimp for canning

Once the time is up, drain the shrimp, and transfer them to a large bowl.

Rinse it with cold water and allow it to sit in it for a few minutes until it cools down completely, then drain it.

Peel the shrimp, and make sure to remove the veins in the back. You can store the shrimp shells and heads to make shrimp stock.

### Step 6 – Packing

Pour 1 gallon of water into a large jug, then stir into it 1 ½ tablespoon of salt.

Pack the shrimp tightly into half-pint or pint jars, then cover them with the salted boiling water while leaving ½ to 1 inch of empty space at the top.

Put on the lids and seal them tightly.

Wipe the sides of the jars with a clean and slightly wet rag, then put on the lids and secure them tightly. Press the center of the lids to ensure they are sealed properly.

### Step 7 – Pressure canning the shrimp

- Slowly lower the jars into the pressure canner to sit on the trivet.
- Put on the lid and seal it, then bring the pressure canner to pressure.
- Once the pressure canner comes up to pressure, allow the steam to continue to vent for 10 minutes to make sure there are no air pockets left in the canner.
- Process the shrimp jars for 40 minutes for pint jars, and half pint jars at 10 pounds of pressure for a weight gauge pressure canner, and 11 pounds for 40 minutes for pint jars, and half pint jars if you are using a dial gauge pressure canner at an altitude of 1000 ft and less.
- Remember to adjust the processing time and pressure according to your altitude

### Step 8 – Releasing the pressure

- Once the processing time is up, turn off the heat and allow the pressure canner to sit undisturbed until the pressure reaches 0.
- Do not move or attempt to open the pressure canner at all until all the pressure is released.

### Step 9 – Letting the jars rest

Once the pressure is released, open the pressure canner, and use thongs to gently remove the jars from the pot.

- Place them on a large towel, and let them cool down completely. They might take 12 to 24 hours.

### Step 10 – Storing

Double check the jars to make sure they are sealed then you can store them in a cool and dark place for up to 3 months.

If you find some jars that are not sealed properly, you can store them in the fridge or the freezer and use them in the next 2 days.

## Smoked Fish

|Intro|: Smoking takes a lot of time, but it gives your foods especially fish an impeccable taste that you can't find anywhere else. Pressure canning makes it even better because, after a day or two of smoking, you can preserve your smoked fish for up to 1 year, saving a lot of time and money.

### Equipment:

- Pressure Canner
- Rack/Trivet
- Thongs
- Towel
- Pint Jars
- Funnel

**Nutrition Facts** per 1 tablespoon

| Calories | 7 kcal |
|----------|--------|
| Carbs | 1.4g |
| Protein | 0.1g |

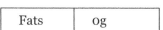

| Fats | 0g |
|------|-----|

## Core Ingredients

Smoked Fish (salmon, blue, mackerel, trout)

### Step 1 – Preparing the smoked fish

Cut the smoked fish meat into medium size chunks. If you are using smoked tuna, use the white meat only, because dark meat doesn't taste good when canned.

Make sure to remove the bones, fins, and blood vessels...you can use them later to make fish stock.

### Step 2 – Sterilizing The Pint Jars

- To sterilize the jars, bring a large pot of water to a boil, then turn off the heat, place the jars in it, and let them sit in it for 5 to 10 minutes.
- Use thongs to pull them out then place them with the lid down on a towel to dry.

### Step 3 – Preparing the pressure cooker

- Start by placing a trivet at the bottom of your pressure canner.
- Fill the pressure canner with enough water to cover the jars completely, and bring it to a simmer.

### Step 4 – Packing

Pack the fish meat chunks tightly into half-pint or pint jars, and be careful not to press it to mush and ruin the meat, and make sure to leave ½ to 1 inch of space on top.

You don't have to add any liquid because the fish is cooked, so it will release its own oil and juices.

Put on the lids and seal them tightly.

Wipe the sides of the jars with a clean and slightly wet rag, then put on the lids and secure them tightly. Press the center of the lids to ensure they are sealed properly.

### Step 5 – Pressure canning the smoked fish

- Slowly lower the jars into the pressure canner to sit on the trivet.
- Put on the lid and seal it, then bring the pressure canner to pressure.
- Once the pressure canner comes up to pressure, allow the steam to continue to vent for 10 minutes to make sure there are no air pockets left in the canner.
- Process the smoked fish jars for 1 hour 50 minutes for pint jars and half pint jars at 10 pounds of pressure for a weight gauge pressure canner, and

at 11 pounds for 1 hour 50 minutes for pint jars and half pint jars if you are using a dial gauge pressure canner at an altitude of 1000 ft and less.

- Remember to adjust the processing time and pressure according to your altitude

### Step 6 – Releasing the pressure

- Once the processing time is up, turn off the heat and allow the pressure canner to sit undisturbed until the pressure reaches 0.
- Do not move or attempt to open the pressure canner at all until all the pressure is released.

### Step 7 – Letting the jars rest

Once the pressure is released, open the pressure canner, and use thongs to gently remove the jars from the pot.

- Place them on a large towel, and let them cool down completely. They might take 12 to 24 hours.

### Step 8 – Storing

Double check the jars to make sure they are sealed then you can store them in a cool and dark place for up to 12 months.

If you find some jars that are not sealed properly, you can store them in the fridge or the freezer and use them the next day.

## Trout

|Intro|: Trout is yet another fantastic fish to pressure can. The salt and natural oils that the trout releases when canned make it much more scrumptious when you finally serve it.

### Equipment:

- Pressure Canner
- Rack/Trivet
- Thongs
- Towel
- 3 Pint Jars
- Funnel

#### Nutrition Facts per 1 Pint Jar

| Calories | 805.85 kcal |
|----------|-------------|
| Carbs | 0g |
| Protein | 113.96g |
| Fats | 35.32g |

## Core Ingredients

- 6 pounds of trout fish meat
- 3 teaspoons of salt

### Step 1 – Preparing the trout

- Start by cutting open the trout's stomach, then clean it, remove the viscera, and clean it thoroughly with water until no blood is left.
- Cut off the heat, tail, and fins, and discard the scales, then cut the trout fish in half lengthwise.
- If you are using a half-pint jar, cut the trout halves into two so they can fit the jars.

### Step 2 – Soaking the trout in salt brine

Depending on how much fish you have, fill a large bowl with water, then add to salt with a ratio of 1 cup per 1 gallon.

Add to it the trout pieces, and let them sit for 65 minutes.

### Step 3 – Preparing the trout meat

Once the time is up, rinse the trout meat with fresh water, then place it in a colander and let it drain completely for 12 to 15 minutes.

### Step 4 – Packing

Pack the trout chunks into half-pint or pint jars with the skin side facing the side of the jars, and make sure to leave ½ to 1 inch of empty space at the top.

Do not add any liquid, because the trout meat will release its own juices and oil when canned.

Put on the lids and seal them tightly.

Wipe the sides of the jars with a clean and slightly wet rag, then put on the lids and secure them tightly. Press the center of the lids to ensure they are sealed properly.

### Step 5 – Pressure canning the trout

- Slowly lower the jars into the pressure canner to sit on the trivet.
- Put on the lid and seal it, then bring the pressure canner to pressure.
- Once the pressure canner comes up to pressure, allow the steam to continue to vent for 10 minutes to make sure there are no air pockets left in the canner.
- Process the trout jars for 1 hour 40 minutes for pint jars and half pint jars at 10 pounds of pressure for a weight gauge pressure canner, and at 11 pounds for 1 hour 40 minutes for pint jars and half pint jars if you are using a dial gauge pressure canner at an altitude of 1000 ft and less.
- Remember to adjust the processing time and pressure according to your altitude

### Step 6 – Releasing the pressure

- Once the processing time is up, turn off the heat and allow the pressure canner to sit undisturbed until the pressure reaches 0.
- Do not move or attempt to open the pressure canner at all until all the pressure is released.

### Step 7 – Letting the jars rest

Once the pressure is released, open the pressure canner, and use thongs to gently remove the jars from the pot.

- Place them on a large towel, and let them cool down completely. They might take 12 to 24 hours.

### Step 8 – Storing

Double check the jars to make sure they are sealed then you can store them in a cool and dark place for up to 12 months.

- If you find some jars that are not sealed properly, you can store them in the fridge and use them the next day.

# |Part 4| Pickling Intro

## Section 1: What is pickling?

A time-honored food preservation technique is pickling, which has been used for millennia. The word "pekel" in Dutch, meaning to "brine" or "salt" that are essential components of the pickling process—is where the name "pickle" originates. Pickling gives food its distinctive sour taste by preserving it in an acidic solution (which could be vinegar) & salt. Because the pH level is maintained at a safe level and any microbial development is controlled, food lasts much longer. Pickles soaked in liquids help keep them from spoiling.

## Section 2: The science of pickling

Pickling magic is a change in color, texture, and taste that results from all the components working together harmoniously and all the correct processes being followed in accordance with a dependable recipe.

With the inclusion of salt, other spices, & vinegar, pickled foods acquire unique characteristics. A fresh cucumber will ultimately decay and become mushy if kept in the refrigerator for a number of days. Because they contain natural enzymes, raw & fresh foods deteriorate over time. All living things include natural proteins called enzymes, and they alter food and ultimately cause deterioration if left uncontrolled.

Pickled foods do not go bad quickly because of the vinegar's acidity and the salt's ability to preserve food holds the key. Combined, salt & vinegar inactivate the natural enzymes present in food and stop the development of new microbes, such as yeasts and molds. Adding vinegar increases the acidity, while salt absorbs more moisture.

The secret to effective pickling is to raise the food's acidity which means lowering the pH to 4.6 or below.

Refrigerator pickles stay longer than rapid process pickles because of the extra step of processing them, such as soaking them in hot water. The high temperature of boiling water at 212 F, which also effectively seals the jar and its contents, further destroys any microbes. Food is further preserved in an anaerobic (oxygen-free) environment found in sealed jars.

## Section 3: Ingredients needed for pickling

### Vinegar

The most crucial consideration when choosing vinegar is to make sure it has at least 5% of acetic acid, and this guarantees the ideal degree of acidity for pickling. You may pickle using different types of vinegars, the 2 most popular being apple cider & white vinegar.

White vinegar is often chosen since it doesn't change the color of food (it only turns red onion to pink color). The taste of apple cider vinegar is more subdued and mildly fruity. The drawbacks include a higher cost and frequent food coloring.

Do not use vinegar that has less than 5 percent of acetic acid. Also DO NOT use non-food-graded vinegar, and DOT NOT use any industrial or cleaning vinegar of course. Homemade vinegar

shouldn't be used for safe pickling since it often has an undetermined acetic acid content.

## Salt

Table salt should be saved for supper. Pickling salt, often known as canning salt, is something different. The noncaking chemicals included in the majority of regular table salts cause pickle brine to become murky.

## Seasonings & Spices

When pickling, always use entire spices; examples include whole peppercorns & dill. Whole spices not only last longer in vinegar, but they also seem more attractive in jars. Seasonings & spices that are powdered can obscure the pickling solution.

Pre-mixed spice packets are available at the shop. Among the best seasonings & spices available there are:

- Bay leaves
- Cinnamon sticks
- Mustard seeds
- Cardamom pods
- Black peppercorns
- Coriander seeds
- Whole cloves
- Fresh dill sprigs
- White sugar
- Garlic cloves
- Crushed red pepper

## Water

A lot of novice picklers often forget the significance of water. Water is only water, after all. No, not always. The industry norm is distilled water. In jars, water that is hard or chlorinated often becomes hazy. Consider purchasing distilled or bottled water if your neighborhood has hard tap water.

This is a quick tip to make your chlorinated water suitable for pickling: Chlorinated water should be poured into multiple clean containers. Give it 48 hours to rest. The chlorine normally evaporates throughout this period.

## Sugar

Brown or Granulated white sugar is used in most recipes. Use only these sugar unless the recipe specifies differently. Other sweets, such as corn syrup or honey, could have unexpected effects.

## Produce

Only the freshest, unblemished fruits and vegetables should be used for pickling. Freshly collected food should ideally be used within 24 hours, so store it in the refrigerator until you're ready to utilize it. Make sure all fruits and veggies are unwaxed before using. Stick to fresh from the garden or food bought at farmers' markets since most products available in supermarket shops have been waxed.

## Section 4: Categories of pickling

Pickles may be divided into two primary groups. Pickles from the first category are kept in vinegar, where germs cannot thrive. The majority of the kosher cucumber pickles sold in bottles at the grocery store are kept in vinegar.

The second group consists of pickles that have been steeped in salt water to promote fermentation, which weakens the ability of "bad" bacteria to ruin food. Many cucumber dill pickles & kimchi are typical examples of fermented pickles.

Fermentation & vinegar are normally the two major methods for doing this.

Vinegar: Foods that have been pickled in vinegar may be canned and kept in cabinets or in the fridge. The "quick-process" methods are other names for this one. As vinegar is acidic, it is vinegar that keeps the food from spoiling. This is the process that most professionally manufactured pickles are prepared with, and it is also the one that many people today most often identify with pickling.

Fermentation: Through this method (see dedicated section), you may also prepare pickles "the old-fashioned manner." When food is allowed to rest for a while, naturally existing sugars begin to break down. This process is known as fermentation. When making pickles, some foods may be fermented by soaking them in a saltwater solution and letting them stand until the sugars dissolve and produce lactic acid. The introduction of vinegar is not essential since the lactic acid transforms into the acidic solution required for pickling.

For most people, pickling with vinegar is arguably the simplest, fastest, and least daunting option, but fermentation offers far more health advantages. Fermentation also produces alcohol. Health advantages are also many. The lactic acid in fermenting pickles creates a variety of healthy enzymes, nutrients, and good bacteria that support intestinal health. While there is no

superior or worse way of pickling, you may prefer one over the other depending on the degree of familiarity and expertise with pickling & canning.

### Refrigerator pickles

These Pickles are made quickly. These pickles are intended to be kept in the fridge and have a limited shelf life (for three months). Vegetables & fruits are cleaned, trimmed, and placed in jars. On the burner, a hot brine is prepared and poured over the canned food. The jars may be kept in the refrigerator when they have cooled.

Pickles that are kept in a refrigerator enable you to be a little more creative with the spices you use since they are kept chilly rather than on a shelf at ambient temperature.

Pickles made quickly using hot water have a longer shelf life. They are made with the additional step of processing them later for extended shelf life (for 12 months). Before making the vinegar brine, some recipes ask for a salty soak or brining for many hours to remove any extra moisture. These are general instructions, for optimum results, it's crucial to follow the recipe meticulously.

## Section 5: Types of Pickled Products

Pickles that have been brined or fermented are preserved for one to several weeks in a brine solution. The product's color, taste, and consistency are altered during curing. If the product has undergone fermentation, the lactic acid created during the process aids in its preservation. To retain the food, acid in the form of vinegar is afterward added to brined dishes that are curing but not fermenting.

Pickles that have undergone a quick process are doused with scalding hot vinegar, seasonings & spices. The product may occasionally be brined for many hours, drained, and then coated with pickling liquid. These pickles taste tart and are simple to make. After being packed in jars, freshly pack or fast pickles taste best when let to stand for a few weeks.

Fruit pickles are formed by simmering whole or cut-up fruits in a hot, sweet or sour sauce composed of vinegar or lemon juice.

Relishes: These are prepared by cooking chopped vegetables and fruits in a hot vinegar solution till the appropriate consistency.

The amount of acidity in a pickled food affects both flavor and texture as well as safety. Never change a recipe's vinegar, water or salt ratios. Use only authentic recipes. By doing this, you may aid in preventing the development of the bacterium Clostridium botulinum, which creates a very lethal toxin in meals with low acidity.

## Section 6: Do & Don't of pickling

### Do's

Adhere to a tried-and-true pickling recipe for a secure and delectable final result.

Adhere to suggested canning processes from a reliable source to guarantee a healthy and delectable final product.

Use types of vinegar that are made commercially. Pickling may be done with either apple cider or white vinegar. Although it has a stronger flavor, white vinegar won't stain the pickled goods. Although it has a milder flavor, apple cider vinegar may discolor produce. Whatever vinegar you select, it must have a 5 percent acidity level.

Making use of professionally made (store-bought) vinegar is the simplest approach to guarantee this.

Put pickles that have been opened in the fridge. Pretty basic.

Give home pickling a try. One can pickle pretty much anything, and there are a bunch of different methods to accomplish it.

### Don'ts

Be inventive with your cooking. To guarantee that the food you preserved is safe to consume, it's crucial to follow a tried-and-true recipe. Don't tamper with the salt to vinegar ratio or proportions since they are crucial to the process of pickling.

As you gain experience, you may experiment with other spices & herbs, but even these might compromise the safety and flavor of the pickles if you use too much or too little of any one ingredient. Get the pickle-making feet wet with authentic recipes if you're a beginner before trying to add your own flair.

Use obsolete canning techniques. Similar to following written recipes, it's crucial to use the most recent safe canning techniques as advised by a reliable source. Even if your grandma or another relative may claim, "We

never cooked our pickles jars in a hot-water bath," it is still advised that you use modern methods to be safe.

Season pickles with normal table salt. Use sea salt if you have no other options, since most pickle recipes ask for kosher or pickling salt. Although adding table or iodized salt isn't inherently fatal, it may build up, cloud the water, and alter the color of whatever you're preserving.

## Section 7: Precautions about pickling

Use sterilized, clean jars while working. Sterilize jars by putting them in simmering water for ten minutes if you're preparing refrigerated pickles.

Warm up jars before using. They may be kept in the washer on the heat and taken out as necessary. A chilly jar could fracture if boiling brine is put in it.

Remember to cut off a minimum of 1/16" from the blossom side of cucumbers if you want to use them. The cucumber won't soften and deteriorate before its time as a result of this.

Always follow an accurate recipe. Even though pickling dates back centuries, some of the old recipes are not be reliable.

Avoid brining with any brass or copper since this might stain the food. Alternatively, you may use pots & utensils made of glass, enamel, or steel.

Giving pickles some crunch: There are a couple of firming agents you may apply if you desire more crunch. Food-grade lime: The calcium in lime helps dishes stay more firmly set. Rinse and soak. And then do it again. When processing, be sure to properly rinse all of the lime. Firming agents available in stores: to keep pickles crisp, several canning businesses offer pre-packaged goods. These calcium chloride granules are more convenient than lime since they don't need to be soaked and rinsed beforehand.

## Section 8: Shelf Life for Different Types of Pickle

Pickles for the refrigerator are produced using vinegar, occasionally with salt & sugar. They are meant to be kept in the refrigerator and often only last between two and four weeks.

Higher ratios of vinegar, sugar & salt are used to make vinegar pickles that are canned. Following that, the jars are treated in a hot water bath. These pickles have a shelf life of 6-12 months, or more and are often kept in a cabinet because of their shelf stability.

Only salt or a brine comprised of water & salt is used to make lacto-ferment pickles. Lactic acid is created by bacteria when they ferment fruits or vegetables. Before being kept in the refrigerator, these pickles ferment at room temp for 1-2 weeks. These usually last 4-6 months

Chutneys and relishes include sugar in addition to vinegar and resemble vinegar pickles the most. They are often treated in a water bath, but not always. These pickles have a shelf life or refrigerator life of a few months to a year or longer.

# |Part 5| Pickling Recipes

## Section 1: Vegetables Pickling Recipes

### Pickled Carrots

|Intro|: I hate to say it, but who doesn't have a bunch of carrots lying around in the fridge, and don't know what to do with them? I know I do, but I have them right now. This recipe will save you from them. These pickled carrots turn out very flavorful, and crispy and will make eat them in no time, and look for more.

### Equipment:

Glass container

Knife

Cutting Board

Towel

Saucepan

**Nutrition Facts** per 2 baby carrots

| Calories | 29 kcal |
|----------|---------|
| Carbs | 6.9g |
| Protein | 0.5g |
| Fats | 0.1g |

### Core Ingredients

- 1 ½ pound of carrots

### Pickling Solution

- 1 cup of apple cider vinegar
- 1 cup of water
- 1 ½ tablespoon of organic cane sugar
- ¾ teaspoon of salt

### Step 1 - Preparation

- Start by peeling the carrots, washing them, then removing the tops, and trimming their ends.
- If your carrots are small, keep them as they are.
- If your carrots are big, cut them in half and remove the yellow innard, then cut them into thick stripes.

- Place the carrots in a large glass container then place it aside.

### Step 2 – Preparing the pickling solution

- Place a saucepan over medium heat then stir in it all the pickling solution ingredients.
- Bring it to a simmer while stirring the sugar until dissolves.

### Step 3 – Pickling the carrots

- Pour the pickling solution on top of the carrots, then cover the container and allow it to cool down completely.
- Once done, transfer the container to the fridge and allow it to sit for 24 hours or more to absorb the flavor.
- Once the time is up, serve your carrots and enjoy. Or you can store them in the fridge for up to 3 weeks.

### Pickled Cauliflower

|Intro|: Cauliflower is a very nice vegetable, but a lot of people don't know how to use it or the best way to cook it, so it often remains sitting in the fridge for days. This pickled cauliflower recipe will introduce cauliflower to your life in a delicious way. It turns out crunchy with a hint of sweetness and a load of flavor.

### Equipment:

Saucepan

Knife

Cutting Board

Towel

Funnel

2 Quart jars or 4-pint jars

**Nutrition Facts** per ¼ cup

| Calories | 11 kcal |
|----------|---------|
| Carbs | 1g |
| Protein | 0g |
| Fats | g |

### Core Ingredients

- 2 Pounds of cauliflower
- 4 cloves of garlic, peeled and sliced

- 3 teaspoons of kosher salt
- 3 teaspoons of white granulated sugar
- 2 teaspoons of mustard seeds
- 2 teaspoons of black peppercorns
- 2 teaspoons of coriander seeds
- 4 sprigs of fresh dill

## Pickling Solution

- 3 cups of water
- 1 ½ cup of white vinegar
- 3 teaspoons of kosher salt
- 3 teaspoons of white granulated sugar

## Step 1 - Preparation

- Start washing the cauliflower, remove the stem and cut it into florets.
- Divide the cauliflower florets between the jars along with the dill sprigs, coriander seeds, black peppercorns, and mustard seeds.

## Step 2 – Preparing the pickling solution

- Place a saucepan over medium heat then stir in it all the pickling solution ingredients.
- Bring it to a simmer while stirring the sugar until dissolves.

## Step 3 – Pickling the cauliflower

- Pour the pickling solution on top of the cauliflower florets until they are completely covered. Add hot water if needed.
- Seal the jars, and allow them to sit in the fridge for at least 24 hours before serving them.
- You can store it for up to 4 weeks in the fridge and enjoy it!

## Summer Pickled Cucumbers

|Intro|: These cucumber pickles are very simple, you can prepare them in 5 minutes and enjoy them as a great snack, or side dish in spring and summer.

## Equipment:

Saucepan

Knife

Cutting Board

Towel

Funnel

Jars

**Nutrition Facts** per 1/3 cup

| Calories | 33kcal |
|----------|--------|
| Carbs | 6.2g |
| Protein | 1g |
| Fats | 0.1g |

## Core Ingredients

- 2 cups of cucumbers, sliced
- ½ cup of green onions, sliced

## Pickling Solution

- 1 cup of water
- 1/3 cup of apple cider vinegar
- 2 tablespoons of white granulated sugar
- 1 teaspoon of salt

## Step 1 - Preparation

- Start by washing and slicing the cucumbers and spring onions, then pack them into jars.

## Step 2 – Preparing the pickling solution

- Place a saucepan over medium heat then stir in it all the pickling solution ingredients.
- Bring it to a simmer while stirring the sugar until dissolves.

## Step 3 – Pickling the cucumber

- Pour the pickling solution on top of the cucumber and onions until they are completely covered. Add hot water if needed.
- Seal the jars, and allow them to sit in the fridge for at least 24 hours before serving them.
- You can store it for up to 4 weeks in the fridge and enjoy it!

## Spicy Radish Pickles

|Intro|: These radish pickles yield nice crunchy radishes that taste spicy with a hint of sweetness, and make for a nice side dish to spice up your meals, and add a unique flavor to them.

## Equipment:

Knife

Cutting Board

Towel

Funnel

Saucepan

Jars

**Nutrition Facts** per ¼ cup

| Calories | 53 kcal |
|----------|---------|
| Carbs | 12g |
| Protein | 0.6g |
| Fats | 0.1g |

## Core Ingredients

- 2 pounds of small and fresh radishes

## Pickling Solution

- 1 ½ cup of apple cider vinegar
- 1 ½ cup of water
- 6 tablespoons of honey
- 4 teaspoons of salt
- 1 teaspoon of red pepper flakes

## Step 1 - Preparation

- Start by washing and thinly slicing the radishes, then transferring them into jars.

## Step 2 – Preparing the pickling solution

- Place a saucepan over medium heat then stir in it all the pickling solution ingredients.
- Bring them to a boil, then stir them until the honey completely dissolves.

## Step 3 – Pickling the radishes

- Pour the pickling solution on top of the radishes, then put the lids, and store them in the fridge for at least 48 hours before serving them.
- You can store it for up to 3 weeks in the fridge and enjoy it!

## Roasted Pickled Beets

|Intro|: Side, snack, or salad when combined with other veggies. The pickled beets are very versatile and last for up to 5 weeks in the fridge. They come out crispy, flavorful, and taste fantastic.

### Equipment:

Saucepan

Knife

Cutting Board

Towel

Funnel

Jars

Oven

Baking sheet

**Nutrition Facts** per 1/8 of the recipe

| Calories | 77 kcal |
|----------|---------|
| Carbs | 17g |
| Protein | 1g |
| Fats | 1g |

## Core Ingredients

- 4 medium red beets

## Pickling Solution

- 1 cup of apple cider vinegar
- 1 cup of water
- 1/3 cup of white granulated sugar
- 1 teaspoon of salt
- ¼ teaspoon of ground mustard
- 5 whole black peppercorns

## Step 1 - Preparation

- Start by washing and trimming the tops of the beets.

## Step 2 – Roasting the beets

- Preheat the oven to 400 F.
- Place each beet in a piece of foil and wrap it around it, then place them on a baking sheet.
- Transfer them to the oven, and roast them for 1 hour until they become soft.

## Step 3 – Preparing the beets for pickling

- Once the beets are roasted, place them aside and allow them to cool down completely.
- Peel the beets and cut them into slightly thick rounds, then transfer them to the storing jars.

## Step 4 – Preparing the pickling solution

- Place a saucepan over medium heat then stir in it all the pickling solution ingredients.
- Bring them to a boil, then stir them until the sugar completely dissolves.

### Step 5 – Pickling the beets

- Pour the pickling solution on top of the beets, then put the lids, and store them in the fridge for at least 48 hours before serving them.
- You can store it for up to 6 weeks in the fridge and enjoy it!

## Pickled Sweet Zucchini

**|Intro|:** If you have some zucchini lying in the fridge that you don't know what to do, the recipe will give you crispy pickled zucchini slices that are full of flavors. You can serve them as a side dish, or burger toppings, and add them to a salad.

### Equipment:

Saucepan

Knife

Cutting Board

Towel

Funnel

Jars

### Nutrition Facts per 1 Pint Jar

| Calories | 13 kcal |
|----------|---------|
| Carbs | 2g |
| Protein | 0g |
| Fats | 0g |

### Core Ingredients

- 1 ½ pound of fresh zucchini

### Pickling Solution

- 1 cup of rice wine vinegar
- ½ cup of water
- 2 tablespoons of white granulated sugar
- 1 ½ teaspoon of pickling spice
- Salt

### Step 1 - Preparation

- Start by washing and trimming the ends of the zucchini, then slice them into ribbons.
- Season it generously with salt, then place it in a colander, and let it drain for 14 to 16 minutes.
- Once the time is up, drain the zucchini, transfer it to a towel, then pat it dry.

### Step 2 – Preparing the pickling solution

- Place a saucepan over medium heat then stir in it all the pickling solution ingredients.
- Bring them to a boil, then stir them until the sugar completely dissolves.

### Step 3 – Pickling the zucchini

- Pack the zucchini ribbons into the jars.
- Pour the pickling solution on top of the zucchini, then put the lids, and store them in the fridge for at least 48 hours before serving them.
- You can store it for up to 3 weeks in the fridge and enjoy it!

## Crunchy Pickled Cabbage

**|Intro|:** Pickled cabbage makes a great addition to your pickles collections. The cabbage comes out crunchy, full of flavors, and simply delicious.

### Equipment:

Knife

Cutting Board

Towel

Funnel

Jars

Bowl

### Nutrition Facts per 1 Cup

| Calories | 22 kcal |
|----------|---------|
| Carbs | 4.6g |
| Protein | 0.5g |
| Fats | 0g |

### Core Ingredients

- ½ of a red cabbage
- 2 cloves of garlic, peeled and sliced
- 1 cup of water
- 1 cup of red wine vinegar
- 2 tablespoons of white granulated sugar
- 2 teaspoons of salt
- ½ teaspoon of black pepper

### Step 1 - Preparation

- Start by washing and finely chop the cabbage.

### Step 2 – Making the pickled cabbage

- Combine all the ingredients in a large bowl, then toss them until well combined.
- Cover the bowl, and let it sit for at least 8 hours in the fridge.
- Once the time is up, you can serve it and enjoy, or store it for up to 3 weeks in the fridge.

## Chili Pickled Brussels Sprouts

|Intro|: There are many ways to enjoy Brussels sprouts, and this recipe is one of the best. The brussels sprouts come crunchy, delicious, and full of flavor. You can serve it as a side dish, toss it with some veggies to make a salad, and simply serve it as a snack.

### Equipment:

Saucepan

Knife

Cutting Board

Towel

Funnel

Jars

**Nutrition Facts** per 1 Pint Jar

| Calories | 17 kcal |
|----------|---------|
| Carbs | 3g |
| Protein | 1g |
| Fats | 0g |

### Core Ingredients

- 2 pounds of brussels sprouts
- 40 peppercorns
- ½ teaspoon of yellow mustard seeds
- Red Pepper flakes
- 4 bay leaves
- 4 cloves of garlic, peeled and sliced

### Pickling Solution

- 3 cups of apple cider vinegar
- 1 cup of water
- 2 tablespoons of salt

### Step 1 - Preparation

- Start by washing and trimming the stems of the brussels sprouts.
- If the brussels sprouts you have are small, cut them in half, if they are big, cut them into quarters.

### Step 2 – Preparing the pickling solution

- Place a saucepan over medium heat then stir in it all the pickling solution ingredients.
- Bring them to a boil, then stir them until the sugar completely dissolves.

### Step 3 – Pickling the brussels sprouts

- Pack the brussels sprouts into jars, then add to them the peppercorns, bay leaves, garlic, mustard seeds, and if you wish, some red pepper flakes to taste.
- Pour the pickling solution on top of the brussels sprouts, then put the lids, and store them in the fridge for at least 48 hours before serving them.
- You can store it for up to 3 weeks in the fridge and enjoy it!

## Instant Pickled Asparagus

|Intro|: If you found a great deal on asparagus, or if you bought more than you need, this quick asparagus recipe will enable you to preserve it in a matter of minutes which will make a great addition to your meals.

### Equipment:

Saucepan

Knife

Cutting Board

Towel

Funnel

Jars

**Nutrition Facts** per 1 Asparagus spear

| Calories | 6 kcal |
|----------|--------|
| Carbs | 1g |
| Protein | 0.2g |
| Fats | 0g |

### Core Ingredients

- 2 pounds of fresh asparagus

### Pickling Solution

- 6 cups of water

- 3 cups of white vinegar
- 4 tablespoons of salt
- 2 tablespoons of pickling spice
- 2 tablespoons of white granulated sugar
- 4 cloves of garlic, peeled and sliced

## Step 1 - Preparation

- Start by washing and trimming the hard stems of the asparagus enough to make them fit into the jars.

## Step 2 – Preparing the pickling solution

- Place a saucepan over medium heat then stir in it all the pickling solution ingredients.
- Bring them to a boil, then stir them until the sugar completely dissolves.

## Step 3 – Pickling the asparagus

- Pack the asparagus spears tightly into jars.
- Pour the pickling solution on top of the asparagus, then put the lids, and store them in the fridge for at least 48 hours before serving them.
- You can store it for up to 2 weeks in the fridge and enjoy it!

## Vinegary Pickled Mushrooms

|Intro|: Pickled mushrooms are very tasty and super versatile. You can use them as a topping for sandwiches, as a side dish, or as a snack. They will add unique and delicious flavor to your meals.

### Equipment:

Saucepan

Knife

Cutting Board

Towel

Funnel

Jars

### Nutrition Facts per 1 Pint Jar

| Calories | 26 kcal |
|----------|---------|
| Carbs | 4g |
| Protein | 2g |
| Fats | 1g |

### Core Ingredients

- 2 pounds of fresh mushrooms

### Pickling Solution

- 2 cups of water
- ¾ cup of white vinegar
- 1 tablespoon of salt
- 1 tablespoon of white granulated sugar
- 6 bay leaves
- 8 black peppercorns

## Step 1 - Preparation

- Start by washing and trimming the hard stems of the mushrooms.
- If the mushrooms that you are using are small, leave them as they are.
- If the mushrooms you are using are big, cut them into quarters.

## Step 2 – Cooking the mushrooms

- Place the mushrooms in a pot and cover them with water.
- Add to them ½ cup of vinegar and bring them to a boil over high heat.
- Keep the mushrooms cooking for 16 minutes until they become soft and tender.

## Step 3 – Preparing the pickling solution

- Place a saucepan over medium heat then stir in it all the pickling solution ingredients including the remaining vinegar.
- Bring them to a boil, then stir them until the sugar completely dissolves.

## Step 4 – Pickling the mushrooms

- Once the time is up, drain the mushrooms then pack them into the jars.
- Pour the pickling solution on top of the mushrooms, then put the lids, and store them in the fridge for at least 48 hours before serving them.
- You can store it for up to 3 weeks in the fridge and enjoy it!

## Pickled Summer Green beans

### Equipment:

Saucepan

Knife

Cutting Board

Towel

Funnel

Jars

**Nutrition Facts** per 1 Pint Jar

| Calories | 227kcal |
|----------|---------|
| Carbs | 49g |
| Protein | 11g |
| Fats | 3g |

## Core Ingredients

- 3 pounds of fresh green beans
- 6 sprigs of fresh dill
- 2 teaspoons of mustard seeds
- 2 teaspoons black peppercorns
- 2 cloves of garlic, peeled and sliced

## Pickling Solution

- 4 cups of water
- ½ cup of apple cider vinegar
- 3 tablespoons of salt
- 2 tablespoons of white granulated sugar

### Step 1 - Preparation

- Start by washing the green beans and trimming their ends.
- You can choose if you wish the bean as they are, or cut them into ¼-inch pieces.
- Divide the green beans between two-pint jars, then add to them the black peppercorns, garlic, dill, and mustard seeds.

### Step 2 – Preparing the pickling solution

- Place a saucepan over medium heat then stir in it all the pickling solution ingredients including the remaining vinegar.
- Bring them to a boil, then stir them until the sugar completely dissolves.

### Step 3 – Pickling the green beans

- Pour the pickling solution on top of the green beans, then put the lids, and store them in the fridge for at least 48 hours before serving them.
- You can store it for up to 3 weeks in the fridge and enjoy it!

## Crispy Red Onion Pickles

|**Intro**|: These onions are crispy in flavor, and beautiful. It's the perfect toppings for burgers, sandwiches, tacos...They require very few ingredients and they can be ready in minutes.

## Equipment:

Saucepan

Knife

Cutting Board

Towel

Funnel

Jars

**Nutrition Facts** per 1 Cup

| Calories | 70.78 kcal |
|----------|---------|
| Carbs | 12.73g |
| Protein | 0.93g |
| Fats | 0.07g |

## Core Ingredients

- 2 large red onions

## Pickling Solution

- 1 ½ cup of apple cider vinegar
- ½ cup of water
- 3 tablespoons of honey
- 2 teaspoons of salt

### Step 1 - Preparation

- Start by peeling the onions and washing them, then cut them into think rounds.
- Transfer the sliced onion to two-pint jars and pack them tightly.

### Step 2 – Preparing the pickling solution

- Place a saucepan over medium heat then stir in it all the pickling solution ingredients including the remaining vinegar.
- Bring them to a boil, then stir them until the sugar completely dissolves.

133

### Step 3 – Pickling the onions

- Pour the pickling solution on top of the onions, then put the lids, and store them in the fridge for at least 1 hour before serving it.
- You can store it for up to 2 weeks in the fridge and enjoy it!

## Section 2: Fruits Pickling Recipes

### Spicy Mango Pickles

|Intro|: If you are used to canning sweet mangos, this recipe will make for a nice change as it balances perfectly the sweet and spicy in the mango. It yields delicious pickled mangos that are amazing as a topping to sandwiches, tacos, burgers...or as a side dish with some rice.

### Equipment:

Knife

Cutting Board

Towel

Saucepan

Jars

Saucepan

### Nutrition Facts per 1/3 Cup

| Calories | 188.86 kcal |
|----------|-------------|
| Carbs | 46.14g |
| Protein | 1.29g |
| Fats | 0g |

### Core Ingredients

- 6 Large green mangos

### Pickling Solution

- 3 cups of apple cider vinegar
- 2 cups of granulated white sugar
- 2 Thai chili peppers, finely chopped
- 2 teaspoons of kosher salt

### Step 1 - Preparation

- Start by peeling the mangos, then cut them into 1-inch cubes or strips.

- Transfer the mangos to jars and pack them tightly.

### Step 2 – Preparing the pickling solution

- Place a saucepan over medium heat then stir in it all the pickling solution ingredients.
- Bring it to a simmer while stirring the sugar until dissolves.

### Step 3 – Pickling the mangos

- Pour the pickling solution on top of the mangos, then put on the lids and cover the jars.
- Store them in the fridge for at least 6 hours before serving.
- You can store it for up to 2 weeks in the fridge and enjoy it!

### Jalapeno and Pineapple Pickles

|Intro|: Pineapples are a great spring and summer fruit that makes for a great refreshing drink, and a great addition to baked goods, however, it's not limited. When pickled with some jalapenos, with the perfect amount of salt and sugar, it makes for great pickles to add to your pizza, tacos, burgers...

### Equipment:

Knife

Cutting Board

Towel

Saucepan

Jars

### Nutrition Facts per 1/3 Cup

| Calories | 87 kcal |
|----------|---------|
| Carbs | 21g |
| Protein | 1g |
| Fats | 1g |

### Core Ingredients

- 2 fresh medium pineapples
- 2 fresh jalapenos

### Pickling Solution

- 2 cups of apple cider vinegar
- ½ cup of fresh lemon juice
- ½ cup of water

- 1 tablespoon of salt
- 10 fresh sprigs of cilantro

### Step 1 - Preparation
- Start by peeling the pineapple into 1-inch cubes.
- Peel the jalapenos, discard the seeds then dice them.
- Transfer the pineapple and jalapenos, then top with the cilantro sprigs.

### Step 2 – Preparing the pickling solution
- Place a saucepan over medium heat water with vinegar and bring them to a boil.
- Next, turn off the heat, then salt with lemon juice and stir them well.

### Step 3 – Pickling the pineapple
- Pour the pickling solution on top of the pineapple, then put on the lids and cover the jars.
- Store them in the fridge for at least 12 hours before serving.
- You can store it for up to 3 weeks in the fridge and enjoy it!

## Southern Pickled Peaches

|Intro|: These pickled peaches are a classic southern recipe that has a festive smell to remind you of the holiday, and a fantastic taste thanks to the combination of cloves, and cinnamon.

### Equipment:
Knife

Cutting Board

Towel

4-quart Jars

Saucepan

Bowl

Pot

### Nutrition Facts per ½ Cup

| Calories | 110.04 kcal |
|----------|-------------|
| Carbs | 28.03g |
| Protein | 0.1g |
| Fats | 0g |

### Core Ingredients
- 4 pounds of fresh peaches, ripe
- 5 cinnamon sticks
- 2 tablespoons of cloves

### Packing Syrup
- 4 cups of granulated white sugar
- 1 cup of water
- 1 cup of white vinegar

### Step 1 - Preparation
- Bring a large pot of water to a boil. Add to it the peaches and blanch them for 4 to 5 minutes.
- In the meantime, fill a large bowl with cold water and some ice.
- Drain the peaches and add them to the bowl, then allow them to cool down until they become cool to the touch.
- Drain them, peel them, and cut them in half.

### Step 2 – Preparing the packing syrup
- Place a saucepan over medium heat then stir in it all the syrup ingredients.
- Bring it to a simmer while stirring the sugar until dissolves.
- Add the peaches to the syrup, then bring them to a rolling boil for 20 to 23 minutes until the peach becomes soft.

### Step 3 – Pickling the peaches
- Gently transfer the peaches to the jars, then add to them the cinnamon sticks and cloves.
- Pour the remaining syrup on top, then put on the lids and cover the jars.
- Store them in the fridge for at least 24 hours before serving.
- You can store it for up to 2 weeks in the fridge or water bath can them for 10 minutes while adjusting the time depending on your and enjoy!

## Sweet and Tangy Pickled Tomatoes

|Intro|: If you haven't tried pickled tomatoes, you have to give them a try. These tomatoes are completely different from regular canned tomatoes, they hold much more flavor because of all the herbs and fragrant seeds used with them. You can serve them as a snack or topping.

## Equipment:
Knife

Cutting Board

Towel

4 Quart Jars

Saucepan

**Nutrition Facts** per 1/3 Cup

| Calories | 188.86 kcal |
|----------|-------------|
| Carbs | 46.14g |
| Protein | 1.29g |
| Fats | 0g |

## Core Ingredients
- 3 ½ pounds of fresh Roma tomatoes or cherry tomatoes
- 8 cloves of garlic, peeled and sliced
- 4 bay leaves
- 4 sprigs of fresh parsley
- 4 sprigs of fresh dill
- 6 tablespoons of salt
- 2 tablespoons of white wine vinegar
- 2 tablespoons of black peppercorns

## Pickling Solution
- 2 tablespoons of white granulated sugar
- 4 Quarts of water
- 6 tablespoons of salt
- 2 tablespoons of white wine vinegar

## Step 1 - Preparation
- Start by washing the tomatoes nicely then pack them into the jars with garlic, bay leaves, parsley, dill, and peppercorns

## Step 2 – Preparing the pickling solution
- Place a saucepan over medium heat then stir in it all the pickling solution ingredients.
- Bring it to a simmer while stirring the sugar until dissolves.

## Step 3 – Pickling the tomatoes
- Pour the pickling solution on top of the tomatoes until they are completely covered, then put on the lids and cover the jars.

- Store them in the fridge for at least 2 weeks before serving.
- You can store it for up to 6 weeks in the fridge and enjoy it!

## Vanilla Pickled Grapes

|Intro|: Grapes might not be the first fruit to come to your mind when you think of pickles, but this recipe is a great way to attempt it. The sweet flavor of the sugar and vanilla, combined with the peppercorns, and mustard balances the best of both worlds. You can serve them as a snack, with crackers, or cheese, or add them to a salad.

## Equipment:
Knife

Cutting Board

Towel

2 Quarts Jars

Saucepan

**Nutrition Facts** per 1 Quart Jar

| Calories | 57 kcal |
|----------|---------|
| Carbs | 14g |
| Protein | 0g |
| Fats | 0g |

## Core Ingredients
- 2 pounds of red grapes
- 2 cinnamon sticks
- ¼ teaspoon of cloves
- ¼ teaspoon of black peppercorns
- 1/8 teaspoon of mustard seeds

## Pickling Solution
- 2 cups of apple cider vinegar
- 2 cups of white granulated sugar
- ½ cup of water
- ½ vanilla bean scraped

## Step 1 - Preparation
- Start by washing the grapes, and removing their stems.
- Transfer them to jars and pack them tightly with cinnamon sticks, cloves, peppercorns, and mustard seeds.

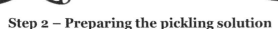

### Step 2 – Preparing the pickling solution

- Place a saucepan over medium heat then stir in it all the pickling solution ingredients.
- Bring it to a simmer while stirring the sugar until dissolves.

### Step 3 – Pickling the grapes

- Pour the pickling solution on top of the grapes, then put on the lids and cover the jars.
- Store them in the fridge for at least 24 hours before serving.
- You can store it for up to 3 weeks in the fridge and enjoy it!

## Golden Pickled Pears

|Intro|: These pickled pears are very easy to prepare, and taste amazing! The use of festive seasonings like cloves and cinnamon makes them perfect to serve on their own as a lovely snack, add to a cheese platter, baked goods, or even a great companion to meat dishes.

### Equipment:

Saucepan

Knife

Cutting Board

Towel

Funnel

Jars

### Nutrition Facts per ½ pound

| Calories | 453.87 kcal |
|---|---|
| Carbs | 114.15g |
| Protein | 0.63g |
| Fats | 0.29g |

### Core Ingredients

- 2.5 pounds of fresh pears (of your choice)
- Cloves (2 cloves per pear)

### Pickling Solution

- 1 pound of granulated white sugar
- 2 tablespoons of fresh ginger, peeled and grated
- 1 ½ cup of cider vinegar
- 1 cinnamon stick
- 1 teaspoon of allspice berries

### Step 1 - Preparation

- Start by washing the pears then place them aside.

### Step 2 – Preparing the pickling solution

- Place a saucepan over medium heat then stir in it all the pickling solution ingredients.
- Bring them to a boil, then stir them until the sugar completely dissolves.

### Step 3 – Cooking The pears

- Peel the pears, then push into each pear 2 cloves. You can choose to leave them whole, or slice them.
- Add the pears to the boiling pickling solution then lower the heat and let them cook until they start to soften for 10 to 15 minutes.

### Step 4 – Pickling the pears

- Once the time is up, use a spoon to transfer the pears into the sterilized jars.
- Pour the remaining pickling solution on top of the pears, then put the lids, and store them in the fridge for at least 1 month before serving them.
- You can water bath can them and store them for up to 1 year and enjoy!

## Sweet Pickled Blueberries

|Intro|: This recipe will give a whole new taste to your blueberries. It is sweet and spicy at the same time which makes it so versatile and a great companion to all dishes. You can enjoy it for up to 6 months.

### Equipment:

Pot

Knife

Cutting Board

Towel

Funnel

Jars

### Nutrition Facts per ½ pound

| Calories | 955.98 kcal |
|---|---|
| Carbs | 235.5g |
| Protein | 1.75g |
| Fats | 0.78g |

### Core Ingredients

- 2 pounds of fresh blueberries

### Pickling Solution

- 4 cups of apple cider vinegar
- 4 cups of white granulated sugar
- 2 cups of water
- 2 tablespoons of kosher salt
- ½ tablespoon of fresh ginger, peeled and grated
- 8 black peppercorns
- 4 juniper berries
- 2 bay leaves
- 2 fresh sprigs of thyme

### Step 1 - Preparation

- Start by washing picking and washing the blueberries.

### Step 2 – Preparing the pickling solution

- Place a large saucepan or pot over medium heat then stir in it all the pickling solution ingredients.
  - Bring them to a boil, then stir them until the sugar completely dissolves.

### Step 3 – Cooking The blueberries

- Add the perries to the pot and stir them well, then bring them to a boil.

### Step 4 – Pickling the blueberries

- Once the blueberries boil, turn off the heat, then use a spoon to transfer the blueberries into the sterilized jars.
- Pour the remaining pickling solution on top of the berries, then put the lids, and store them in the fridge for at least 1 month before serving them.
- You can water bath can them and store them for up to 6 months and enjoy!

# Section 3: Other Food to Pickle

## Pickled Ginger

|Intro|: Pickled ginger is a classic Japanese dish that is served with sushi and a variety of other dishes. It's a little bit strong, but it enhances the flavor of whatever food you serve it and gives a nice kick.

### Equipment:

Knife

Cutting Board

Towel

Jars

Saucepan

Bowl

### Nutrition Facts per 8 ounces

| Calories | 13.7 kcal |
|----------|-----------|
| Carbs | 3.3g |
| Protein | 0.1g |
| Fats | 0.1g |

### Core Ingredients

- 8 ounces of fresh ginger, peeled
- ½ teaspoon of sea salt

### Pickling Solution

- 1 cup of rice vinegar
- 1/3 cup of white sugar

### Step 1 - Preparation

- Start by peeling the ginger, then cut it into bite-size pieces.
- Toss the ginger pieces with salt in a bowl, then let it sit for 25 minutes.
- Once the time is up, pack the ginger chunks into the storing jars.

### Step 2 – Preparing the pickling solution

- Place a saucepan over medium heat then stir in it the vinegar with water.

### Step 3 – Pickling the mangos

- Pour the pickling solution on top of the mango, then put on the lids and cover the jars.
- Store them in the fridge for at least 1 week before serving.
- You can store it for up to 5 weeks in the fridge and enjoy it!

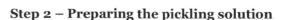

## Pickled Eggs

|**Intro**|: Eggs are a staple ingredient in every house, however, there is only so much that you can do with them. If your chickens are laying more eggs than you know what to do with, or if you got a great deal on a big amount of eggs, this is the perfect recipe to use it. The spices seep into the eggs and give them a fantastic flavor that makes them a great snack, sandwich toppings…

### Equipment:

Knife

Cutting Board

Towel

Saucepan

2 Quart Jars

Saucepan

### Nutrition Facts per 1 Egg

| Calories | 82 kcal |
|----------|---------|
| Carbs | 2g |
| Protein | 6g |
| Fats | 2g |

### Core Ingredients

- 24 eggs, hard-boiled
- 6 sprigs of fresh dill
- 2 cloves of garlic, peeled and sliced
- 2 bay leaves

### Pickling Solution

- 2 large yellow or white onion
- 6 cups of white vinegar
- 2 cups of water
- 2/3 cups of sugar
- 2 tablespoons of pickling spice
- 2 teaspoons of salt

### Step 1 - Preparation

- Start hard boiling the eggs, then place them aside or use an ice water bath to cool them down.
- Once the eggs are cool enough to handle peel them.
- Next, pack the eggs with fresh dill, bay leaves, and garlic into the storing jars.

### Step 2 – Preparing the pickling solution

- Peel the onions and wash them, then cut them to thin slices.
- Place a saucepan over medium heat then stir in it all the pickling solution ingredients with onion.
- Bring it to a boil, then lower the heat and let them cook for 6 minutes.

### Step 3 – Pickling the eggs

- Pour the pickling solution on top of the eggs, then put on the lids and cover the jars.
- Store them in the fridge for at least 1 week before serving.
- You can store it for up to 4 weeks in the fridge and enjoy it!

## Pickled Garlic

|**Intro**|: If you love pickles, this pickled garlic will make for a perfect addition to your fridge. You can use it for all your recipes that require garlic, it will enhance their flavor and add a nice kick to them.

### Equipment:

Knife

Cutting Board

Towel

Saucepan

Jars

Saucepan

### Nutrition Facts per ¼ Cup

| Calories | 52 kcal |
|----------|---------|
| Carbs | 10g |
| Protein | 2g |
| Fats | 1g |

### Core Ingredients

- 2 pounds of garlic
- 4 sprigs of fresh dill

### Pickling Solution

- 5 cups of white vinegar
- ¼ cup of canning salt
- 1 teaspoon of red pepper flakes

### Step 1 - Preparation

- Start by peeling the garlic cloves, and remove their tops.
- Pack the garlic into the jars with fresh dill

### Step 2 – Preparing the pickling solution

- Place a saucepan over medium heat then stir in it all the pickling solution ingredients.
- Bring it to a boil while stirring the sugar until dissolves.

### Step 3 – Pickling the garlic

- Pour the pickling solution on top of the garlic, then put on the lids and cover the jars.
- Store them in the fridge for at least 4 weeks before serving.
- You can store it for up to 6 months in the fridge and enjoy it!

# |Part 6| Fermenting Intro

## Section 1: What is fermentation?

Enzymatic conversion of food components & managed microbial growth is used to create fermented meals and drinks. The breakdown of some dietary components into other compounds by microbes like bacteria or yeast is what is referred to as the fermentation process. Glucose, for instance, may be converted into organic gases, alcohol, or acids.

Lactic acid fermentation & fermentation by Ethyl alcohol are the two basic forms of fermenting. Both entail the breakdown of the carbohydrates that the organism consumes in order to extract the oxygen that contributes to the formation of every carbohydrate molecule. In the instance of bacteria, they create lactic acid as a byproduct, while in the case of yeast, they create a mixture of $CO_2$ & ethyl alcohol.

During the fermentation of ethyl alcohol, yeast cells eat sugar to create Carbon dioxide gas that makes bread rise, and ethyl alcohol gives beer, spirits & wine their kick.

The microorganisms in yogurt, such as lactobacillus acidophilus, perform lactic acid fermentation. The bacteria do this by consuming milk sugar and lactose and using the lactic acid that is produced as a by-product to turn lactose into $O_2$ for themselves. The sour taste of yogurt is due to this acid. Many everyday foods and drinks, including sourdough bread, beer, wine & Greek yogurt are products of fermentation. Among the other well-known fermented foods are:

- Sauerkraut
- Tempeh
- Miso
- Kombucha
- Kimchi

## Section 2: Benefits of fermented foods

Fermentation has a huge number of advantages. Numerous fermented foods and drinks include probiotics, living organisms that promote improved digestion and intestinal health. Lower risk of diabetes, high blood pressure, inflammation, cardiovascular disease, and other diseases are also associated with the consumption of fermented foods.

Improved digestion: Complex carbs must be broken down by healthy bacteria, which is why gut health is crucial to digestion. Your digestion may be kept regular by including a few fermented foods in the diet.

Better gut health - By lowering intestinal pH, healthy bacteria battle disease-causing bacteria in the digestive system. This may stop food-borne infections brought on by daily bacterial ingestion.

Promotes the health of the immune system - In regard to strengthening the immune system, the probiotics included in many fermented products may aid in the body's production of the vitamins B1, K B3, B5, B2, B6, B12.

Reduced risk of illness - Overweight, asthma, and inflammatory diseases are more common in those with less varied gut microbiotas. More diversified gut microbiota is produced by fermented foods, and this lowers the risk of inflammatory illness.

Reduction in food waste - Each and every day, the United States wastes around 1 pound of food for each person. You may reduce food waste by extending the shelf life of fruit, dairy products, and other items by fermenting food at home.

## Section 3: Lactic Acid Fermentation

A kind of "friendly" bacteria called lactic acid specializes in eating the lactose found in milk and food products and turning it into lactic acid as well as other substances. Lactic acid bacteria transform milk into an entirely new product by altering its taste and flavor. When fermented foods such as sauerkraut, and kimchi are made, lactic acid fermentation takes place. Items like cabbage are dipped in salty brine to make it work. Lactobacillus bacteria, which are found almost

everywhere, even on meals like cabbage as well as other foods, are not harmed by salt, which destroys bacteria that cause food deterioration. After a time of soaking in this salty brine, the veggies' carbohydrates are transformed into lactic acid by the lactobacillus, which further assists in the preservation and gives the food a tangy taste. Additionally, other products resulting from lactic acid fermentation are miso, soy sauce, tofu, ketchup & pepperoni.

## Section 4: Ethyl Alcohol Fermentation

Beer, spirit, wine, and bread are all products of the fermentation of ethanol. Keep in mind that sourdough bread employs both ethyl alcohol & lactic acid fermentation. The sour taste of the bread is imparted by the lactobacillus, whereas the yeast gives it its rise. Secondary and primary fermentation are the two phases of fermentation that are generally involved with wine & beer. While the secondary phase is slower and aids in the development of more complex tastes, the main stage initiates a quick creation of alcohol.

## Section 5: Acetic Acid Fermentation

Although it is debatably a variation of ethyl alcohol fermentation, some individuals see this fermentation as a third form of fermentation.

According to how it operates, certain bacteria called acetic acid bacteria decompose alcohol & sugar to create acetic acid that, when much diluted, is just regular vinegar. This procedure, which comes after the first step of ethyl alcohol production, is also used to make vinegar and kombucha.

## Section 6: Key ideas of fermentation

The methods needed for certain ferments differ greatly across traditions & cultures. For example, the conventional method for creating kimchi differs greatly from the one used to make Indian lime pickles. When it comes to pickling, some fundamental ideas never change.

### Eliminate Air

The weighs used to keep the cabbage submerged in the water & brine and the water-channel air lock that usually keeps oxygen out are both visible in a fermentation crock of sauerkraut.

A classic fermentation crock, such as this one, often has weights to hold the food out of the brine and a liquid path all around the rim that, whenever the lid is on, prevents oxygen-rich air from entering while allowing carbon dioxide to escape.

The establishment of an anaerobic environment is crucial for any effective lactic acid fermentation. Because there is little to no oxygen present, yeast and other bacteria can't grow and could spoil the taste of the ferment.

Depending on your degree of comfort and the tools at hand, there are a variety of methods to remove air. The simplest technique is immersing food in salt brine. Anything below the brine's surface is oxygen-deprived. A second approach involves combining or crushing a substance to produce a mash (such as a hot pepper mash). Making a mash usually releases fluids in addition to dramatically increasing the possible surface area exposed to germs. The liquid covers any openings or spaces left by air when the mash is packed securely in a fermentation tank and secured with a weight. This effectively eliminates oxygen from the atmosphere.

Then there are more advanced techniques like an airtight that physically removes oxygen. Any mechanism that permits carbon dioxide to leave the vessel while preventing oxygen from entering is considered an airlock. Carbon dioxide builds up during fermentation, displaces any oxygen in the container, and exits, maintaining an oxygen-free environment.

A vacuum sealer is a perfect tool for eliminating oxygen if you're truly into kitchen gadgets. Keep a watch on it, however, as lengthier ferments may ultimately result in bags exploding like overinflated balloons, as it also produces an excellent solution for storing the CO2 produced during fermentation. Open any excessively inflated vacuum bags and move their contents to fresh ones to prevent this.

### Choose the Right Ingredients

Good ferments need high-quality ingredients. The quality of the components and how they were handled have an impact on how well a ferment turns out. Use good peppers for producing spicy sauce. To avoid these practices, choose food that hasn't been wax-coated,

surface-treated, and irradiated with pesticides to prolong its shelf life.

Organic produce usually checks these criteria, but a label isn't an assurance of that. You could come across some chilies that have been preserved by being coated in oil or another substance. Many individuals could have problems with it without even realizing it. All of these surface treatments reduce the number of microorganisms that are present and necessary for starting fermentation.

Even the freshwater you use matters when utilizing a brine. It is preferable to use distilled or filtered water since lightly chlorinated; untreated water may limit microbial activity. Before utilizing tap water in a ferment, you should at the very least let it out in the open for a whole night in a jar.

### Added salt

In most circumstances, salt is both beneficial and necessary for fermentation. It prevents the development of harmful microorganisms and promotes the survival of salt-tolerant microbes. But really, what salt concentration is ideal? The salt content of around 2 percent is enough for many recipes when fermenting at home.

If the salt concentration is low:

- it lessens total microbial activity suppression, allowing for quicker fermentation. More appropriate for colder climates, where microbial activity is less suppressed & slower
- Increases the likelihood of spoiling because hazardous microorganisms are not as well controlled
- It can lead to mushy ferments, particularly if they are heated during fermentation.

An abundance of salt:

- Significantly reduces total microbial activity while lowering spoiling risk
- Stifles fermentation, which is advantageous in warm environments
- May guarantee crisper & firmer results since pectin cell walls are less microbial degraded.

In conclusion, how much salt you use depends mostly on the kind of fruit or vegetable you're utilizing. However, at a specific concentration, certain advantageous bacteria, like P. cerevisiae, simply cannot ferment. Additionally, a pickle with a 10% salt content could taste too salty.

### The temperature

The pace and quality of fermentation are significantly influenced by temperature. In speaking, fermentation proceeds more quickly at higher temperatures, whereas it moves more slowly at lower ones. Likewise, different temperatures encourage certain microbial populations.

So what temperature is best for fermentation? It's room temp, 50 to 70°F. A variety of bacteria flourish in this range, with the high end leaning more toward Lactobacillus. Due to the greater generation of acetic acid at low temp, sharper, less vinegar-like tastes tend to be preferred; higher temperatures provide gentler acidity but almost dairy-like overtones. But once again, picking a temperature mostly relies on the substance you're fermenting, how soon you want the fermentation to complete, and how mushy and broken you want the final result to be.

### Timing and Inspection

You're nearing the finish line. Pickled plums, cucumbers, peppers, and cabbage are fermenting. How can a healthy ferment be ensured? Fermentation is all about upkeep and supervision. You put time, effort, and money into this protracted procedure. You must not disregard it. It may even include tasting and smelling the product as it develops in certain circumstances. Maintain a diary for your fermentation. It's incredibly easy to do, and it's a really valuable thing to have. However, because situations are always changing, it's helpful to refer to them when things go well or poorly.

A ferment is finished when? Acidified foods are required to have a pH under 4.6 in order to be considered safe for consumption, while many commercial manufacturers aim for a pH of 4.2 as well. The majority of the lactic acid fermentation is technically finished in 1-3 weeks. Most of the carbohydrates present in the ferment have already been digested by bacteria at this point.

The time is ultimately up to you. Ferment for a longer period of time if you want your sauerkraut tender and crumbly. Fermentation should be stopped sooner if you want the sauerkraut crisp and very sour.

## Section 7: Fermenting Vs. Pickling

Since both are methods of preserving food and both result in foods with a sour taste, pickling & fermentation are sometimes misunderstood. The key difference between the two is that during fermentation,

lactobacillus bacteria produce acetic acid, which is what gives the meal its sour taste. Pickling involves submerging food in a vinegar-based solution that gives it a sour taste even if fermentation is not really occurring.

# |Part 7| Fermenting Recipes

## Section 1: Fermented Veggies Recipes & Salsas

### Fermented Sauerkraut

(Prep time: 20 minutes | Cook time: 0 | Processing time: 1 week | Servings: 1 jar)

#### Ingredients

- 1 tbsp. of sea salt
- 1 cabbage head
- 4 cups of water mixed with 1 tbsp. of salt

#### Instructions

- Rinse the cabbage & take out all the dirty leaves.
- Cut the cabbage into fours with the core, & slice thinly.
- Toss the cabbage with sea salt & let it rest for 15 minutes. Massage & knead with hands for 8 to 10 minutes.
- Take a clean glass jar & add the cabbage, and pack it down. Mash it as you go & leave a two-inch space from the top.
- If the liquid does not cover the cabbage, mix the 4 cups of water with salt.
- Add enough to the jar so that all cabbage is submerged. Leave one inch of headspace. Make sure no cabbage is out of the liquid; otherwise, it can't be used.

- Place the lid & set the jar for one week at room temperature in a shaded area. Place a tray underneath.
- After one day, open & release any gasses.
- After 1 week, taste & smell. If it has achieved desired taste, move it to the fridge.

**Nutrition: Kcal 34 | Protein 1 g | Fiber 7 g | Carbs 1 g | Fat 0 g**

### Fermented Asparagus with Ginger

(Prep time: 20 minutes | Cook time: 5 minutes | Processing time: 1 week | Servings: 3 (12 oz.) jars)

#### Ingredients

- 3 Tbsp. pickling salt
- 1½ tsp. yellow mustard seeds
- 2 ½ lbs. asparagus
- 3 garlic cloves
- 2½ cups rice vinegar
- 3 fresh ginger slices

#### Instructions

- In a water bath, boil the jars & lids. Cut the asparagus according to the jar size.
- Rinse & blanch the asparagus for 60 seconds. Drain & dry on a tea towel.
- Add pickling salt and vinegar to a pan, place on flame, let it come to a boil, then turn the heat low.
- Add the asparagus to the jars, and add the rest of the ingredients equally to each jar.
- Add the hot vinegar mixture to the jars, and leave the half-inch space from the top.
- Place lids & seal.
- Process in the water bath for 10 minutes. Let them rest undisturbed for 12-24 hours & open after one week.

**Nutrition: Kcal 20 | Protein 1 g | Fiber 4 g | Carbs 1 g | Fat 2 g**

### Fermented Cauliflower

(Prep time: 20 minutes | Cook time: 0 minutes | Processing time: 1 week | Servings: 3 pints)

#### Ingredients

- 2 tbsp. pickling salt
- 3 cloves garlic
- 1 head cauliflower, broken into small florets

- 4 cups of water
- 3 hot peppers

## Instructions

- Wash the jars.
- In a bowl, mix salt & water, and mix until dissolved.
- In each jar, add garlic clove & pepper.
- Add cauliflower to each jar equally.
- Add salt mixture & make sure to cover. Use water if brine is not enough.
- Add some weight to the top of the jar & place the lid.
- Place in a cool, dry place for 3 to 5 minutes.
- Open & taste test after a week, and store in the fridge.

**Nutrition: Kcal 16 | Protein 1 g | Fiber 1 g | Carbs 3 g | Fat 0 g**

## Fermented peppers

(Prep time: 10 minutes | Cook time: 0 minutes | Processing time: 5 days | Servings: 32 oz. jar)

## Ingredients

- 4 cups of water
- 1 tbsp. of apple cider vinegar
- 1 1/2 tbsp. of sea salt
- Enough fresh jalapeno peppers to fill a jar

## Instructions

- Rinse the jar and lids with soap & water.
- Mix the salt & water, and heat until dissolved. Let it cool for a bit.
- Cut the jalapenos into rounds. Add to the jar & press.
- Add vinegar & cover the peppers; leave one" of space from the top.
- Make sure the peppers are submerged. Place the lid.
- Place at room temperature away from sunlight. Open the jar daily to let the gasses out.
- Let it rest for 1 week, open & test taste.
- Store in the fridge.

**Nutrition: Kcal 4 | Protein 0 g | Fiber 0 g | Carbs 1 g | Fat 0 g**

## Fermented Carrots

(Prep time: 15 minutes | Cook time: 10 minutes | Processing time: 5 days | Servings: 4)

## Ingredients

- 3/4 lb. carrots
- 1 tsp. dill seed
- Half tsp. sea salt
- 3/4 cup vinegar
- 1 tsp. coriander seed
- Half cup water
- 1 tsp. peppercorns
- 1 onion, sliced
- 1 tsp. mustard seed

## Instructions

- Peel & slice the carrots.
- In a pan, add sugar, vinegar, water & salt. Let it come to a boil.
- Add the rest of the ingredients & boil. Simmer for 10 minutes, add to the prepared jars, and leave one" space from headspace.
- Place the lids & seal. Boil the jars in a water bath for 15 minutes.
- Take the jars out & cool them on the counter, undisturbed for 24 hours.
- Open after one week to taste test & store the open jars in the fridge.

**Nutrition: Kcal 21 | Protein 2 g | Fiber 6 g | Carbs 6 g | Fat 0 g**

## Fermented Kimchi

(Prep time: 15 minutes | Cook time: 0 minutes | Processing time: 5-7 days | Servings: 2 quarts)

## Ingredients

- 2-3 turnips
- 3 tbsp. of sweet paprika
- 12 scallions, chopped
- 1 to 2 tbsp. of red pepper flakes
- 8 garlic cloves, minced
- 2 heads cabbage
- 3 tbsp. of salt

## Instructions

- Slice the rinsed cabbage thinly.
- In a bowl, add all the ingredients & mix well.
- Pound the mixture to release juices.

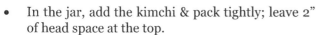

- In the jar, add the kimchi & pack tightly; leave 2" of head space at the top.
- The mixture should be under the liquid, and place a weight on top. If there's not enough liquid, add brine to cover.
- Place the lid on top & seal. Let it rest at room temperature for 3 weeks.
- Open the jars once a day to release the gasses.
- Store in the fridge after opening.

**Nutrition: Kcal 33.3 | Protein 1 g | Fiber 6 g | Carbs 1 g | Fat 0 g**

## Zucchini relish

(Prep time: 30 minutes | Cook time: 30 minutes | Processing time: 10 minutes | Servings: 8 half-pints)

### Ingredients

- 2 cups of sliced bell peppers
- 2 cups of sliced onions
- 2 cups of 5% apple cider vinegar
- 1/8 cup of pickling salt
- 4 cups of chopped zucchini
- 2 tsp. yellow mustard seed
- 3 1/2 cups of cane sugar
- 1 tbsp. celery seed

### Instructions

- Toss the vegetables in a bowl with salt.

- Add crushed ice & water on top. Let it rest for 2 hours.
- Wash & boil the jars for 10 minutes; keep them hot.
- Drain & rinse the vegetables.
- In a pot, add the rest of the ingredients, boil & add vegetables. Simmer for 10 minutes.
- Add the relish into hot, dry jars, leaving half" of space.
- Wipe the rims & place lids. Add the filled jars to the water bath & boil for 10 minutes as per your altitude.
- Dry the jars at room temperature without disturbing them for 12-24 hours.
- Keep in the fridge & use within 1 week.

**Nutrition: Kcal 200 | Protein 4 g | Fiber 8 g | Carbs 14 g | Fat 4 g**

## Lacto-fermented Salsa

(Prep time: 2 weeks & 30 minutes | Cook time: 30 minutes | Processing time: 20 minutes | Servings: 18-20 pints)

### Ingredients

- 7 quarts of chopped tomatoes
- Half cup of diced jalapeños
- 4 cups of green chilies, chopped
- 10 grated garlic cloves
- 2½ tbsp. salt
- 5 cups of diced onions
- 2 tbsp. ground cumin
- 3 tbsp. fresh cilantro
- 1 tbsp. black pepper
- 3 tbsp. oregano

### Instructions

- 1st week: toss all vegetables with salt & spices (do not add tomatoes yet).
- Add to a jar, and let it ferment for 1 week.
- 2nd week: In a pot, add tomatoes to a pot, and place on medium flame.
- Let it come to a boil, and simmer for 10 minutes.
- Add the fermented vegetables, boil & simmer for 20 minutes.
- Add to cleaned & hot sterilized jars.
- Place in a water bath and process for 20 minutes.
- Take the jars out & cool them on the counter, undisturbed for 24 hours.
- Store in a cool & dry place.

**Nutrition: Kcal 101 | Protein 8 g | Fiber 3 g | Carbs 10 g | Fat 4 g**

## Lacto fermented cherry salsa

(Prep time: 2 weeks & 30 minutes | Cook time: 0 minutes | Processing time: 1-5 days | Servings: 1 gallon)

### Ingredients

- 2 cups of chopped cilantro
- 6 cups of diced sweet onion
- 1 cup of chopped mint
- 4 pounds of sweet & dark cherries, pitted
- 1 cup of diced jalapeno pepper
- 1 cup of lime juice
- 1/3 cup of salt
- 1/4 cup of sugar
- 1 cup whey

### Instructions

- In a bowl, add all ingredients except for whey & salt.
- Taste & adjust seasoning & vegetables. Keep in mind there's more salt to come.
- Add whey & salt to the salsa.
- Add salsa to sterilized jars, and place lids. Leave one" space from the top.
- Make sure salsa is covered in liquid, and add more water if necessary.
- Place lids & do not make them too tight.
- Let them rest at room temperature for 1 to 5 days.
- Taste salsa each day & when it has reached the desired taste, keep it in the fridge.

**Nutrition: Kcal 109 | Protein 9 g | Fiber 5 g | Carbs 19 g | Fat 4 g**

## Section 2: Fermented Fruit Recipes

### Lacto-fermented peach chutney

(Prep time: 30 minutes | Cook time: 0 minutes | Processing time: 2 days | Servings: 1 jar)

### Ingredients

- 2 tsp. cinnamon
- 2 to 3 lemon wedges, unpeeled & diced
- 1 cup of chopped pecans
- 1 cup of dried raisins

- 3 cups of peeled & chopped peaches
- 1 Tbsp. of sugar
- 1 tsp. cloves

### Instructions

- In a bowl, add all ingredients, mix & press to release juices.
- Let it rest for 20-30 minutes, covered.
- Add to clean jars, pressing as you go. Make sure the contents are submerged in juices; if not, add water.
- Place lid & let it rest for 48-72 hours at room temperature, away from light & draft.
- Open & taste test, use within 2 weeks.

**Nutrition: Kcal 214 | Protein 4 g | Fiber 0.8 g | Carbs 4 g | Fat 4 g**

## Honey-Fermented Cranberries

(Prep time: 20 minutes | Cook time: 0 minutes | Processing time: 30 days | Servings: 16)

### Ingredients

- 2 cups raw honey or more
- 1-inch piece of ginger
- 3 cups of fresh cranberries, crushed lightly
- 1 cinnamon stick
- 1 orange's juice

### Instructions

- Process the cranberries in a food processor lightly, and transfer them to a jar (one quart).
- Add the rest of the ingredients & stir.
- The mixture should cover the cranberries or add more honey.
- Place the lid loosely & place it in a dark place. Let it rest for 1 week. Meanwhile, give a shake after tightening the lid & losing the lid afterward.

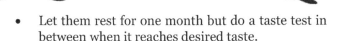

- Let them rest for one month but do a taste test in between when it reaches desired taste.

**Nutrition: Kcal 146 | Protein 4 g | Fiber 5 g | Carbs 12 g | Fat 6 g**

## Fermented Berries

(Prep time: 20 minutes | Cook time: 0 minutes | Processing time: 2-3 days | Servings: 2 cups)

### Ingredients

- 2 tsp chia seeds
- 2 tbsp. culture (kefir grains)
- 1 Tbsp. water, or more
- 2 cups fresh berries (without pit)
- 1 tbsp. sugar

### Instructions

- Slice the big berries. Add to a clean glass jar.
- Add the rest of the ingredients. Add water to cover the ingredients.
- Place a weight to submerge the berries. Place the lid.
- Let it ferment for 2 to 3 days in a cool & dark place.
- Keep in the fridge for 3 months.

**Nutrition: Kcal 276 | Protein 3.9 g | Fiber 4 g | Carbs 11 g | Fat 3.9 g**

## Lacto-Fermented Watermelon Radishes

(Prep time: 20 minutes | Cook time: 0 minutes | Processing time: 8-10 days | Servings: 1 half gallon)

### Ingredients

- 10 small watermelon radishes (about 10 small to large)
- Water
- Kosher salt, 1 tbsp.

### Instructions

- Trim the radish, wash & dry.
- Slice with a mandolin into thin slices, add salt & mix.
- Place plastic wrap on top, removing all air. Place a towel on top.
- Take the plastic off & mix well; cover it like previously for 1 to 3 days.
  - On day 4th, transfer to a jar with liquids.

- Press it down & submerge it in enough water, cover with plastic, remove air & place towel on top.
- Keep the jar in a pan to collect any juices if they spill.
- On days 5 to 7, check the mixture & the contents should be submerged. If not, add more water on top.
  - On day 8th, check the radishes, keep checking every day & stop when they reach a sour enough taste.

- Store in the fridge.

**Nutrition: Kcal 43 | Protein 1 g | Fiber 2 g | Carbs 0 g | Fat 0 g**

## Fermented Cinnamon Apple Chutney

(Prep time: 20 minutes | Cook time: 0 minutes | Processing time: 1-3 days | Servings: 6)

### Ingredients

- 1/4 to half cup whey
- 1 cup chopped pecans
- 1 cup pure water or more
- 1 cup raisins
- 6 cups apples
- Half cup lemon juice
- 1 tsp. sea salt
- 1/4 cup palm sugar
- 4 tsp. 5-spice blend

### Instructions

- Core the apple & chop them.
- Add the rest of the ingredients & mix.
- Add to a clean jar, pack down & make sure it is covered in liquid (or water), leaving half" space from above.
- Place the lid & let it ferment for 2-3 days at room temperature.
- Store in the fridge.

**Nutrition: Kcal 206 | Protein 3.2 g | Fiber 4 g | Carbs 11 g | Fat 3 g**

## Fermented Pear Chutney

(Prep time: 20 minutes | Cook time: 0 minutes | Processing time: 2-4 days | Servings: 1 quart jar)

## Ingredients

- Half cup sun-dried raisins
- 3-4 pears, chopped (peeled or unpeeled)
- 2 tsp. sea salt
- Half a cup of water, or more
- 1-2 lemons' juice
- Half cup chopped pecans
- 1 onion, chopped
- 1 tbsp. grated ginger

## Instructions

- In a bowl, add all ingredients, mix & let it rest for 20-30 minutes.
- Add to a clean, sanitized jar, and pack it down.
- Add water & leave one" space from above.
- Place the lid & let it ferment for 2-4 days away from sunlight at room temperature.
- Store in the fridge.

**Nutrition: Kcal 189 | Protein 3.9 g | Fiber 5 g | Carbs 9 g | Fat 4 g**

## Fermented Raisin Chutney

(Prep time: 20 minutes | Cook time: 0 minutes | Processing time: 2-4 days | Servings: 1 quart jar)

## Ingredients

- 2 cloves garlic, crushed
- 1 tbsp. coriander seeds
- 1-1/2 cups of soaked raisins
- 10 black peppercorns
- 1 tsp. sea salt

- Half cup cilantro leaves
- 1/4 tsp. red pepper flakes
- Half tbsp. cumin seeds
- Half cup water
- Half tbsp. minced ginger
- 2 Tbsp. whey

## Instructions

- In a food processor, add garlic and cilantro & process.
- Add drained raisins with the rest of the ingredients. Pulse until chunky.
- Add to sanitized, clean jars & pressing it down, submerging in juice.
- Add more water if necessary, and place a lid on top.
- Let it ferment at room temperature for 2 to 3 days. Open daily to release gasses.
- Store in the fridge for 2-3 weeks.

**Nutrition: Kcal 211 | Protein 1 g | Fiber 5 g | Carbs 7 g | Fat 4 g**

## Fermented Date Chutney

(Prep time: 20 minutes | Cook time: 20 minutes | Processing time: 2-4 days | Servings: 1-pint jar)

## Ingredients

- 1 minced clove of garlic
- Half onion, chopped
- 1 Chile de Arbol
- 1 1/2 tbsp. whey
- 2 tbsp. olive oil
- Half tsp. cayenne pepper
- 1 tsp brown mustard seed
- 1 oz. raisins, chopped
- Salt, to taste
- Half cup water
- 6 oz. dates, chopped
- 1 tbsp. cider vinegar

## Instructions

- Sauté the garlic in hot oil for a few seconds.
- Add onion & Arbol, and cook for 4 minutes.
- Add mustard seeds, and cook for 60 seconds.
- Add the rest of the ingredients (except for whey). Let it come to a boil, turn the heat low & simmer for 5-10 minutes.
- Add more water to reach your desired consistency.
- Turn the heat off & cool slightly.

- Add whey & mix, and add more water to reach your desired consistency.
- Add to clean jar. Let it rest for 3 days at room temperature.
- Store in the fridge later.

**Nutrition: Kcal 176 | Protein 1 g | Fiber 2 g | Carbs 6 g | Fat 2 g**

# Section 3: Fermented Drinks

## Kombucha

(Prep time: 20 minutes | Cook time: 0 minutes | Processing time: 7-14 days | Servings: 1 jar)

### Ingredients

- 1 scoby, + 3-7 oz. starter liquid
- 2 green tea bags
- 3.5-7 oz. of granulated sugar
- 2 black tea bags

### Instructions

- In a pan, add 1.8 liters of water & boil, and turn the heat off. Add sugar & tea bags, and let it steep for 6 to 10 minutes.
- Take the tea bags out, cool & pour them into a 3-liter jar.
- Add starter liquid & SCOBY; leave at least 1-inch space from the top.
- Do not place lid; cover with a muslin cloth or tea towel & secure with a rubber band.
- Ferment at the counter for 1-2 weeks at room temperature.
- After 7 days, taste it every day. As it reaches desired flavor, take out scoby & 3.5-7 oz. for another batch as starter liquid.
- Drink & serve chilled.
- Customize by adding lemon juice, ginger, and berries & serve.

**Nutrition: Kcal 33 | Protein 0.1 g | Fiber 0 g | Carbs 8 g | Fat 0 g**

## Fermented Apple Juice

(Prep time: 20 minutes | Cook time: 0 minutes | Processing time: 3 days | Servings: 1 quart)

### Ingredients

- 2 tbsp. whey
- 9 apples
- Sea salt, a pinch

### Instructions

- In a juicer, add apples & juice them.
- Add whey & salt. Mix & add to the quart size.
- Place a lid & let it rest for 3 days at room temperature.
- Store in the fridge for 1 month.

**Nutrition: Kcal 87 | Protein 0 g | Fiber 1 g | Carbs 3 g | Fat 0 g**

## Fermented Kefir Dairy-based

(Prep time: 10 minutes | Cook time: 0 minutes | Processing time: 2-3 days | Servings: 1 cup)

### Ingredients

- 1 tsp. active kefir grains
- 1 cup of full-fat milk

### Instructions

- In a jar, add milk & grains. Mix.
- Place muslin cloth & cover the jar, secure with a rubber band.
- Let it ferment for 12-48 hours. Taste test if it has thickened & tastes sour, it is done.
- Add new grains if it has not been fermented for 48 hours.
- Strain & serve chilled.
- Store in the fridge for 1 week.

**Nutrition: Kcal 109 | Protein 7 g | Fiber 0 g | Carbs 1 g | Fat 1 g**

Nutrition: Kcal 45 | Protein 2 g | Fiber 0 g | Carbs 6 g | Fat 1 g

## Fermented Kefir Coconut Water based

(Prep time: 10 minutes | Cook time: 0 minutes | Processing time: 2 days | Servings: 1 liter)

### Ingredients

- ¼ cup of Milk kefir grains
- 1 liter of coconut water

### Instructions

- Add coconut water to clean jar & leave two" from above.
- Leave room for gasses to build up.
- Add culture, mix & place the lid.
- Let it ferment on the counter, at room temperature for 12 to 18 hours.
- After hours taste the coconut water, as it has reached to preferred sourness if it done.
- Or give 6 to 10 hours more.
- Strain & store in the fridge & enjoy.

**Nutrition: Kcal 23 | Protein 0 g | Fiber 0 g | Carbs 1 g | Fat 1 g**

## Sour Beer

(Prep time: 20 minutes | Cook time: 2 hours | Processing time: 6 months & 14 days | Servings: 5 Gallon)

### Ingredients

- 5 lb. of Wheat Malt
- 1 packet of Ale Yeast
- 6 lb. of Pilsner Malt
- 1 pouch of Lambic Blend Wyeast 3278 (secondary)
- 3.75 AAU Hallertauer hops (instance)

### Instructions

- Add 5-gallon water to a large pan & heat at 152 F for half an hour with malts & yeast.
- Let it come to a boil, add hops.
- Boil for 1 hour & 30 minutes, turn the heat off & chill it in a vessel.
- Add dry yeast & close for 14 days.
- Then, add the secondary culture, let it rest for 6 months.
- Taste test & enjoy.

## Fermented Beet Kvass

(Prep time: 20 minutes | Cook time: 2 hours | Processing time: 6 months & 14 days | Servings: 5 Gallon)

### Ingredients

- ¼ cup pickle brine
- 3 cups water
- 2 cups unpeeled diced beets
- 1 tbsp. sea salt

### Instructions

- In a jar, add brine & beets.
- Mix the salt & water, add to the jar leaving one" space from the top.
- Mix & place the lid. Let it ferment for 2 weeks, open & close the lid after 3 to 4 or 5 to 7 days after.
- Test taste after 2 weeks, if you like the flavor strain & store in the fridge. Or, let it ferment for longer.

**Nutrition: Kcal 44 | Protein 1 g | Fiber 2 g | Carbs 11 g | Fat 1 g**

# |Part 8| Dehydrating Intro

## Section 1: Why should you dehydrate food?

Despite the fact that techniques for drying food have advanced through time, dehydration is still one of the oldest ways of food preservation. Food may be conveniently preserved at home by dehydrating it.

Dehydrating food is perhaps the simplest method of food preservation. Drying is one of the quickest and most affordable methods to preserve produce and has been used for hundreds of years to make food last longer without refrigeration. Additionally, it may reduce the weight of meals designed for camping and trekking, protecting both your budget and the back.

The food's moisture content is drastically reduced during dehydration, extending its shelf life while maintaining its excellent flavor; this is due to the fact that drying the food lowers its water content to 5 to 20%. The bacteria that cause food to rot cannot exist inside that range.

## Section 2: Methods of dehydration

There are many methods of dehydrating food; some are more effective than others. This is because contemporary equipment has improved the pace of dehydration, decreasing the likelihood that the food would rot. Here are some of today's most popular techniques.

### Sun drying

It is perhaps the oldest and simplest method of food preservation. The fruit has been cut into slices and set out in the sun on shelves or lines for roughly 12,000 years. In regions where the sun shines for extended periods, solar drying is particularly efficient. Due to the Mediterranean environment, the ancient Romans consumed dried raisins & figs often. However, it will function in any place that has the lowest temperature of 86 F with a humidity of 60%. Just keep in mind that fruit needs many days to completely dry. To keep other insects & flies away, place on a mesh screen, keeping everything galvanized to a minimum, then cover with another screen.

### Air Drying

It is a traditional technique of food dehydration, much like sun drying. The primary distinction is that air drying often occurs in the shadow. This is so that everything that requires shielding from the sun's rays may be preserved. It is particularly effective for herbs and fragile greens that you are keeping for culinary blends or herbal teas.

### Solar drying

Solar drying is an improvement over sun drying since it employs a dehydrator driven by the sun to cure food passively. Solar drying consumes no power since there is no heating element or blower to move the air. Solar dryers are often shaped like a little tabletop greenhouse and operate outside.

### A drying oven

In the oven, food is gently dried at the heat of around 140 °F. Electric ovens are not the most effective dryers since they are so big. But if you want speedy drying, they may save you the effort of purchasing additional equipment. But you'll have to keep the door open to allow the moisture out, and they may also warm up the home. If you're considering drying food in the oven, be sure it has a low enough setting. Anything over 140 F will cause the food to cook rather than dry out.

### Electric dehydrator

Electric dehydrators are what you get when you combine contemporary technology with traditional drying methods. These little workhorses include fans and heating components that can swiftly and effectively dry the food. That guarantees almost minimal spoiling and a delicious final product. The majority of electric dehydrators also include an adjustable temperature indicator with the dial. Based on what is

being processed, this might assist speed up or slow down the drying process. Consider utilizing the food dehydrator in the shed or another room where noise won't be an issue if it has a fan. This tip is also applicable if you wish to avoid overheating the living area while using a food dehydrator in the summer.

### Dehydrator Excalibur

With an Excalibur dehydrator, you can easily dry veggies, fish, fruits, and herbs, make jerky, fruit leathers, and soaking grains & nuts.

### Using a microwave to dehydrate

If you like cooking in the microwave and just have a little quantity of food to dehydrate, you can think about drying herbs & fruits in the microwave using the "defrost" setting. Generally speaking, microwaved fruits will require 20-40 minutes to completely dry, but be sure to check on them often to avoid overdoing them. It takes 2-3 minutes to microwave herbs.

## Section 3: Foods to dehydrate

Nearly all fresh foods can be dried. However, certain foods dehydrate better than others. Here are a few of our favorites:

- Fruits such as bananas, pears, apricots, apples, blueberries, peaches, and cherries, for making fruit leather, dehydrated as purees for snacking, or diced in trail mixes or granola.
- Vegetables such as carrots, onions, tomatoes, peas, mushrooms, and beans, for adding to backpacking meals, soups & stews.
- Fish & meat such as ground chicken, turkey, or beef; thin-cut meats; fresh fish; meat jerky, and cured meats for enhancing the flavor of backpacking meals or packing for stews & soup ingredients.
- Nuts & seeds such as hazelnuts, walnuts, pecans, macadamia, and almonds, after sprouting or soaking, make them easier to consume.
- Sprouted grains such as buckwheat, rice, quinoa, amaranth, and barley, in order to store food for granola, baking, or flour while keeping the nutrients.
- Herbs such as oregano, hyssop, basil, dill, fennel, parsley, mint, and lemon balm for using them in teas, cooking & baking.
- Crackers, granolas & bread for raw food diets.

## Section 4: How to prepare food for dehydration?

In the this and following sections, we will explain and introduce some general guidelines. Please refer to the recipes part for the detailed instructions

### Tools

To achieve an equal thickness, food preparation for dehydration is an important step. In this manner, everything will dehydrate uniformly, giving you a consistent outcome. Incomplete drying of one or two thicker parts might lead to deterioration while being stored.

Use the proper instrument for the task to ensure you obtain the finest outcome possible. The apple slicing mechanism is one item that has existed for a very long time. The cast-iron model is more than 20 years old & still working. Slice, core & peel fruits at the same time for processing fruit like pears and apples.

Choose one without any plastic components. Select tools that are sealed to the counter by the suction cup on the bottom. Some versions have a clamp, and however, if the countertop isn't a conventional size it might be a bit tricky.

When peeling & slicing fruit and vegetables, a peeler with a sharp, paring knife comes in handy.

To slice, dice, and chop items for stews, soups & snacks, you can use a food processor or sharp grater.

### Slice thickness

For optimal results, slice vegetables & fruits between 1/4th to half inch thick before dehydrating. Where possible, cut the meat more thinly.

### Consider peeling.

Not every item you dehydrate has to be peeled. Vegetables & fruits are often skinned in order to eliminate impurities that might impact flavor and appearance. To reduce exposure to pesticides, you could also decide to peel the skins off non-organic fruit.

Fruits like apricots, tomatoes & peaches may have their skins removed by dipping them in hot water for 1 minute. Place next for 1 minute in cold water or until the skins begin to wrinkle and lift. Now you can simply remove the skins by hand.

Vegetables that typically take longer to cook may be blanched by steaming for 2-5 minutes. Prior to drying, this will assist in maintaining nutrients and preventing taste loss.

## Blanching is optional

When something is "blanched," it means that it has been heated up before being put into a dehydrator. Typically, people blanch their veggies because it helps minimize taste loss before drying out, especially with vegetables that take more time to cook. The simplest method for blanching is to put the steamer's basket of veggies in the water that has been heated below. Vegetables should be steamed for 2-5 minutes until they are well cooked.

The most often blanched veggies are:

- Blanch Broccoli for 3 to 5 minutes
- Blanch spinach & kale until wilted
- Blanch Peas for 3 minutes
- Blanch Cabbage for 2 to 3 minutes
- Blanch Carrots for 3 to 4 minutes
- Blanch Corns for 1 to 3 minutes
- Blanch Asparagus for 3 to 5 minutes
- Blanch Green beans for 4 to 5 minutes.

## Dip for taste and color

There is a reason why dried fruit that has been processed professionally keeps its color and texture. Preservatives have most likely used. The preservatives help preserve the fresh fruit's appearance and texture when put to the fruit's surface.

That doesn't imply that one must soak their food in a preservative prior to drying it, but it is important to think about ways to increase the shelf life of the food. Here are a few remedies that work particularly well to prevent light-colored fruits from becoming black.

Ascorbic acid: Mix 0.95 liters of water with 1 tbsp. of pure ascorbic acid. C hop or sliced food should be added to the mixture. The mixture should rest for no more than an hour. Before putting to dehydrator trays, drain & gently rinse. Ascorbic acid is often available at your neighborhood supermarket or health food shop.

Citric acid: Mix one tbsp. of crystalline citric acid. Chop or sliced food should be added to the mixture. The mixture should rest for no more than an hour. Before putting to dehydrator trays, drain, & gently rinse. The food will taste tarter if you use citric acid, which is just 1/8 as efficient as ascorbic acid. Purchase citric acid from the neighborhood supermarket or health food shop.

Fruit juice: Mix 0.95 liters of water with one cup of lemon juice. Fruit should be dipped for 10 minutes, then thoroughly drained. Lemon juice will leave a sour flavor on fruit and, like citric acid, is only about 1/6 as efficient as ascorbic acid.

Sodium bisulfite: One tsp. of sodium bisulfite powder should be dissolved in 0.95 liters of water. Cut fruit should be soaked for two minutes, then drained and rinsed. Avoid reusing sodium bisulfite solution since doing so will reduce its effectiveness. The frequent sulfite allergy should also be taken into consideration.

## Section 5: How to dry your food?

### Fruits

Apple slices should be on a dehydrator tray. Select high-quality, ripe-picked produce for the tastiest dried fruit. Fruit that is ripe has the most sugar content, making for sweeter treats. Watch out for anything that is very ripe or damaged since it might turn black when dried. If you choose to keep the skins on, wash them first.

Slice it into uniform slices of thickness. Put on dehydrating trays and dehydrate until malleable at 135-145 F.

Drying periods for fruits, including bananas, peaches, nectarines & apples, will be between 6 to 16 hours. Grapes, apricots, figs, and pears may be ready in 20-36 hours. Within those time frames, check every two to three hours, changing trays as required.

If an older batch of fruit is already drying in the dehydrator, avoid adding fresh fruit since it will retain water.

### Drying out veggies

Vegetables ripen more slowly than fruits but also dry up more rapidly. Be cautious while preparing and take all necessary precautions to maintain freshness before drying.

This involves preparing everything for at least one batch, rinsing it in cold water, and keeping it in the fridge or a cooler place.

Simply cut any hard skin or stem fragments, as well as any bruises or blemishes. Spiralizer or use a food processor to cut to the same length & thickness. To hasten to dry, choose short lengths over bigger ones. Only blanch when it is required. Dehydrate at 125 F and put on dehydrator trays without touching. The only exceptions are onions & tomatoes, which should be dried at 145 F. Based on the vegetable and the size of the pieces, drying periods might vary from 4-10 hours.

If at all possible, avoid drying vegetables with strong aromas at the same time as those with more delicate

aromas. Garlic, onions, Brussels sprouts & peppers all leave their own flavor in other cuisines.

## Methods for drying seafood & meat

Only use fresh, low-fat fish and lean meat varieties while drying because fat will quickly go bad. Avoid dehydrating pork unless you're using cured & sliced ham.

Before dehydrating, trim the fat from the cooked meat and cut it into 1-inch-long cubes.

On trays, distribute out and dehydrate at 145 F. Most cooked meats will require 6 to 12 hours to dry thoroughly. During the preparation process, if any oil develops, pat it dry. Dehydrating prepared ground beef can be done using the same procedure.

To make jerkies for camping trips and snacks, the pork must be sliced into thin, even strips. After that, use a salted "rub" to brine or dry cure the meat for 6–12 hours in the refrigerator. After curing, brush the strips off, then dry them at 160 degrees. Strips should be cooled to 145 F until they still break but can be bent easily.

## Nuts and seeds

When seeds and nuts are already delicious raw, why would anybody dehydrate them? Soaking and then drying nuts and seeds might help some individuals with digestive problems find them easier to manage. That is a result of enzyme inhibitors found in raw nuts. Seeds & nuts become easier to digest after soaking since it assists in breaking down those inhibitors.

Soaked nuts in water & salt solution overnight to get them ready for dehydration (1 tbsp. sea salt in 4 cups of nuts soaked in water). Drain, then spread in one layer. Dry at 145 F. for 12-24 hours Almonds, pumpkin seeds, pecans, Cashews & walnuts all work in this manner.

## Herbs being dried

One of the simplest and fastest things to dry is herbs. They need minimal preparation and retain their taste for a long period in storage. Morning is the best time of day to harvest your preferred herbs, ideally before the flowers emerge. If you're looking for seeds, like coriander & celery, harvest them on a dry day when the sunlight is out. Cut the stems into single-stem sections, bundle them, and hang them in the shade. Alternately, spread out in one layer on the dehydrator trays and dehydrate for 2-4 hours at 95-105 F. When herbs are completely dried, they become crumble & brittle readily.

The quantity of food dried, its water content, the ambient temperature, humidity level, and, in the event of oven drying, the usage of fans all affect how long it takes to dry the food in traditional ovens. Some meals take a few hours, while others might take up to a day. Typical principles include:

- Herbs should dehydrate at 95 to 105 F
- Vegetables should dehydrate at 115 to 130 F
- Fruits should dehydrate at 125 to 135 F
- Meat/or jerky should dehydrate at 155 F

Spoiling might occur if the drying process is interrupted or prolonged by employing lower temperatures. Foods may be dried together if they demand comparable drying periods and temperatures. Onion, pepper & Garlic are examples of vegetables that should be dried individually.

## Section 6: Dehydrated vs. canned food

High heat is exposed to the food when you are preserving it by canning it. Depending on the diet, this results in a loss of 60-80 percent of the micronutrients. In contrast, roughly 3-5 percent of nutrients are typically lost via dehydration.

Dehydrating typically requires less work than canning. That's because it entails processing syrups & brines as well as preparing the food, sterilizing jars, and producing syrups and brines. Since canned food is already wet, it may often be consumed raw. Dehydrated meals preparation times may be extended by the requirement to soak or reconstitute certain dried items.

## Section 7: Tips about dehydrating

Select a time when your product is at its best: Fruits and vegetables should be picked when they are at their best. This is because as soon as you select the vegetable or fruit, it will begin to lose nutrients and alter in taste. Although certain goods, particularly fruit, sometimes seem sweeter when removed from their packaging.

Prepare: You should start preparing the product as soon as it is harvested. Before putting them on sheets, juicy vegetables & fruits need to be chopped.

When preparing your fruits and vegetables for drying, thinly slice them. Clean, de-stemmed leafy greens like chard & kale and break into large pieces that are approximately the size of a hand. After that, you may season them and make them into chips. They do shrink up quite a bit. A complete head of kale measures around two cups, or the amount of a small bag of chips that you may get at the local health food store. On the other hand, green beans don't need cutting. They may be washed, and have the ends trimmed.

Improve Flavor & Color: Drying may be as simple or as complicated as you want, if you don't mind exerting a little more work, you may also improve the taste and safeguard more the color.

Apples, potatoes & pears may take on a dark yellow or brownish hue. Nevertheless, you may immediately soak them in an acidic medium comprising of lemon juice mixed with water if you want them to remain white without any brown or yellow marks. It won't impact the taste if you rapidly dry them off after dipping.

Buying The Correct Equipment: A dehydrator is a must; the Excalibur is a recommended model. Once you have it, the following other crucial tools may help the process go more smoothly. Reusable nonstick sheets are helpful; no matter what type you have, one will need some high-quality sheets to lay the food on. You'll save a ton of future hassles if you do get these. Because of the fan on the rear of these machines, using parchment paper in their place might be a bit challenging. Sometimes they can wind the paper about, and you don't want that. You should be aware that the environment you're drying in will influence how long things take to dry. Your vegetables will dry quicker the dryer the air is.

## Section 8: FAQs about Dehydrating

### What is the shelf life of dehydrated food?

Although properly prepared and kept dried food has indeed been known to survive five to 10 years, it's preferable to utilize yours between four months to 12 months.

### Are nutrients lost (or preserved) when food is dehydrated?

Food may lose some nutrients when it is dried, but not as much as when it is preserved in another way. Vitamins break down because of light & heat. In other words, canning results in a greater loss of nutrients than low-humidity & heat dehydration. By blanching select veggies, you may lessen the quantity of vitamins A, C & thiamine that are lost from your diet.

### Does food dehydration eradicate bacteria?

You may get rid of the bacteria that make food rot by drying the veggies and fruits until their moisture content is between 5-20 percent. The USDA suggests first cooking raw meat to 160 F and then drying at a specific temp of 145 F if you're concerned about germs on meat.

### Does the food that has been dried have more sugar?

As dehydrating concentrates sugar while eliminating water vapor, dried fruit feels sweeter. Dried fruit has more sugar per g than fresh fruit, although total sugar content is not increased by drying fruit.

### Does food dehydration destroy enzymes?

Yes, in certain instances. Yes, enzymes do die when food is dried at extreme temps. Denser foods can endure greater temps without losing enzymes, but when temps above 140-158 F, most enzymes ultimately lose their activity.

### Can you use an Instant Pot to dehydrate food?

Sadly, no. Even though an Instant Pot is a fantastic multi-tool that can slow cook, cook under pressure, and make yogurt, it is too damp to dry anything. Despite the lid being open.

### Can cooked food be dehydrated?

You can, indeed. Even meals can be dried, but certain cooked foods dry better than some others.

### How should I keep dry goods stored?

Pack the food into silicone bags or freezer-safe containers with tight-fitting covers, or keep it in dry, clean jars (simple mason jars or canning jars can work well).

# |Part 9| Dehydrating Recipes

## Section 1: Dehydrated Fruit Recipes

### Caramel Apple Chips

|Intro|: Next time you are in the mood for some chips, these sweet apple chips will satisfy your cravings for sure. They are very simple to make, healthy, and delicious.

#### Equipment:

Knife

Cutting Board

Dehydrator

Bowl

Oven

Baking sheet

Storing Jars

#### Nutrition Facts per 1/6 serving

| Calories | 46.13 kcal |
|----------|------------|
| Carbs | 12.56g |
| Protein | 0.31g |
| Fats | 0.14g |

#### Core Ingredients

- 4 large firm apples of your choice
- 2 cups of water
- 2 tablespoons of fresh lemon juice
- 1 tablespoon of cinnamon powder

#### Step 1 - Preparation

- Combine the water with lemon juice and cinnamon in a large bowl.
- Peel the apples and thinly slice them.

#### Step 2 – Soaking the apples

- Mix the water with lemon juice and cinnamon in a large mixing bowl.
- Add the apple slices and toss them until well-coated.
- Allow them to soak for 10 to 14 minutes to absorb the flavor.

#### Step 3 – Dehydrating the apples in a dehydrator

- Prepare the dehydrator according to the manufacturer's instructions.
- Place the apple slices in a single layer on the dehydrating trays.
- Adjust the temperature to 145F, then dehydrate the apples for 10 to 14 hours until they become crisp and crunchy.

#### Step 4 – Dehydrating the apples in the oven

- Preheat the oven to 200 F.
- Spread the apple slices evenly on lined-up baking sheets.
- Bake them for 60 minutes to 100 minutes until the apple slices become crunchy and crispy.

#### Step 5 – Storing the apple chips

- Allow the chips to cool down completely, then transfer them to jars or containers.
- Seal the containers tightly to be able to store them for 8 months to 1 year, and enjoy!

### Dry Apricot Bites

|Intro|: Dry apricots are a very versatile fruit that tastes fantastic on its own as a snack, or in a salad, chutney, and salsas. In some countries, it makes a great addition to meat stews that combine both savory and sweet tastes.

#### Equipment:

Knife

Cutting Board

Dehydrator

Storing Jars

#### Nutrition Facts per 1 medium apricot

| Calories | 17 kcal |
|----------|---------|
| Carbs | 4g |
| Protein | 0g |
| Fats | 0g |

#### Core Ingredients

- Apricots

### Step 1 - Preparation

- Start by washing and drying the apricots.
- Cut them in half, discard the pit, then slice them into ¼-inch thick slices.

### Step 2 – Dehydrating the apricots in a dehydrator

- Prepare the dehydrator according to the manufacturer's instructions.
- Place the apricot slices in a single layer on the dehydrating trays.
- Adjust the temperature to 135F, then dehydrate the apricots for 6 to 8 hours until they become crisp and crunchy.

### Step 5 – Storing the apricot chips

- Allow the chips to cool down completely, then transfer them to jars or containers.
- Seal the containers tightly to be able to store them for years, and enjoy!

## Chewy Banana Chips

|Intro|: Who doesn't like bananas? These chewy banana chips are healthy and delicious and make for a great replacement for regular candy. You can eat them as a snack, incorporate them into your baked goods, or use them to decorate your cakes.

### Equipment:

Knife

Cutting Board

Dehydrator

Storing Jars

Bowl

### Nutrition Facts per 1 per gram

| Calories | 204 kcal |
|----------|----------|
| Carbs    | 52g      |
| Protein  | 2g       |
| Fats     | 0g       |

### Core Ingredients

- Bananas, ripe
- Fresh or bottled lemon juice

### Step 1 - Preparation

- Start by peeling the bananas, then cut them into ¼-inch thick slices.

### Step 2 – Soaking the bananas

- Transfer the bananas to a large bowl.
- Add to them the lemon juice with a ratio of ½ cup of 1 ½ tablespoon of lemon juice per pound.

### Step 3 – Dehydrating the bananas in a dehydrator

- Prepare the dehydrator according to the manufacturer's instructions.
- Place the banana slices in a single layer on the dehydrating trays.
- Adjust the temperature to 135F, then dehydrate the banana slices for 8 to 10 hours until they become completely dry and chewy.

### Step 4 – Dehydrating the banana in the oven

- Preheat the oven to 200 F.
- Spread the banana slices evenly on lined-up baking sheets.
- Bake them for 60 minutes to 100 minutes until the apple slices become crunchy and crispy.

### Step 5 – Storing the banana chips

- Allow the chips to cool down completely, then transfer them to jars or containers.
- Seal the containers tightly to be able to store them for 8 months to 1 year, and enjoy!

## Blueberry Bites

|Intro|: Dehydrating blueberries is a very simple task and a great healthy snack that you can carry around wherever you go. You can enjoy it with granolas, cereal, baked goods, and trail mixes, and also makes for a decoration for cakes.

### Equipment:

Knife

Cutting Board

Dehydrator

Storing Jars

### Nutrition Facts per 1 ounce

| Calories | 139 kcal |
|----------|----------|
| Carbs    | 32.74g   |

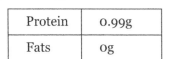

| Protein | 0.99g |
|---------|-------|
| Fats | 0g |

## Core Ingredients

- Fresh blueberries

## Step 1 - Preparation

- Start by washing the blueberries and discarding the stems.

## Step 2 – Blanching the blueberries

- Depending on the number of blueberries you have, bring a pot of water to a boil.
- Add in the blueberries and blanch them for 30 seconds, then drain them and transfer them to a lined-up baking sheet to dry for a few minutes.
- This step will help the blueberries retain their shape after you dehydrate them.

## Step 3 – Dehydrating the blueberries in a dehydrator

- Prepare the dehydrator according to the manufacturer's instructions.
- Place the blueberries in an even layer on the dehydrating trays.
- Adjust the temperature to 135F, then dehydrate the blueberries for 8 to 12 hours until they become dry and chewy.

## Step 4 – Storing the blueberries bites

- Allow the blueberries to cool down completely, then transfer them to jars or containers.
- Seal the containers tightly to be able to store them for 8 months to 1 year, and enjoy!

## Homemade Red Grapes Raisins

|Intro|: Dehydrated grapes makes for amazingly delicious homemade raisins that are definitely much better than the store-bought ones. They come out chewy and very flavorful making for a delicious snack and a great addition to your salads and baked goods.

## Equipment:

Knife

Cutting Board

Dehydrator

Storing Jars

Pot

**Nutrition Facts** per ½ Cup

| Calories | 218 kcal |
|----------|----------|
| Carbs | 57g |
| Protein | 2g |
| Fats | 0g |

## Core Ingredients

- Red Grape

## Step 1 - Preparation

- Start by washing the grapes, and discarding the stems.

## Step 2 – Blanching the grapes

- Depending on the number of grapes you have, bring a pot of water to a boil.
- Add in the grapes and blanch them for 30 seconds, then drain them and transfer them to a lined-up baking sheet to dry for a few minutes.
- This step will help the grapes retain a nice shape after you dehydrate them.

## Step 3 – Dehydrating the grapes in a dehydrator

- Use a fork to poke holes in the grapes, it will enable them to dry quickly, and taste better.
- If you have big grapes, you can slice them in half instead.
- Prepare the dehydrator according to the manufacturer's instructions.
- Place the grapes in an even layer on the dehydrating trays.
- Adjust the temperature to 135F, then dehydrate them for 17 to 48 hours until they become dry and chewy.
- Dehydrating grapes takes a long time because they are very juicy, and the time required increases when depending on their size as well.

## Step 4 – Storing the grapes

- Allow the grapes to cool down completely, then transfer them to jars or containers.
- Seal the containers tightly to be able to store them for 2 years, and enjoy!

## Blackberries Bites

**|Intro|:** Blackberries are a very delicious fruit on their own, however, if you happen to have some leftover blackberries on your hand that you don't know what to do, dehydrating them is the perfect way to preserve them and enjoy them every day.

**Equipment:**

Knife

Cutting Board

Dehydrator

Storing Jars

**Nutrition Facts** per 1/4 Cup

| Calories | 38 kcal |
|----------|---------|
| Carbs | 9g |
| Protein | 1g |
| Fats | 0.4g |

**Core Ingredients**

- Fresh Blackberries

**Step 1 - Preparation**

- Start by washing the blackberries then place them on a lined-up baking sheet to dry for 15 minutes.

**Step 2 – Dehydrating the blackberries in a dehydrator**

- Prepare the dehydrator according to the manufacturer's instructions.
- Place the blackberries in a single layer on the dehydrating trays.
- Adjust the temperature to 125F, then dehydrate them for 20 to 36 hours until they become totally dry and chewy.

**Step 3 – Dehydrating the blackberries in the oven**

- Preheat the oven to 155 to 175 F depending on which one is the lowest setting in your oven.
- Spread the blackberries evenly on lined-up baking sheets.
- Bake them for 6 to 8 hours while flipping the blackberries every 2 hours to prevent them from burning.

**Step 4 – Storing the blackberries**

- Allow the blackberries to cool down completely, then transfer them to jars or containers.
- Seal the containers tightly to be able to store them for 8 months to 1 year, and enjoy!

## Toasted Coconut Flakes

**|Intro|:** Dehydrated coconut chips are a delicacy that makes for the perfect way to preserve coconuts. With this recipe, you can make regular coconut chips, or toasted coconut chips if you love that nice, crunchy, and tasty toast smell.

**Equipment:**

Knife

Cutting Board

Dehydrator

Storing Jars

Oven

Vegetable Peeler

**Nutrition Facts** per ¼ cup

| Calories | 200 kcal |
|----------|----------|
| Carbs | 7g |
| Protein | 2g |
| Fats | 19g |

**Core Ingredients**

- Fresh Coconuts

**Step 1 - Preparation**

- Start by washing the coconuts, drill a hole in them to remove the coconut water first, then remove the tough brown outer layer.
- Use a knife and a vegetable peeler to remove the brown layer that is stuck to the coconut flesh.
- When done, use a vegetable peeler to slice the coconut flesh into slivers.
- Rinse the coconut slivers with some water, then drain them and place them on a baking sheet to dry for 30 minutes before using them.

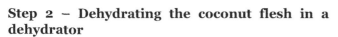
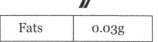

### Step 2 – Dehydrating the coconut flesh in a dehydrator

- Prepare the dehydrator according to the manufacturer's instructions.
- Place the coconut slivers in a single layer on the dehydrating trays.
- Adjust the temperature to 105F, then dehydrate them for 4 to 6 hours until they become crispy and crunchy. If you prefer them to be toasted, continue to dehydrate them and stir them every 1 hour until they gain a nice golden color.

### Step 3 – Dehydrating the coconut

- Preheat the oven to 140 F.
- Spread the coconut slivers evenly on lined-up baking sheets.
- Bake them for 60 to 70 minutes while checking on them every minute, and stirring them so they don't burn. If you prefer them to remain white, pull them out once they become crispy and crunchy, if you prefer them toasted, then bake them a little longer while checking and stirring them every 5 minutes.

### Step 4 – Storing the coconut flakes

- Allow the flakes to cool down completely, then transfer them to jars or containers.
- Seal the containers tightly to be able to store them for 8 months to 1 year, and enjoy!

## Dry Dates

|Intro|: Dates are a very underrated fruit that a lot of people are missing on, so if you happen to get some dates, don't hesitate to incorporate them into your diet, and the best way to do this is by dehydrating them. They taste chewy but sweet, delicious, and very filling.

### Equipment:

Knife

Cutting Board

Dehydrator

Storing Jars

Bowl

### Nutrition Facts per 1 date

| Calories | 20 kcal |
|----------|---------|
| Carbs | 5.33g |
| Protein | 0.17g |
| Fats | 0.03g |

### Core Ingredients

- Fresh dates of your choice

### Step 1 - Preparation

- Start by washing the dates with cold water.

### Step 2 – Blanching the dates

- Depending on the number of dates you have, bring a pot of water to a boil.
- Add in the dates and blanch them for 30 to 60 seconds, until their skin starts to blister.
- Drain them and transfer them to a large bowl, cover them with cold water and let them sit for a few minutes to cool down.
- Drain them, slice them in half, then discard the pits.

### Step 3 – Dehydrating the dates in a dehydrator

- Prepare the dehydrator according to the manufacturer's instructions.
- Place the dates with the open sides facing down in an even layer on the dehydrating trays.
- Adjust the temperature to 125F, then dehydrate them for 24 hours.
- Once the time is up, if you wish to cut the dates into small pieces you can do it now, or you can keep them as they are.
- Dehydrate the dates for another 24 until they become dry and chewy.
- The dates are loaded with natural sugar which is why they take a long time to dry.

### Step 4 – Storing the dates

- Allow the dates to cool down completely, then transfer them to jars or containers.
- Seal the containers tightly to be able to store them for 8 months to 1 year, and enjoy!

## Dry Figs

|Intro|: Just like dates, figs are a very special and underrated fruit that is packed with natural sugar. Dehydrating them takes a while because they are sweet and juicy, however, the end result is absolutely worth it.

### Equipment:

Knife

Cutting Board
Dehydrator
Storing Jars
Oven

**Nutrition Facts** per 1 Fig

| Calories | 46.13 kcal |
|---|---|
| Carbs | 12.56g |
| Protein | 0.31g |
| Fats | 0.14g |

## Core Ingredients

- Fresh black or green figs

### Step 1 - Preparation

- Start by washing the figs, then cut them in half.

### Step 2 – Dehydrating the figs in a dehydrator

- Prepare the dehydrator according to the manufacturer's instructions.
- Place the fig halves in a single layer on the dehydrating trays with the open side facing up.
- Adjust the temperature to 135F, then dehydrate the figs for 7 to 12 hours until they become completely dry and chewy.

### Step 3 – Dehydrating the figs in the oven

- Preheat the oven to 140 F.
- Spread the fig halves evenly on lined-up baking sheets with the open side facing up.
- Bake them for 8 to 12 hours.

### Step 4 – Storing the figs

- Allow figs halves to cool down completely, then transfer them to jars or containers.
- Seal the containers tightly to be able to store them for up to 1 year, and enjoy!

## Lemon Wheels

|Intro|: Dehydrating lemons is a very special way to preserve and use them to add a nice flavor and kick to your tea, lemonade, and drinks. They also make for very cute and beautiful decorations for your baked goods.

**Equipment:**
Knife
Cutting Board
Dehydrator
Storing Jars
Oven

**Nutrition Facts** per 1 piece

| Calories | 7 kcal |
|---|---|
| Carbs | 2g |
| Protein | 1g |
| Fats | 0g |

## Core Ingredients

- Lemons, limes, or oranges

### Step 1 - Preparation

- Start by washing your lemons, the cut them into ¼-inch rounds.

### Step 2 – Dehydrating the lemons in a dehydrator

- Prepare the dehydrator according to the manufacturer's instructions.
- Place the lemon rounds in a single layer on the dehydrating trays.
- Adjust the temperature to 135F, then dehydrate the lemons for 6 to 8 hours until they become completely dry and chewy.

### Step 3 – Dehydrating the lemons in the oven

- Preheat the oven to 200 F.
- Spread the lemon slices evenly on lined-up baking sheets.
- Bake them for 3 to 4 hours until the lemon slices while flipping them halfway through.

### Step 4 – Storing the lemon wheels

- Allow the lemon wheels to cool down completely, then transfer them to jars or containers.
- Seal the containers tightly to be able to store them for 8 months to 1 year, and enjoy!

## Mango Chips

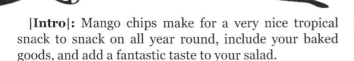

**|Intro|:** Mango chips make for a very nice tropical snack to snack on all year round, include your baked goods, and add a fantastic taste to your salad.

**Equipment:**

Knife

Cutting Board

Dehydrator

Storing Jars

Oven

**Nutrition Facts** per 1 piece

| Calories | 30 kcal |
|----------|---------|
| Carbs | 7g |
| Protein | 0.50g |
| Fats | 0g |

**Core Ingredients**

- Fresh Mangos, ripe

### Step 1 - Preparation

- Start by washing the mangos, then peel them.
- Cut the mangos in half, then slice them into ¼-inch thick pieces

### Step 2 – Dehydrating the mango in a dehydrator

- Prepare the dehydrator according to the manufacturer's instructions.
- Place the mango slices in a single layer on the dehydrating trays.
- Adjust the temperature to 135F, then dehydrate the mango pieces for 10 to 14 hours until they dry completely.

### Step 3 – Storing the mango chips

- Allow the mango chips to cool down completely, then transfer them to jars or containers.
- Seal the containers tightly to be able to store them for up to 1 year, and enjoy!

## Nectarines Bites

**|Intro|:** If you have some nectarines on hand or a nectarine tree that yielded more than you know to do with, dehydrating them preserves them for you all year. You can serve them as a snack, add them to a salad, granola...They taste sweet and delicious.

**Equipment:**

Knife

Cutting Board

Dehydrator

Storing Jars

Oven

Baking Sheet

**Nutrition Facts** per 1/8 cup

| Calories | 73 kcal |
|----------|---------|
| Carbs | 16.67g |
| Protein | 1.33g |
| Fats | 0g |

**Core Ingredients**

- Fresh Nectarines

### Step 1 - Preparation

- Start by washing and drying nectarines.
- Cut them in half, discard the stones, then slice them into ¼-inch thick pieces

### Step 3 – Dehydrating the nectarines in a dehydrator

- Prepare the dehydrator according to the manufacturer's instructions.
- Place the nectarine slices in a single layer on the dehydrating trays.
- Adjust the temperature to 120F, then dehydrate them for 5 to 10 hours until they become completely dry and chewy.

### Step 4 – Dehydrating the nectarines in the oven

- Preheat the oven to the lowest setting.
- Spread the nectarine slices evenly on lined-up baking sheets.
- Bake them for 3 to 5 hours while flipping them halfway through.

### Step 5 – Storing the nectarine bites

- Allow the nectarine bites to cool down completely, then transfer them to jars or containers.
- Seal the containers tightly to be able to store them for 8 months to 1 year, and enjoy!

## Peach Bites

**|Intro|:** Dehydrated peach slices make for a scrumptious snack that will please all palates. It's also a great way to preserve your peaches for up to 6 months since they tend to go bad quickly. If you like making jams and jellies, you can cut up some dry peach slices and mix them, they make for a nice surprise.

### Equipment:
Knife

Cutting Board

Dehydrator

Storing Jars

Pot

**Nutrition Facts** per 1 peach

| Calories | 59 kcal |
|----------|---------|
| Carbs | 14g |
| Protein | 1g |
| Fats | 1g |

### Core Ingredients
- Fresh peaches

### Step 1 - Preparation
- Start by washing peaches.

### Step 2 – Blanching the peaches
- Depending on the number of peaches you have, bring a pot of water to a boil.
- Add in the peaches and blanch them for 30 seconds, then drain them and transfer them to a large bowl.
- Cover the peaches with cold water, and allow them to cool down until they become cool enough to handle.
- Drain the peaches, peel them, discard the pits, then cut them into ½-inch thick slices.

### Step 3 – Dehydrating the peaches in a dehydrator
- Prepare the dehydrator according to the manufacturer's instructions.
- Place the peaches in an even layer on the dehydrating trays.
- Adjust the temperature to 125F, then dehydrate them for 10 to 12 hours until they become dry and chewy.

### Step 4 – Storing the peach slices
- Allow the peach slices to cool down completely, then transfer them to jars or containers.
- Seal the containers tightly to be able to store them for 6 months, and enjoy!

## Pineapple Chips

**|Intro|:** There is no better way to celebrate the summer than with pineapple chips. They are naturally sweet, healthy, and natural candy that will also make a great addition to elevate your dishes.

### Equipment:
Knife

Cutting Board

Dehydrator

Storing Jars

**Nutrition Facts** per 1 Cup

| Calories | 501 kcal |
|----------|----------|
| Carbs | 130g |
| Protein | 2.3g |
| Fats | 0.8g |

### Core Ingredients
- Fresh Pineapple

### Step 1 - Preparation
- Start by washing the pineapple and core it.
- Slice the pineapple into ¼-inch thick rounds, then cut them into bite-size pieces.

### Step 2 – Dehydrating the pineapple in a dehydrator
- Prepare the dehydrator according to the manufacturer's instructions.
- Place the pineapple slices in a single layer on the dehydrating trays.
- Adjust the temperature to 135F, then dehydrate the pineapple slices for 10 to 14 hours until they become completely dry and slightly chewy.

### Step 3 – Storing the pineapple chips

- Allow the chips to cool down completely, then transfer them to jars or containers.
- Seal the containers tightly to be able to store them for 8 months to 1 year, and enjoy!

## Strawberry Chips

|Intro|: Who doesn't miss strawberries when they stop being in season? With this recipe, you won't miss them anymore because when dried they taste fantastic, and will become your new addiction.

### Equipment:

Knife

Cutting Board

Dehydrator

Storing Jars

### Nutrition Facts per ½ cup

| Calories | 19 kcal |
|----------|---------|
| Carbs | 4g |
| Protein | 1g |
| Fats | 0g |

### Core Ingredients

- Fresh and firm Strawberries

### Step 1 - Preparation

- Start by washing the strawberries, then transfer them to a baking sheet and allow them to dry for 15 to 20 minutes.
- Slice the strawberries into ¼-inch thick slices lengthwise.

### Step 2 – Dehydrating the strawberries in a dehydrator

- Prepare the dehydrator according to the manufacturer's instructions.
- Place the strawberry slices in a single layer on the dehydrating trays.
- Adjust the temperature to 160F, then dehydrate them for 7 to 9 hours until they become completely dry and slightly chewy.

### Step 3 – Storing the strawberry chips

- Allow the chips to cool down completely, then transfer them to jars or containers.
- Seal the containers tightly to be able to store them for 6, and enjoy!

## Section 2: Dehydrated Vegetable Recipes

## Dehydrated Asparagus

|Intro|: Dehydrating asparagus is yet another incredible method to preserve asparagus all year round, and save a lot of money. To use it you just have to soak it in some hot water. Also, you can ground it into powder, then easily use it to make asparagus soup.

### Equipment:

Knife

Cutting Board

Dehydrator

Bowl

Storing Jars

Pot

Colander

### Nutrition Facts per 1 cup

| Calories | 26.88 kcal |
|----------|------------|
| Carbs | 25.21g |
| Protein | 2.96g |
| Fats | 0.16g |

### Core Ingredients

- Asparagus

### Step 1 - Preparation

- Start by washing the asparagus spears, then trim off the tough ends, then cutting the stalks and leaving the tender parts on their own.
- If you are using big asparagus spears, peel the outer layer of their stems.
- Separate the 3 types of asparagus pieces.

## Step 2 – Blanching the asparagus

- Depending on the amount of asparagus you have, bring a pot of water to a boil.
- Add to it one part of the asparagus and bring it to another boil, then cook them for 3 minutes over high heat.
- Once the time is up, drain it, and transfer it to a bowl. Cover it with cold water and let it sit for 2 to 3 minutes until it becomes cool to the touch.
- Drain it and transfer it to a colander to dry for 15 to 20 minutes.
- When done, repeat the process with the remaining 2 asparagus parts, each part on its own.
- This step is important because asparagus has 3 different textures, so each one of them needs to be dehydrated for a certain amount of time.

## Step 3 – Dehydrating the asparagus in a dehydrator

- Prepare the dehydrator according to the manufacturer's instructions.
- Place each asparagus part in an even layer on the dehydrating trays.
- Adjust the temperature to 135F.
- Dehydrate the asparagus tips for 6 to 9 hours until they become completely dry.
- Dehydrate the asparagus stalks for 8 to 12 hours until they become completely dry.
- Dehydrate the tough asparagus ends for 11 to 14 hours until they become completely dry.

## Step 4 – Storing the asparagus

- Allow the asparagus pieces to cool down completely, then transfer them to jars or containers.
- Seal the containers tightly to be able to store them for 6 months, and enjoy!

## Avocado Chips

|Intro|: It is an established fact that it's really hard to preserve avocados because they go bad quickly. This recipe is super simple and easy to make avocado chips and store them for up to 6 months. You can serve them with a dipping sauce, or you can ground them, and use them later to make the salsa by adding hot water to it.

## Equipment:

Knife

Cutting Board

Dehydrator

Storing Jars

Bowl

## Nutrition Facts per 1 cup

| Calories | 238.69 kcal |
| --- | --- |
| Carbs | 12.72g |
| Protein | 2.98g |
| Fats | 21.87g |

## Core Ingredients

- Fresh and ripe avocado

## Step 1 - Preparation

- Start by washing the avocados, then cut them in half.
- Discard the pit, then slice the avocado into ¼-inch thick pieces.
- Transfer them to a bowl, then toss them gently with a splash of lemon or line juice.

## Step 2 – Dehydrating the avocado in a dehydrator

- Prepare the dehydrator according to the manufacturer's instructions.
- Place the avocado slices in a single layer on the dehydrating trays.
- Adjust the temperature to 135F, then dehydrate the apples for 8 to 12 hours until they become crisp and crunchy.

## Step 4 – Dehydrating the avocados in the oven

- Preheat the oven to 140 F.
- Spread the avocado slices evenly on lined-up baking sheets.
- Open the oven door slightly for about 3 inches, then bake in it the avocado slices for 10 to 12 hours until they become completely dry and crispy.

## Step 5 – Storing the avocado chips

- Allow the chips to cool down completely, then transfer them to jars or containers.
- Seal the containers tightly to be able to store them for 6 months, and enjoy!

## Beetroot Chips

|Intro|: Beetroot chips are the ultimate beautiful, crunchy, and tasty chips. They tick all boxes and make for a great delicious and healthy alternative to regular potato chips.

### Equipment:
Knife

Cutting Board

Dehydrator

Storing Jars

Oven

Baking sheet

### Nutrition Facts per 1/5 of the recipe

| Calories | 35 kcal |
|----------|---------|
| Carbs | 8g |
| Protein | 1g |
| Fats | 1g |

### Core Ingredients
- Red beetroots

### Step 1 - Preparation
- Start by washing and peeling the beetroots, then slice then into 1/8 inch rounds.

### Step 2 – Dehydrating the beetroots in a dehydrator
- Prepare the dehydrator according to the manufacturer's instructions.
- Place the beetroot slices in a single layer on the dehydrating trays.
- Adjust the temperature to 125F, then dehydrate them for 8 to 14 hours until they become crisp and crunchy.

### Step 3 – Dehydrating the beetroots in the oven
- Start by tossing the beet slices in a large bowl with a generous sprinkle of salt.
- Place the beetroot slices in a colander, and let them drain for 18 to 24 minutes to drain.
- Once the time is up, pat the chips dry. This step is important because it drains the liquid from the beetroots so they can dry faster.
- Preheat the oven to 300 F.

- Spread the beetroot slices evenly on lined-up baking sheets.
- Bake them for 30 minutes to 60 minutes until the beetroot slices become crunchy and crispy.

### Step 4 – Storing the beetroot chips
- Allow the chips to cool down completely, then transfer them to jars or containers.
- Seal the containers tightly to be able to store them for 3 months, and enjoy!

## Broccoli Bites

|Intro|: Dehydrating broccoli is a really nice way to preserve it in its original form without adding any spices. You can store it for up to 12 months, and when ready to use, you just have to cover it with hot water and let it sit for 15 to 20 minutes.

### Equipment:
Knife

Cutting Board

Dehydrator

Storing Jars

Pot

Colander

### Nutrition Facts per 1 cup

| Calories | 30.86 kcal |
|----------|-----------|
| Carbs | 6.03g |
| Protein | 2.56g |
| Fats | 0.34g |

### Core Ingredients
- Fresh broccoli

### Step 1 - Preparation
- Start by washing the broccoli with warm water, then cut it into florets of the same size.
- Cut the broccoli stems into bite-size pieces then keep them in a separate bowl.

### Step 2 – Blanching the broccoli
- Depending on the amount of broccoli you have, bring a pot of water to a boil.

- Add to it the broccoli florets and bring it to another boil, then cook them for 3 minutes over high heat.
- Once the time is up, drain the florets, and transfer them to a bowl. Cover them with cold water and let them sit for 2 to 3 minutes until they become cool to the touch.
- Drain the florets and transfer them to a colander to dry for 15 to 20 minutes.
- When done, repeat the process with the broccoli stems.
- This step is important because broccoli has 2 different textures, so they need to be separated while dehydrating.

## Step 3 – Dehydrating the broccoli in a dehydrator

- Prepare the dehydrator according to the manufacturer's instructions.
- Place each broccoli part in an even layer on the dehydrating trays.
- Adjust the temperature to 125F, then dehydrate them for 8 to 14 hours until they become completely dry.

## Step 4 – Storing the broccoli

- Allow the broccoli florets and pieces to cool down completely, then transfer them to jars or containers.
- Seal the containers tightly to be able to store them for 6 months, and enjoy!

## Brussels Sprouts Bites

|Intro|: Dehydrating is a very cool method along with pickling to enjoy brussels sprouts. This recipe uses balsamic vinegar and salt with them which adds a very nice flavor, and makes them addictive. The Brussels sprout leaves come out crunchy and tasty just like chips.

## Equipment:

Knife

Cutting Board

Dehydrator

Storing Jars

Oven

Baking sheets

Bowl

**Nutrition Facts** per 1 cup

| Calories | 42.51 kcal |
|----------|------------|
| Carbs | 8.78g |
| Protein | 3g |
| Fats | 0.26g |

## Core Ingredients

- Fresh Brussels Sprouts
- Balsamic Vinegar
- Sea Salt

## Step 1 - Preparation

- Start washing the brussels sprouts and peel their leaves.
- Transfer the leaves to a large bowl, then toss them with a splash of balsamic vinegar and salt to taste.

## Step 2 – Dehydrating the brussels sprouts in a dehydrator

- Prepare the dehydrator according to the manufacturer's instructions.
- Place the brussels sprout leaves in a single layer on the dehydrating tray.
- Adjust the temperature to 140F, then dehydrate the figs for 6 to 8 hours until they become dry and crunchy.

## Step 3 – Dehydrating the brussels sprouts in the oven

- Preheat the oven to 350 F.
- Spread the brussels sprouts leaves evenly on lined-up baking sheets and bake them for 6 minutes while tossing them every 2 minutes.

## Step 4 – Storing the brussels sprouts

- Allow Brussels sprouts to cool down completely, then transfer them to jars or containers.
- Seal the containers tightly to be able to store them for up to 3 months, and enjoy!

## Cabbage Chips

|Intro|: Dehydrated cabbage leaves make for fantastic chips to add to your collections, and serve with a salsa or a sauce. They also make for a tasty snack that you toss with some salt and enjoy on its own. Or you can simply

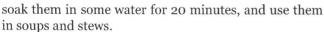

soak them in some water for 20 minutes, and use them in soups and stews.

**Equipment:**

Knife

Cutting Board

Dehydrator

Storing Jars

**Nutrition Facts** per 1 cup

| Calories | 19.91 kcal |
|---|---|
| Carbs | 4.62g |
| Protein | 1.02g |
| Fats | 0.08g |

**Core Ingredients**

- Fresh green or red cabbage

**Step 1 - Preparation**

- Start by washing the cabbage, and remove the damaged outer leaves.
- Core the cabbage, and cut them into quarters.
- Next, slice the cabbage into ½ wide strips.

**Step 2 – Dehydrating the cabbage in a dehydrator**

- Prepare the dehydrator according to the manufacturer's instructions.
- Place the cabbage slices in a single layer on the dehydrating trays.
- Adjust the temperature to 125F, then dehydrate them for 8 to 12 hours until they become crisp and crunchy.

**Step 3 – Storing the cabbage chips**

- Allow the chips to cool down completely, then transfer them to jars or containers.
- Seal the containers tightly to be able to store them for up to 18 months, and enjoy!

## Carrot Chips

|Intro|: Carrots are very healthy, and tasty when cooked right, however, it's one of those veggies that you won't find yourself reaching out for it a lot, and might also have a hard time getting your kids to eat it. If you dehydrate it though, you won't have an issue with it at all it's gonna disappear within hours because the slices come out salty with a nice hint of sweetness, and crispy.

**Equipment:**

Knife

Cutting Board

Dehydrator

Storing Jars

Pot

Baking sheet

**Nutrition Facts** per 1 pound

| Calories | 186 kcal |
|---|---|
| Carbs | 43g |
| Protein | 4g |
| Fats | 1g |

**Core Ingredients**

- 1 pound of fresh carrots

**Step 1 - Preparation**

- Start by washing the carrots, then cut off the heads, and trim the ends.
- Slice them into 1/8 thick coins.

**Step 2 – Blanching the carrots**

- Depending on the number of carrots you have, bring a pot of water to a boil.
- Add in the blueberries and blanch them for 4 minutes, then drain them and transfer them to a large bowl.
- Cover the carrots with cold water and allow them to sit in them for 1 to 2 minutes until they cool down.
- Drain the carrot coins than transfer them to a lined-up baking sheet and let them dry.

**Step 3 – Dehydrating the carrots in a dehydrator**

- Prepare the dehydrator according to the manufacturer's instructions.
- Place the carrots in an even layer on the dehydrating trays.
- Adjust the temperature to 125F, then dehydrate the carrot coins for 6 to 10 hours until they become dry and crunchy.

### Step 5 – Storing the carrot chips

- Allow the carrots to cool down completely, then transfer them to jars or containers.
- Seal the containers tightly to be able to store them for 8 months to 1 year, and enjoy!

## Cauliflower Bites

|Intro|: Dehydrating cauliflower makes for an easy and simple method to preserve it instead of letting it sit in the fridge until turns bad. When ready to use it, you just have to soak it in some hot water for up to 20 minutes, then you can add it to your soups and stews and enjoy.

### Equipment:

Knife

Cutting Board

Dehydrator

Storing Jars

**Nutrition Facts** per ¼ cup

| Calories | 30.03 kcal |
|----------|------------|
| Carbs | 3.8g |
| Protein | 0.8g |
| Fats | 0g |

### Core Ingredients

- Head of cauliflower (s)

### Step 1 - Preparation

- Start by washing the cauliflower with warm water, then cut it into florets of the same size.
- Cut the broccoli stems into bite-size pieces then keep them in a separate bowl.

### Step 2 – Blanching the cauliflower

- Depending on the amount of cauliflower you have, bring a pot of water to a boil.
- Add to it the cauliflower florets and bring it to another boil, then cook them for 3 minutes over high heat.
- Once the time is up, drain the florets, and transfer them to a bowl. Cover them with cold water and let them sit for 2 to 3 minutes until they become cool to the touch.

- Drain the florets and transfer them to a colander to dry for 15 to 20 minutes.
- When done, repeat the process with the cauliflower stems.
- This step is important because just like broccoli, cauliflower has 2 different textures, so they need to be separated while dehydrating.

### Step 3 – Dehydrating the cauliflower in a dehydrator

- Prepare the dehydrator according to the manufacturer's instructions.
- Place each cauliflower part in an even layer on the dehydrating trays.
- Adjust the temperature to 125F, then dehydrate them for 8 to 14 hours until they become completely dry.

### Step 4 – Storing the cauliflower

- Allow the cauliflower florets and pieces to cool down completely, then transfer them to jars or containers.
- Seal the containers tightly to be able to store them for 6 months, and enjoy!

## Edamame Popcorn

|Intro|: Popcorn is already amazing on its own, but Edamame is a nice change from the regular corn. When seasoned with salt and dehydrated, it comes out crunchy, slightly chewy, and delicious. You can serve them on their or add them to a salad and enjoy.

### Equipment:

Knife

Cutting Board

Dehydrator

Storing Jars

Colander

Baking Sheet

**Nutrition Facts** per ¼ cup

| Calories | 42.18 kcal |
|----------|------------|
| Carbs | 2.94g |
| Protein | 4.34g |
| Fats | 1.83g |

### Core Ingredients

- Edamame beans

### Step 1 - Preparation

- Start by washing the edamame beans, then transfer them to a colander and allow them to drain for 15 minutes.
- Once the time is up, transfer the beans to lined-up baking sheets and allow them to dry completely.

### Step 2 – Dehydrating the edamame in a dehydrator

- Prepare the dehydrator according to the manufacturer's instructions.
- Place the edamame beans in a single layer on the dehydrating trays.
- Adjust the temperature to 135F, then dehydrate the beans for 10 to 14 hours until they become crisp and crunchy.

### Step 3 – Storing the edamame beans

- Allow the edamame beans to cool down completely, then transfer them to jars or containers.
- Seal the containers tightly to be able to store them for 8 months to 1 year, and enjoy!

## Green Beans Chips

|Intro|: Green beans make for a great addition to stews, or a simple nice side dish tossed with butter and some seasoning, however, they are one of those vegetables that are very hard to get when they are not ins season. Aside from canning them, dehydrating them is the best option to preserve them and enjoy them all year long. When you wish to use them again, you can just soak them in hot water.

### Equipment:

Knife

Cutting Board

Dehydrator

Storing Jars

Colander

Pot

Bowl

**Nutrition Facts** per ¼ pound

| | |
|---|---|
| Calories | 35 kcal |
| Carbs | 7.9g |
| Protein | 2.1g |
| Fats | 0.2g |

### Core Ingredients

- Green beans
- Salt

### Step 1 - Preparation

- Start by washing the green beans and draining them.
- Trim off their ends, and cut them into 1-inch pieces. This way, when you wish to use them, you don't have to cut them up.

### Step 2 – Blanching the green beans

- Bring a large pot of water to a boil, and prepare an ice bath.
- Add in the beans with salt. The ratio of salt should be 1 teaspoon of salt per pound of green beans.
- Bring the pot to another boil, then blanch the beans for 3 minutes.
- Once the time is up, drain the beans and transfer them to the ice bath.
- Allow them to sit for a few minutes until they become cool to the touch then transfer them to a colander to drain.

### Step 3 – Dehydrating the green beans in a dehydrator

- Prepare the dehydrator according to the manufacturer's instructions.
- Place the green beans in a single layer on the dehydrating trays.
- Adjust the temperature to 125F, then dehydrate them for 8 to 14 hours until they become crisp and completely dry.

### Step 4 – Storing the green beans

- Allow the green beans to cool down completely, then transfer them to jars or containers.
- Seal the containers tightly to be able to store them for 8 months to 1 year, and enjoy!

## Kale Chips

**|Intro|:** Kale tastes amazingly fresh with salads, in stews, and in soups, however, and it tastes just as good when it's dehydrated and seasoned with salt. You can serve it as chips with a dip or salsa, it will not disappoint you. If you wish to use it for stews and soup instead, you have to dehydrate it without the seasonings. When ready to use with stew or soup, you just have to soak in water for an hour or two and enjoy!

## Equipment:

Knife

Cutting Board

Dehydrator

Storing Jars

Colander

Bowl

### Nutrition Facts per ½ cup

| Calories | 44 kcal |
|----------|---------|
| Carbs | 3g |
| Protein | 1g |
| Fats | 4g |

## Core Ingredients

- 2 cups of fresh kale leaves
- 2 tablespoons of nutritional yeast
- 3 teaspoons of olive oil
- ¾ teaspoon of salt

## Step 1 - Preparation

- Start by removing and discarding the hard stems, stalks, and ribs of the kale leaves.
- Tear the kale leaves into chip size pieces, then wash them, and place them on lined-up baking sheets to air dry.

## Step 2 – Seasoning the kale

- Whisk the oil with nutritional yeast and salt in a large mixing bowl.
- Add the kale pieces then toss until they are completely coated.

## Step 3 – Dehydrating the kale in a dehydrator

- Prepare the dehydrator according to the manufacturer's instructions.

- Place the kale leaves in a single layer on the dehydrating trays.
- Adjust the temperature to 145F for 60 minutes.
- Once time is up, lower the temperature to 115 F, then dry the kale leaves for 3 to 5 hours until they become crispy and crunchy.

## Step 4 – Storing the kale chips

- Allow the chips to cool down completely, then transfer them to jars or containers.
- Seal the containers tightly to be able to store them for 8 months to 1 year, and enjoy!

## Pumpkin Bites

**|Intro|:** Dehydrating pumpkin is one of the most popular ways of preserving it. You can choose to can it, but this method also helps the pumpkin keeps it's flavor when stored for a long time. When ready to use it, you just have to soak it for a few hours, then you can enjoy it with stews, soups, or you can use with your baked goods.

## Equipment:

Knife

Cutting Board

Dehydrator

Storing Jars

### Nutrition Facts per 1/6 of the recipe

| Calories | 7.53 kcal |
|----------|-----------|
| Carbs | 1.88g |
| Protein | 0.29g |
| Fats | 0.03g |

## Core Ingredients

- Ripe Pumpkin

## Step 1 - Preparation

- Start by washing the pumpkin, the slice it in half.
- Remove the strings and seeds attached, then use a spoon to scrap out the remaining attached strings.
- Slice the pumpkin into 1-inch thick slices, then peel them, and dice them.

## Step 2 – Dehydrating the pumpkin in a dehydrator

- Prepare the dehydrator according to the manufacturer's instructions.
- Place the pumpkin cubes in a single layer on the dehydrating trays.
- Adjust the temperature to 150F, then dehydrate them for 10 to 14 hours until they become completely dry.

## Step 3 – Dehydrating the pumpkin in the oven

- Preheat the oven to 140 F.
- Spread the pumpkin cubes evenly on lined-up baking sheets.
- Bake them for 3 to 5 hours until the pumpkin cubes become completely dry.

## Step 4 – Storing the pumpkin cubes

- Allow the pumpkin pieces to cool down completely, then transfer them to jars or containers.
- Seal the containers tightly to be able to store them for 8 months, and enjoy!

## Tomato Chips

|Intro|: Tomato chips makes for a nutritious and yummy snack. The seasoning gives it so much more flavor so you can eat it on its own or serve it with some sauce or salsa. Or, you can break them into pieces, soak them in some hot water until it softens then serve it in a salad, or add it to your pasta.

**Equipment:**

Knife

Cutting Board

Dehydrator

Storing Jars

Oven

Baking Sheets

**Nutrition Facts** per ¼ cup

| Calories | 8.1 kcal |
|----------|----------|
| Carbs | 1.75g |
| Protein | 0.4g |
| Fats | 0.09g |

## Core Ingredients

- Ripe fresh tomatoes
- Italian seasoning (to taste)

## Step 1 - Preparation

- Start by washing the tomatoes, and discarding the stems.
- Slice the tomatoes into ¼-inch thick, then season the tomato wheels on both sizes with Italian seasoning or any seasoning blend that you prefer.

## Step 2 – Dehydrating the tomato in a dehydrator

- Prepare the dehydrator according to the manufacturer's instructions.
- Place the tomato slices in a single layer on the dehydrating trays.
- Adjust the temperature to 125F, then dehydrate them for 10 to 12 hours until they become crisp and crunchy.

## Step 3 – Dehydrating the tomatoes in the oven

- Preheat the oven to 170 F or your lowest settings.
- Spread the tomato slices evenly on lined-up baking sheets.
- Bake them for 3 to 4 hours until the tomato slices become crunchy and crispy.

## Step 4 – Storing the tomato chips

- Allow the chips to cool down completely, then transfer them to jars or containers.
- Seal the containers tightly to be able to store them for 18 months, and enjoy!

## Zucchini Chips

|Intro|: Zucchini is one of the easiest vegetables to plant and harvest, it's guaranteed to find it in all small and big gardens, which means that you are bound to end up with a lot of zucchini that you need to preserve, and there is no better way to preserve it than dehydrating it. Zucchini chips come out crips and crunchy, which makes for amazing, healthy, and tasty chips.

**Equipment:**

Knife

Cutting Board

Dehydrator

Storing Jars

Oven

Baking sheets

**Nutrition Facts** per ¼ cup

| Calories | 9 kcal |
|----------|--------|
| Carbs    | 1.9g   |
| Protein  | 0.7g   |
| Fats     | 0.1g   |

## Core Ingredients

- Fresh Zucchini

## Step 1 - Preparation

- Start by washing the zucchini, and cutting off the tops.
- Cut the zucchini into ¼-inch rounds.

## Step 3 – Dehydrating the zucchini in a dehydrator

- Prepare the dehydrator according to the manufacturer's instructions.
- Place the zucchini slices in a single layer on the dehydrating trays.
- Adjust the temperature to 125F, then dehydrate them for 4 to 10 hours until they become crisp and crunchy.

## Step 4 – Dehydrating the zucchini in the oven

- Preheat the oven to 200 F.
- Spread the zucchini slices evenly on lined-up baking sheets.
- Bake them for 1 to 4 hours until the zucchini slices become crunchy and crispy.

## Step 5 – Storing the zucchini chips

- Allow the chips to cool down completely, then transfer them to jars or containers.
- Seal the containers tightly to be able to store them for 1 year, and enjoy!

## Section 3: Dehydrated Crackers, Bread and Chips Recipes

### Crunchy Corn Chips

|Intro|: Crunchy, tasty chips that make for a great alternative to regular chips. They are vegan, healthy, and delicious, so you enjoy them on their own as a snack, salsa, or a dipping sauce of your choice.

**Equipment:**

Knife

Cutting Board

Dehydrator

Bowl

Storing Jars

Food Processor

**Nutrition Facts** per 1/4 cup

| Calories | 63.57 kcal |
|----------|------------|
| Carbs    | 13.3g      |
| Protein  | 2.42g      |
| Fats     | 0.98g      |

## Core Ingredients

- 4 cups of corn kernels
- ½ cup of water
- ½ teaspoon of onion powder
- ½ teaspoon of garlic powder
- Salt

## Step 1 - Preparation

- Combine the water with corn kernels, onion powder, garlic powder, and a pinch of salt to taste in a blender, then process them until they become smooth and thick.

## Step 2 – Dehydrating the corn chips in a dehydrator

- Prepare the dehydrator according to the manufacturer's instructions.
- Spread the corn mixture to make a ¼-inch single layer on the dehydrating trays.
- Adjust the temperature to 155F, then dehydrate the corn chips for 2 hours.
- Once the time is up, cut the chips into the size that you desire.
- Dehydrate the chips for another 6 to 9 hours until they become crisp and crunchy.

### Step 3 – Storing the corn chips

- Allow the chips to cool down completely, then transfer them to jars or containers.
- Seal the containers tightly to be able to store them for 8 months to 1 year, and enjoy!

## Almond crackers

### Equipment:

Knife

Cutting Board

Dehydrator

Storing Jars

**Nutrition Facts** per 1 square cracker

| Calories | 63.28 kcal |
|----------|-----------|
| Carbs | 2.62g |
| Protein | 2.71g |
| Fats | 5.11g |

### Core Ingredients

- 4 cups of almonds, soaked and drained
- 2 cups of water
- ½ cup of nutritional yeast
- ½ cup of flaxseed meal, ground
- ¼ cup of fresh rosemary leaves, finely chopped
- 1 teaspoon of salt, to taste

### Step 1 - Preparation

- Combine the almonds with nutritional yeast, flaxseed meal, rosemary, and salt in a food processor then pulse them several times until they become well combined.
- Add in the water gradually while mixing until the mixture becomes thick and smooth.

### Step 2 – Dehydrating the crackers in a dehydrator

- Prepare the dehydrator according to the manufacturer's instructions.
- Spread the crackers mixture on dehydrating trays to make about a ¼-inch thick layer.
- Adjust the temperature to 115F, then dehydrate the crackers for 2 hours.

- Once the time is up, cut the crackers into the shape you desire, then dehydrate them for another 6 to 8 hours until they become crisp and crunchy.

### Step 3 – Storing the crackers

- Allow the crackers to cool down completely, then transfer them to jars or containers.
- Seal the containers tightly to be able to store them for 3 months, and enjoy!

## Toasted Croutons

|**Intro**|: If you have some stale bread sitting around in your kitchen, you can easily benefit from it by turning it into toasted croutons that you can serve as a snack with a dipping sauce, or you can add it to a salad and enjoy.

### Equipment:

Knife

Cutting Board

Dehydrator

Storing Jars

Oven

Baking sheets

**Nutrition Facts** per 1/6 of the recipe

| Calories | 47 kcal |
|----------|---------|
| Carbs | 8.15g |
| Protein | 1.83g |
| Fats | 0.78g |

### Core Ingredients

- Stale bread

### Step 1 - Preparation

- Start by cutting your bread into small bite-size cubes.

### Step 2 – Dehydrating the bread in a dehydrator

- Prepare the dehydrator according to the manufacturer's instructions.
- Place the bread pieces in a single layer on the dehydrating trays.
- Adjust the temperature to 155F, then dehydrate the bread for 5 to 8 hours until they become crunchy and golden.

### Step 3 – Dehydrating the bread in the oven

- Preheat the oven to 375 F.
- Spread the bread pieces evenly on lined-up baking sheets.
- Bake them for 14 to 20 minutes until the bread pieces become crunchy and acquire a nice golden color.

### Step 4 – Storing the croutons

- Allow the croutons to cool down completely, then transfer them to jars or containers.
- Seal the containers tightly to be able to store them for 8 months to 1 year.
- When ready to serve them, toss them with some parmesan cheese, oil, and some herbs of your choice and enjoy!

## Crunchy Flax Seed Crackers

|Intro|: These flax seed crackers make for a delicious sweet snack that has a tasty combination of bananas and dates. They're naturally sweet, so they go amazing with some hot chocolate, coffee, sweet sauce, or whipped cream.

### Equipment:

Knife

Cutting Board

Dehydrator

Storing Jars

Food processor

Bowl

### Nutrition Facts per 1/6 of the recipe

| Calories | 159.17 kcal |
|----------|-------------|
| Carbs    | 21.23g      |
| Protein  | 4.78g       |
| Fats     | 6.97g       |

### Core Ingredients

- 8 cups of water
- 4 cups of whole golden flax seed
- 2 cups of ground flax seed
- 4 ripe bananas, peeled
- 3 cups of Medjool dates, pitted
- 1 teaspoon of sea salt

- ½ teaspoon of cinnamon powder

### Step 1 - Preparation

- Start by combining the whole and ground flax seed in a large bowl, then add to them the water.
- Cover the bowl, and allow them to soak overnight.

### Step 2 – Soaking the dates

- The next day, place the dates in a bowl and cover them with water.
- Allow them to sit for 2 hours until they become soft, then drain them and discard the water.

### Step 3 – Making the crackers mixture

- Add the soaked flaxseed mixture with it's soaking water to a large food processor.
- Add to it the dates with the remaining ingredients, then process until the mixture becomes smooth and thick.

### Step 4 – Dehydrating the crackers in a dehydrator

- Prepare the dehydrator according to the manufacturer's instructions.
- Pour the crackers mixture into the dehydrating trays, and spread it to make a ¼ to ½ inch thick layer.
- Adjust the temperature to 145F, then dehydrate the crackers for 2 hours.
- Cut the crackers into the shape you prefer, then lower the temperature to 105 F.
- Dehydrate the crackers for another 10 to 12 hours until they become completely dry and crispy.

### Step 5 – Storing the crackers

- Allow the crackers to cool down completely, then transfer them to jars or containers.
- Seal the containers tightly to be able to store them for 8 months to 1 year, and enjoy!

## Biscotti

|Intro|: Who doesn't like crispy biscotti to enjoy with hot tea, cocoa, or coffee? In this case, you can turn any type of homemade bread that you like whether it is banana, zucchini, carrot, seed...bread, you can dehydrate it and enjoy it as a nice breakfast or snack!

### Equipment:

Knife

Cutting Board

Dehydrator

Storing Jars

Baking sheets

Oven

**Nutrition Facts** per 2 oz

| Calories | 184.84 kcal |
|----------|-------------|
| Carbs | 30.96g |
| Protein | 2.44g |
| Fats | 5.95g |

## Core Ingredients

- Banana bread (or any other bread of your choice)

## Step 1 - Preparation

- Start by cutting the bread into 1-inch thick sticks.

## Step 2 – Dehydrating the bread in a dehydrator

- Prepare the dehydrator according to the manufacturer's instructions.
- Place the bread sticks in a single layer on the dehydrating trays.
- Adjust the temperature to 150F, then dehydrate them for 4 to 5 hours until they become crisp.

## Step 3 – Dehydrating the bread in the oven

- Preheat the oven to 350 F.
- Spread the bread sticks evenly on lined-up baking sheets.
- Bake them for 14 to 20 minutes until they become crispy.

## Step 4 – Storing the biscotti

- Allow the biscotti sticks to cool down completely, then transfer them to jars or containers.
- Seal the containers tightly to be able to store them for 1 month, and enjoy!

## Crispy Angel Food Cake

|**Intro**|: Yes, you read it right. You can dehydrate cake, and serve it as it is, crunchy and flavorful with some tea, or coffee. Or you can also, ground it, add to some other ingredients and transfer it to cake bites and enjoy!

**Equipment:**

Knife

---

Cutting Board

Dehydrator

Storing Jars

**Nutrition Facts** per 2 oz

| Calories | 146.29 kcal |
|----------|-------------|
| Carbs | 32.77g |
| Protein | 0.35g |
| Fats | 0.45g |

## Core Ingredients

- Angel food cake (homemade or storebought)

## Step 1 - Preparation

- Start by cutting the cake into ½-inch thick slices.

## Step 2 – Dehydrating the cake in a dehydrator

- Prepare the dehydrator according to the manufacturer's instructions.
- Place the cake slices in a single layer on the dehydrating trays.
- Adjust the temperature to 125F, then dehydrate them for 3 to 5 hours until they become crisp and crunchy.

## Step 3 – Storing the angel food cake slices

- Allow the cake slices to cool down completely, then transfer them to jars or containers.
- Seal the containers tightly to be able to store them for 2 months!

## Crispy and Soft Rolls

|**Intro**|: If you love homemade bread, you will love it with this recipe even more. The bread rolls come crispy on the outside, but soft on the inside, and can last you for up to a month.

**Equipment:**

Knife

Cutting Board

Dehydrator

Storing Jars

Food processor

Bowl

**Nutrition Facts** per 1 roll

| Calories | 407 kcal |
|----------|----------|
| Carbs | 52.3g |
| Protein | 9.7g |
| Fats | 18.9g |

## Core Ingredients

- 4 cups of almond flour
- 3 cups of onion, sliced
- 2 cups of psyllium seed husk
- 1 cup of ground flax seed
- 2/3 cup of water
- 1 ¼ teaspoon of fresh lemon juice
- 4 cloves of garlic, peeled and crushed
- 3 teaspoons of salt

## Step 1 - Preparation

- Start by combing the onion with garlic, water, and lemon juice in a food processor then process them, until they become smooth.

## Step 2 – Making the bread

- Mix the almond flour with psyllium seed husk, ground flax seed, and salt in a large bowl.
- Add the onion mixture then mix them well until well combined.
- Cut the dough into 6 pieces, then shape them into small size balls.

## Step 3 – Dehydrating the bread in a dehydrator

- Prepare the dehydrator according to the manufacturer's instructions.
- Place the bread rolls on the dehydrating trays while leaving ample space between them.
- Adjust the temperature to 145F, then dehydrate them for 60 minutes.
- Once the time is up, lower the temperature to 110 F, then dehydrated the bread rolls for 6 to 7 hours until they are done.

## Step 4 – Storing the bread rolls

- Allow the bread rolls to cool down completely, then wrap them tightly with foil, transfer them to a container and store them in the freezer for up to 1 month enjoy!

# Crunchy Potato Chips

|Intro|: Potato chips have become a staple snack in almost homes nowadays, however, it's not a secret how unhealthy it is. This is why this recipe makes for an incredible alternative that you can enjoy for a long time. It's crispy, crunchy, yummy, and healthy.

## Equipment:

- Knife
- Cutting Board
- Dehydrator
- Storing Jars

**Nutrition Facts** per 4.5 oz

| Calories | 77.92 kcal |
|----------|-----------|
| Carbs | 17.71g |
| Protein | 2.08g |
| Fats | 0.09g |

## Core Ingredients

- 2 ¼ pounds of potatoes
- 12 cups of water
- Sea salt

## Step 1 - Preparation

- Start by washing and peeling the potatoes.
- Use a sharp knife or mandoline to slice them into very thin slices.

## Step 2 – Cooking the potatoes

- Combine the water with salt in a large pot, then bring it to a boil.
- Add in the potato slices, then cook them for 5 minutes.
- Once the time is up, drain the potato slices and pat them dry with a towel.

## Step 3 – Dehydrating the potato in a dehydrator

- Prepare the dehydrator according to the manufacturer's instructions.
- Place the potato slices in a single layer on the dehydrating trays.
- Adjust the temperature to 125F, then dehydrate them for 10 to 12 hours until they become crisp and crunchy.

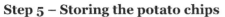

### Step 5 – Storing the potato chips
- Allow the chips to cool down completely, then transfer them to jars or containers.
- Seal the containers tightly to be able to store them for 2 to 3 months, and enjoy!

## Sweet Potato Chips

|Intro|: If you like regular potato chips, then you will love sweet potato chips even more. They are salty but sweet, and crunchy. A perfect sweet and healthy snack to replace your store-bought ones.

### Equipment:
Knife

Cutting Board

Dehydrator

Storing Jars

Bowl

### Nutrition Facts per 1 sweet potato

| Calories | 143 kcal |
|----------|----------|
| Carbs | 26g |
| Protein | 2g |
| Fats | 4g |

### Core Ingredients
- 8 Large sweet potatoes
- 1 tablespoon of avocado oil
- Sea salt (to taste)

### Step 1 - Preparation
- Start by washing and peeling the sweet potatoes.
- Use a sharp knife or mandoline to slice them into very thin slices.

### Step 2 – Seasoning the sweet potatoes
- Place the potato slices in a large bowl, then add the avocado oil, and salt.
- Toss them until well-coated.

### Step 3 – Dehydrating the sweet potatoes in a dehydrator
- Prepare the dehydrator according to the manufacturer's instructions.

- Place the sweet potato slices in a single layer on the dehydrating trays.
- Adjust the temperature to 115F, then dehydrate them for 10 to 16 hours until they become crisp and crunchy.

### Step 5 – Storing the sweet potatoes chips
- Allow the chips to cool down completely, then transfer them to jars or containers.
- Seal the containers tightly to be able to store them for 2 to 3 months, and enjoy!

# Section 4: Dehydrated Side Dishes Recipes

### Veggies Risotto

|Intro|: Risotto is a very delicious dish that can be served as a side or main dish, however, it's even better when you can prepare it before hand, store it for a long time. It's perfect for hiking, traveling, or for you to use on your busy days.

### Equipment:
Knife

Cutting Board

Dehydrator

Bowl

Pot

Storing Jars

### Nutrition Facts per 1 serving (4 servings in total)

| Calories | 604.58 kcal |
|----------|-------------|
| Carbs | 90.04g |
| Protein | 10.64g |
| Fats | 22.04g |

### Core Ingredients
- 5 cups of broth
- 16 mushrooms (of your choice), sliced
- 1 large zucchini, diced
- 1 large white or yellow onion, peeled and diced
- 2 cups of arborio-rice
- ½ cup of green peas, fresh or frozen

- 2 tablespoons of vegetable oil
- Salt and black pepper to taste

## Step 1 - Preparation
- Start by washing the mushrooms, and discarding the stems then slice them.
- Wash the zucchini and dice it.
- Peel the onion, wash it, then dice it or finely chop it.

## Step 2 – Cooking the risotto
- Heat the oil in a large pot then cook in it the onion for 4 to 6 minutes until it becomes translucent.
- Add the rice and cook them for 2 minutes while stirring them the whole time.
- Add 1 cup of broth at a time while stirring the rice until it's absorbed, then continue to add the remaining broth the same way until it's completely absorbed by the rice, and becomes thick and creamy.
- Season the risotto with some salt and pepper to your taste.

## Step 3 – Dehydrating the risotto in a dehydrator
- Prepare the dehydrator according to the manufacturer's instructions.
- Place the veggies in a single layer on the dehydrating trays, then spread the risotto in trays on its own.
- Adjust the temperature to 135F, then dehydrate the veggies and risotto for 5 to 8 hours until they become completely dry.

## Step 4 – Storing the veggies and risotto
- Allow the veggies and risotto to cool down completely, then combine them, and transfer them to jars or containers.
- Seal the containers tightly to be able to store them for 3 months and enjoy!

## Step 5 – Serving the risotto
- When ready to serve your risotto, add to it enough water to cover it, then bring it to a boil.
- Lower the heat and allow the risotto to cook until the rice and veggies become tender.
- Stir in the cheese of your choice until it melts then serve it and enjoy!

## Colorful Primavera

|Intro|: Whether you are hiking, camping, or simply staying at home, this colorful primavera dish will relive you of the stress of making a whole meal. It's perfect for all seasons and takes little to no work to prepare. You can preserve it for up to 4 months.

**Equipment:**

Knife

Cutting Board

Dehydrator

Storing Jars

Pot

**Nutrition Facts** per 1/5 serving

| Calories | 330 kcal |
|----------|----------|
| Carbs | 33g |
| Protein | 9g |
| Fats | 19g |

## Core Ingredients
- 2 pounds of cherry tomatoes
- 2 large zucchinis
- 2 large summer squash
- ¼ cup of parsley leaves, finely chopped
- ¼ cup of capers, drained

## Cooking Ingredients
- 2 ½ cup of pasta shells
- ¼ cup of vegetable oil
- Water

## Seasoning
- ½ tablespoon of ground dry basil
- 1 teaspoon of garlic powder
- 1 teaspoon of dry oregano
- 1 ¼ teaspoon of salt, to taste

## Step 1 - Preparation
- Start by cutting the zucchinis into 4 pieces lengthwise, then slice them into ¼-inch thick pieces.
- Repeat the same process for the summer squash.
- Slice the cherry tomatoes in half.
- Drain the capers and discard their liquid.

### Step 2 – Dehydrating the veggies in a dehydrator

- Prepare the dehydrator according to the manufacturer's instructions.
- Place the zucchini, and summer squash, along with capers, parsley, and tomatoes in a single layer on the dehydrating trays.
- Adjust the temperature to 135F, then dehydrate the apples for 8 to 14 hours until they become completely dry.

### Step 3 – Making the seasoning combo

- Mix the dry basil, with oregano, garlic powder, salt, and a pinch of black pepper into a small bowl.
- Transfer them to a small jar or pack, then seal until ready to use. You can store them for up 3 months as well.

### Step 4 – Storing the primavera veggies

- Allow the veggies to cool down completely, then transfer them to jars or containers. You can store each vegetable on its own, or you can mix them, and store each serving on its one. This way, you can grab one jar whenever you wish to make it.
- Seal the containers tightly to be able to store them for 4 months.

### Step 5 – Assembling the primavera pasta

- When ready to serve your pasta, start by placing it in a large pot with the seasoning mix, oil or butter, and the dehydrated veggies.
- Cover them with water then put on half the lid and let them simmer over low heat until the veggies and pasta become soft, and the water evaporates.
- Stir in the cheese of your choice until it melts then serve it and enjoy!

## Chocolate and Quinoa Chili

|Intro|: This chili is yet another amazing recipe to prepare beforehand, and store for up to 3 months. It's perfect for the winter to warm up your bones, and it's also a very easy dish to throw around for yourself or your family.

### Equipment:

Knife

Cutting Board

Dehydrator

Storing Jars

Large pot

### Nutrition Facts per 1/6 serving

| Calories | 525 kcal |
|----------|----------|
| Carbs | 82g |
| Protein | 22g |
| Fats | 9g |

### Core Ingredients

- 28 ounces of diced tomato, homemade canned or storebought
- 19 ounces of kidney beans, homemade canned or storebought
- 19 ounces of black beans, homemade canned or storebought
- 12 ounces of corn kernels, homemade canned or storebought
- 14 ounces of tomato sauce
- 1 large white or yellow onion
- 2 cups of quinoa, cooked
- 2 tablespoons of olive oil
- 2 ½ tablespoons of chili powder
- 4 cloves of garlic, peeled and finely chopped
- ½ tablespoon of cumin
- ½ tablespoon of cocoa powder
- 1 ½ teaspoon of paprika
- 1 teaspoon of granulated sugar
- ½ teaspoon of ground dry coriander
- Salt and pepper, to taste

### Step 1 - Preparation

- Start by draining the beans.
- Peel the garlic, and finely chop it.

### Step 2 – Cooking the chili

- Place a large pot over hight heat, and heat in it the olive oil.
- Sautee in it the onion for 3 to 5 minutes until it becomes soft.
- Stir in the remaining ingredients except for the corn and beans, them let them cook over low heat with the lid on for 35 minutes.
- Once the time is up, add the corn and beans and stir them well, then let them cook for another 10 minutes until the chili is thoroughly heated.
- Turn off the heat, and allow the chili to cool down completely.

### Step 3 – Dehydrating the chili in a dehydrator

- Prepare the dehydrator according to the manufacturer's instructions.
- Place spread the chili in a single layer on the dehydrating trays.
- Adjust the temperature to 145F, then dehydrate the apples for 8 to 14 hours until it's completely dry.

### Step 4 – Storing the chili

- Allow the dry chili to cool down completely, then scrap it and transfer it to jars or sealable bags.
- Seal the containers or bags tightly to be able to store them for up to 2 months.

### Step 5 – Serving the chocolate chili

- When ready to serve your chili, add it to a saucepan or pot depending on much are you using, then add 1 cup of water per serving to it. For this recipe, you will need 6 cups of water.
- Lower the heat, and bring it to a boil, then put on the lid, and let it cook for 15 to 20 minutes.
- Serve it hot, and enjoy!

## Festive Apple Porridge

|Intro|: This apple porridge preserves nicely, and makes for a great breakfast, or dinner treat. Its ingredients are very simple, and it easily is put together and dehydrated so you can preserve it, and enjoy it for up to 3 months.

### Equipment:

Knife

Cutting Board

Dehydrator

Storing Jars

Pot

### Nutrition Facts per ¼ serving

| Calories | 750 kcal |
|----------|----------|
| Carbs | 114g |
| Protein | 15g |
| Fats | 29g |

### Core Ingredients

- 4 medium apples of your choice, peeled and diced

- 4 cups of water
- 2 cups of quinoa
- ½ cup of maple syrup
- ½ tablespoon of vanilla extract
- ½ tablespoon of cinnamon powder
- Salt, to taste

### Step 1 - Preparation

- Start by peeling the potatoes, then cut them into small cubes.
- Roughly chop the pecans.

### Step 2 – Cooking the porridge

- Stir the water with quinoa, apples, cinnamon, and a pinch of salt in a large pot.
- Bring them to a boil, then put on the lid, and let them cook for 16 to 20 minutes until the quinoa and apples are cooked.
- Once the time is up, turn off them heat, then add the maple syrup with vanilla extract.
- Stir them until well combined, then turn off the heat and allow it to cool down completely.

### Step 3 – Dehydrating the porridge in a dehydrator

- Prepare the dehydrator according to the manufacturer's instructions.
- Spread the porridge on a single layer on the dehydrating trays.
- Adjust the temperature to 135F, then dehydrate the apples for 8 to 14 hours until it becomes completely dry.

### Step 4 – Storing the porridge

- Allow the porridge to cool down completely, then scrap it and transfer it to jars or sealable bags.
- Seal the containers or bags tightly to be able to store them for up to 2 months.

### Step 5 – Serving the porridge

- When ready to serve your porridge, add it to a pot, then add to it 1 cup of water per serving. This recipe is for 4 servings, so it requires 4 cups of water.
- Bring it to a boil, then lower the heat, put on the lid, and let it cook for 10 to 15 minutes until the quinoa and apples become soft.
- You can stir in some milk and chopped nuts, then serve it hot and enjoy!

## Instant Mashed Potato

**|Intro|:** Mashed potato is the ideal side dish to accompany any meal. Dehydrated mashed potato is super easy to prepare, is hassle-free, and will save you a lot of time and money. You can store it and enjoy it for up to 12 months!

## Equipment:

Knife

Cutting Board

Dehydrator

Storing Jars

Pot

### Nutrition Facts per 1 pound

| Calories | 282.76 kcal |
|----------|-------------|
| Carbs | 64.26g |
| Protein | 7.53g |
| Fats | 0.33g |

## Core Ingredients

- Potatoes, of your choice

## Step 1 - Preparation

- Start by washing, and peeling the potatoes, then cut them into large chunks.

## Step 2 – Cooking the potatoes

- Bring a large pot of water to a boil.
- Add to it the potatoes with a pinch of salt, then cook them over low heat for 15 to 20 minutes until they become soft, but still hold their shape.
- Drain the potatoes and mash them while adding to them some of the cooking liquid to make them runny but no to liquid.

## Step 3 – Dehydrating the mashed potatoes in a dehydrator

- Prepare the dehydrator according to the manufacturer's instructions.
- Spread the mashed potato in a single layer on the dehydrating trays.
- Adjust the temperature to 135F, then dehydrate it for 8 to 14 hours until it becomes completely dry and crispy.

## Step 4 – Storing the mashed potato

- Allow the mashed potato to cool down completely, then transfer into jars or containers.
- Seal the containers tightly to be able to store them for 1 year, and enjoy!

## Italian Minestrone Soup

**|Intro|:** This Italian-inspired minestrone is perfect for all seasons, and makes for a great side dish, or a meal. You can prepare it beforehand, and store it for up to 6 months. Assembling it takes 5 minutes, but the outcome is a very delicious and hearty soup.

## Equipment:

Knife

Cutting Board

Dehydrator

Storing Jars

Pot

### Nutrition Facts per 1/4 serving

| Calories | 483 kcal |
|----------|----------|
| Carbs | 69g |
| Protein | 20g |
| Fats | 14g |

## Core Ingredients

- 15 ounces of cannellini beans, homemade or storebought
- 15 ounces of diced tomatoes, homemade canned, or storebought
- 2 stalks of celery, diced
- 1 large zucchini, diced
- 1 large yellow or white onion, peeled and diced
- 1 large carrot, diced

## Cooking Ingredients

- 1 cup of pasta shells
- ¼ cup of olive oil
- Water

## Seasoning

- 4 vegetable bouillon cubes, crushed
- 1 teaspoon of dry ground thyme
- 1 teaspoon of dry oregano

- 1 teaspoon of garlic powder
- ½ teaspoon of red pepper flakes

## Step 1 - Preparation

- Start by washing, and cutting your vegetables, then drain the cannellini beans.

## Step 2 – Dehydrating the vegetables in a dehydrator

- Prepare the dehydrator according to the manufacturer's instructions.
- Place the beans, tomato, celery, zucchini, carrot, and onion in a single layer on the dehydrating trays separately.
- Adjust the temperature to 135F, then dehydrate for 8 to 12 hours until they become completely dry.

## Step 3 – Making the seasoning combo

- Mix the seasoning ingredients in a small bowl.
- Transfer them to a small jar or pack, then seal until ready to use. You can store them for up 3 months as well.

## Step 4 – Storing the minestrone veggies

- Allow the veggies to cool down completely, then transfer them to jars or containers. You can store each vegetable on its own, or you can mix them, and store each serving on its one. This way, you can grab one jar whenever you wish to make it.
- Seal the containers tightly to be able to store them for 6 months.

## Step 5 – Assembling the minestrone soup

- When ready to serve your soup, start by placing the pasta in a large pot with the seasoning mix, oil, and dehydrated veggies.
- Cover them with water about 8 to 9 cups then put on half the lid and let them simmer over low heat until the veggies and pasta and veggies become soft for about 8 to 10 minutes.
- Adjust the seasoning of your soup then serve it hot and enjoy!

## Chili beans and lentils Stew

|Intro|: If you love stew, then this recipe will be a great addition to your chili recipes, and will quickly become a favorite. You can prepare several batches and freeze them, then simply take a minute to prepare and serve it hot like you just made it.

**Equipment:**

Knife

Cutting Board

Dehydrator

Storing Jars

Pot

**Nutrition Facts** per 1/4 serving

| Calories | 520 kcal |
|----------|----------|
| Carbs | 66g |
| Protein | 22g |
| Fats | 19g |

## Core Ingredients

- 14 ounces of diced or roasted tomatoes, homemade canned or storebought
- 14 ounces of kidney beans, homemade canned or storebought
- 3 cups of broth
- 2 cups of zucchini, diced
- 1 cup of red lentils
- 1 cup of white or yellow onion, peeled and diced
- 1 cup of green bell pepper, diced
- 6 cloves of garlic, peeled and finely chopped
- 2 tablespoons of tomato paste
- 3 tablespoons of chili powder
- 1 tablespoon of cumin
- 1 tablespoon of olive oil
- Salt and pepper, to taste

## Cooking Ingredients

- ¼ cup of olive oil
- Water

## Step 1 - Preparation

- Start by washing, and cutting your vegetables, then drain the kidney beans.

## Step 2 – Cooking the stew

- Place a large pot over medium-high heat, and heat in it the oil.
- Sautee in it the onion for 3 to 5 minutes until it becomes soft. Add the pepper and cook them for another 3 minutes.

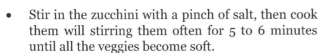

- Stir in the zucchini with a pinch of salt, then cook them will stirring them often for 5 to 6 minutes until all the veggies become soft.
- Add the remaining ingredients and stir them until well combined, then bring them to a boil.
- Lowe the heat, and put on the lid, then cook the stew for 20 to 25 minutes until the chili becomes thick, and the veggies are tender.

### Step 3 – Dehydrating the lentils stew in a dehydrator

- Prepare the dehydrator according to the manufacturer's instructions.
- Spread the chili in a single layer on the dehydrating trays separately.
- Adjust the temperature to 135F, then dehydrate it for 8 to 14 hours until it becomes completely dry

### Step 4 – Storing the lentils stew

- Allow the stew to cool down completely, then scrap it off and transfer it to jars or containers.
- Seal the containers tightly to be able to store them for 4 weeks in a dark place, or up to 3 months in the freezer.

### Step 5 – Assembling the stew

- When ready to serve your stew, heat the oil in a large pot or saucepan.
- Add to it the dry stew and cover it with water, around 4 cups. Bring it to a boil, then put on the lid and let it cook over low heat for 8 to 10 minutes.
- Once the stew becomes thick, and all the veggies soften, serve it hot, and enjoy!

## Roasted Tortilla Soup

|Intro|: This soup turns out very hearty and light, it also makes for a very delicious side dish or dinner for all seasons. It also can be stored for up to 6 months, so it's very handy to have it on hand whenever you don't feel like doing much work in the kitchen.

### Equipment:

Knife

Cutting Board

Dehydrator

Storing Jars

Pot

**Nutrition Facts** per 1/4 serving

| Calories | 545 kcal |
|----------|----------|
| Carbs | 76g |
| Protein | 17g |
| Fats | 18g |

### Core Ingredients

- 30 ounces of black beans, homemade or storebought
- 30 ounces of fire-roasted tomatoes
- 2 cups of roasted corn kernels
- 1 large yellow onion, peeled and diced
- 2 jalapeno pepper, seeded and diced
- ½ cup of fresh cilantro leaves, roughly chopped

### Cooking Ingredients

- ¼ cup of olive oil
- Water

### Seasoning

- 4 vegetable bouillon cubes, crushed
- 1 teaspoon of chili powder
- 1 teaspoon of garlic powder
- 1 teaspoon of cumin
- Salt and black pepper, to taste

### Step 1 - Preparation

- Start by washing and peeling the onion and jalapeno, then dice them.
- Drain the beans.

### Step 2 – Dehydrating the vegetables in a dehydrator

- Prepare the dehydrator according to the manufacturer's instructions.
- Place the beans, tomato, onion, cilantro, and corn in a single layer on the dehydrating trays separately.
- Adjust the temperature to 135F, then dehydrate them for 8 to 14 hours until they become completely dry.

### Step 3 – Making the seasoning combo

- Mix the seasoning ingredients in a small bowl.
- Transfer them to a small jar or pack, then seal until ready to use. You can store them for up 3 months as well.

### Step 4 – Storing the tortilla soup

- Allow the veggies to cool down completely, then transfer them to jars or containers. You can store each vegetable on its own, or you can mix them, and store each serving on its one. This way, you can grab one jar whenever you wish to make it.
- Seal the containers tightly to be able to store them for 6 months.

### Step 5 – Assembling the tortilla soup

- When ready to serve your soup, start by placing the dry veggies in a large pot with the seasoning mix, and oil then bring them to a boil
- Cover them with water about 4 to 5 cups for this 4-serving recipe then put on half the lid and let them simmer over low heat until the veggies become soft for about 8 to 10 minutes.
- Adjust the seasoning of your soup then serve it hot with some tortilla chips and enjoy!

## Potato Stir Fry

|Intro|: This stir fry/warm salad is very simple, yet very scrumptious. The combination of bell pepper with potatoes, and onion is fantastic, for they taste amazing together with simple seasoning.

### Equipment:

Knife

Cutting Board

Dehydrator

Storing Jars

Pan

**Nutrition Facts** per 1/3 serving

| Calories | 201.74 kcal |
|----------|-------------|
| Carbs | 27.08g |
| Protein | 3.22g |
| Fats | 9.48g |

### Core Ingredients

- 3 cups of potatoes, peeled and diced
- 2 tablespoons of green onions, diced
- 2 tablespoons of white or yellow onion, peeled and diced
- 2 tablespoons of red or green bell pepper, diced

### Cooking Ingredients

- 2 tablespoons of olive oil
- Salt and black pepper to taste

### Step 1 - Preparation

- Start by washing, and cutting your vegetables.

### Step 2 – Dehydrating the vegetables in a dehydrator

- Prepare the dehydrator according to the manufacturer's instructions.
- Place the potato, green onions, yellow onion, and bell pepper in a single layer on the dehydrating trays separately.
- Adjust the temperature to 125F, then dehydrate them for 8 to 12 hours until they become completely dry.

### Step 3 – Storing the potato stir fry

- Allow the veggies to cool down completely, then transfer them to jars or containers. You can store each vegetable on its own, or you can mix them, and store each serving on its one. This way, you can grab one jar whenever you wish to make it.
- Seal the containers tightly to be able to store them for 8 months.

### Step 4 – Assembling the potato stir fry

- When ready to serve your stir fry, bring a large pot of water with a pinch of salt to a boil.
- Add to it the potato and bring it to a boil, then lower the heat and cook it for 15 to 20 minutes until it becomes soft.
- In the meantime, combine the green onion, yellow onion, and bell pepper in a medium bowl then cover them with boiling water.
- Allow them to sit for 15 to 20 minutes while preparing the potatoes until they become soft.
- Once the time is up, heat the oil in a large pan, and add the drained potato along with the onion and pepper mixture. Cook them for 6 to 10 minutes while stirring until the potatoes become golden.
- Season them with some salt and pepper then serve it hot and enjoy!

## Spicy Cauliflower Popcorn

|Intro|: Cauliflower is a very underrated veggie that often lies unused in the fridge because not everyone likes it, so this recipe is perfect for it because it will make everyone fall in love with it. It comes out very crunchy

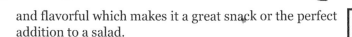

and flavorful which makes it a great snack or the perfect addition to a salad.

## Equipment:

Knife

Cutting Board

Dehydrator

Storing Jars

**Nutrition Facts** per ½ head of cauliflower

| Calories | 264 kcal |
|----------|----------|
| Carbs | 15g |
| Protein | 6g |
| Fats | 22g |

## Core Ingredients

- 2 large heads of cauliflower
- ½ cup of hot sauce
- ¼ cup of coconut oil
- 2 tablespoons of paprika
- ½ tablespoon of cayenne pepper
- 1 teaspoon of cumin
- ½ teaspoon of red pepper flakes

## Step 1 - Preparation

- Start by washing the cauliflower then cut it into bite-size florets.
- Mix the remaining ingredients in a large bowl, then add the cauliflower florets and toss them until they are well coated.

## Step 2 – Dehydrating the cauliflower in a dehydrator

- Prepare the dehydrator according to the manufacturer's instructions.
- Place the cauliflower florets in a single layer on the dehydrating trays separately.
- Adjust the temperature to 130F, then dehydrate them for 8 to 14 hours until they become completely dry and crunchy.

## Step 3 – Storing the cauliflower popcorn

- Allow the cauliflower popcorn to cool down completely, then transfer it to jars or containers.
- Seal the containers tightly to be able to store them for up to 3 months and enjoy.

# Section 5: Dehydrated Grains, nuts, and Seeds Recipes

## Crunchy Almonds

|**Intro**|: There is nothing like dehydrated salted almonds for a healthy snack that will leave you craving more. It's very easy to make and can last you for up to 12 months

## Equipment:

Knife

Dehydrator

Bowl

Storing Jars

**Nutrition Facts** per 1 cup

| Calories | 972.72 kcal |
|----------|-------------|
| Carbs | 36.2g |
| Protein | 35.53g |
| Fats | 83.88g |

## Core Ingredients

- Raw almonds
- Sea salt

## Step 1 - Preparation

- Start by combining the almonds with salt in a large bowl, and cover them with cold water. The ratio of salt is ½ tablespoon per cup.
- Allow them to soak for 8 to 12 hours. This will help the almonds turn out crunchy.
- If you like your almonds slightly salted, keep them as they are, if not, you can rinse them.

## Step 2 – Dehydrating the almonds in a dehydrator

- Prepare the dehydrator according to the manufacturer's instructions.
- Spread the almonds in single layers on the dehydrating trays.
- Adjust the temperature to 150F, then dehydrate them for 14 to 20 hours until they become completely dry and crunchy.

### Step 3 – Storing the almonds

- Allow the almonds to cool down completely, then transfer them to jars or containers.
- Seal the containers tightly to be able to store them for 12 months in the fridge, and enjoy!

## Instant Rice

|Intro|: If you are like me, you love rice a lot, but you think that cooking it can sometimes be an inconvenience because you have to time it, and stay next to it to make sure it's cooked perfectly and doesn't stick or burn, this recipe will absolve you of that. You can dehydrate a big batch, and every time you want to use it, just let it soak in hot water while going about your chores. The end result is fluffy and perfectly cooked rice.

### Equipment:

Knife

Cutting Board

Dehydrator

Storing Jars

Bowl/Saucepan

Pot

### Nutrition Facts per 1 cup of white rice

| Calories | 167.04 kcal |
|----------|-------------|
| Carbs | 36.49g |
| Protein | 3.5g |
| Fats | 0.33g |

### Core Ingredients

- Rice (of your choice)
- Water
- Salt

### Step 1 - Preparation

- Depending on the rice you are using, start by cooking according to the directions on the packages, and season it with a pinch of salt.

### Step 2 – Dehydrating the rice in a dehydrator

- Prepare the dehydrator according to the manufacturer's instructions.
- Spread the cooked rice evenly in a single layer on the dehydrating trays.

- Adjust the temperature to 125F, then dehydrate it for 6 to 10 hours until it becomes completely dry.

### Step 3 – Storing the rice

- Allow the rice to cool down completely, then transfer them to jars or containers.
- Seal the containers tightly to be able to store them for 6 months.

### Step 4 – Serving the rice

- When ready to use your rice, place it in a saucepan or bowl, then add to it boiling water with a ration of 1 cup of boiling water for each 2/3 cup of dry rice.
- Cover it, and let it sit for 10 to 15 minutes until it absorbs the water completely.
- Adjust the seasoning of your rice, heat it through, then serve it and enjoy!

## Spicy Sunflower Seeds

|Intro|: These spicy sunflower seeds make for a very delicious and healthy snack that you can share with your family and friends. It also makes for a nice crunchy addition to salads and adds a lovely flavor.

### Equipment:

Knife

Cutting Board

Dehydrator

Storing Jars

Bowl

### Nutrition Facts per ½ cup

| Calories | 469.38 kcal |
|----------|-------------|
| Carbs | 17.27g |
| Protein | 15.52g |
| Fats | 41.42g |

### Core Ingredients

- 6 cups of sunflower seeds, shelled
- Water

### Marinade Ingredients

- ¼ cup of olive oil
- 1/3 cup of chili powder

- 2 tablespoons of apple cider vinegar
- 2 tablespoons of tamari sauce
- ½ tablespoon of brown sugar
- ½ tablespoon of cumin
- 1 teaspoon of onion powder
- 1 teaspoon of salt
- 1 teaspoon of garlic powder

## Step 1 - Preparation

- Place the sunflower seeds in a large bowl, and cover them with cold water.
- Allow them to soak for 6 hours to overnight, then drain them and discard the soaking liquid. This step is essential because it will make the seeds crunchy when dehydrated.
- The next day, drain and seeds and pat them dry or allow them to dry under the sun.

## Step 2 – Marinating the sunflower seeds

- Combine all the marinade ingredients in the bowl and mix them well until well combined.
- Add the sunflower seeds and toss them until well combined.

## Step 3 – Dehydrating the sunflower seeds in a dehydrator

- Prepare the dehydrator according to the manufacturer's instructions.
- Spread the sunflower seeds in an even layer in a single layer on the dehydrating trays.
- Adjust the temperature to 115F, then dehydrate them for 7 to 10 hours until they become completely dry and crunchy.

## Step 4 – Dehydrating the sunflower seeds in the oven

- Preheat the oven to 115 F.
- Spread the seeds evenly on lined-up baking sheets.
- Bake them for 1 to 2 hours while stirring them every 20 minutes until they become crunchy.

## Step 5 – Storing the sunflower seeds

- Allow the sunflower seeds to cool down completely, then transfer them to jars or containers.
- Seal the containers tightly to be able to store them for 12 months.

## Crunchy Pumpkin seeds

|Intro|: These dehydrated pumpkin seeds make for really yummy snacks that grown-ups and kids can enjoy, and also a nice crunch and flavor to your bread or salad. They are also super cheap because you can save them from your pumpkins when you can them.

## Equipment:

Knife

Cutting Board

Dehydrator

Storing Jars

Bowl

## Nutrition Facts per ½ cup

| Calories | 178.43 kcal |
|----------|-------------|
| Carbs    | 3.42g       |
| Protein  | 9.65g       |
| Fats     | 15.66g      |

## Core Ingredients

- Pumpkin seeds in shells
- Water
- Salt, to taste

## Step 1 - Preparation

- Place the pumpkin seeds in a large bowl, and cover them with cold water with a pinch of salt
- Allow them to soak overnight, then drain them and discard the soaking liquid. This step is essential because it will make the seeds crunchy when dehydrated.
- The next day, drain and seeds and pat them dry or allow them to dry under the sun.

## Step 2 – Dehydrating the pumpkin seeds in a dehydrator

- Prepare the dehydrator according to the manufacturer's instructions.
- Spread the pumpkin seeds as evenly as much as you can in a single layer on the dehydrating trays.
- Adjust the temperature to 150F, then dehydrate them for 16 to 24 hours until they become completely dry and crunchy.

### Step 3 – Storing the pumpkin seeds

- Allow the pumpkin seeds to cool down completely, then transfer them to jars or containers.
- Seal the containers tightly to be able to store them for up to 3 months and enjoy!

## Crunchy Neon Pistachios

|Intro|: If you have a pistachio tree, or found a got a good deal for it, you have to try this recipe. They turn out super crunch with a hint of delicious sweetness and saltiness. You can serve it as a snack, add it to homemade bread dough, salad…

### Equipment:

Knife

Cutting Board

Dehydrator

Storing Jars

Bowl

### Nutrition Facts per ¼ cup

| Calories | 201.39 kcal |
|----------|-------------|
| Carbs | 15.6g |
| Protein | 6.34g |
| Fats | 14.12g |

### Core Ingredients

- 2 cups of pistachios
- Water

### Marinade Ingredients

- ¼ cup of maple syrup
- ½ tablespoon of dry ground coriander
- 1 teaspoon of cumin
- ½ teaspoon of cinnamon powder
- ½ teaspoon of cayenne pepper
- ½ teaspoon of ground ginger
- ½ teaspoon of sea salt

### Step 1 - Preparation

- Place the pistachios in a large bowl, and cover them with cold water.
- Allow them to soak overnight, then drain them and discard the soaking liquid. This step is essential because it will make the seeds crunchy when dehydrated.
- The next day, drain them and pat them dry or allow them to dry under the sun.

### Step 2 – Marinating the pistachios

- Combine all the marinade ingredients in the bowl and mix them well until well combined.
- Add the pistachios and toss them until well combined.

### Step 3 – Dehydrating the pistachios in a dehydrator

- Prepare the dehydrator according to the manufacturer's instructions.
- Spread the pistachios evenly as much as possible on the dehydrating trays.
- Adjust the temperature to 115F, then dehydrate them for 7 to 10 hours until they become completely dry and crunchy.

### Step 4 – Storing the pistachios

- Allow the pistachios to cool down completely, then transfer them to jars or containers.
- Seal the containers tightly to be able to store them for 12 months.

## Cinnamon Pecans

|Intro|: These crunch pecans will put you in the holiday mood from the first taste. They're perfectly sweet, crunchy, and a delicious snack. They are very versatile so you can use them in porridge, with baked goods, cheesecake, cakes, pies…

### Equipment:

Knife

Cutting Board

Dehydrator

Storing Jars

Bowl

### Nutrition Facts per ½ cup

| Calories | 430.86 kcal |
|----------|-------------|
| Carbs | 28.88g |
| Protein | 4.83g |
| Fats | 37.45g |

### Core Ingredients

- 6 cups of pecan halves
- Water

### Marinade Ingredients

- 1 cup of maple syrup
- 1 ½ tablespoon of cinnamon powder
- ¼ teaspoon of nutmeg powder
- Pinch of salt

### Step 1 - Preparation

- Place the pecans in a large bowl, and cover them with cold water.
- Allow them to soak overnight, then drain them and discard the soaking liquid. This step is essential because it will make the seeds crunchy when dehydrated.
- The next day, drain them and pat them dry or allow them to dry under the sun.

### Step 2 – Marinating the pecans

- Combine all the marinade ingredients in the bowl and mix them well until well combined.
- Add the pecan halves and toss them until well combined.

### Step 3 – Dehydrating the pecans in a dehydrator

- Prepare the dehydrator according to the manufacturer's instructions.
- Spread the pecan halves evenly as much as possible on the dehydrating trays.
- Adjust the temperature to 105F, then dehydrate them for 10 to 14 hours until they become completely dry and crunchy.

### Step 4 – Storing the pecans

- Allow the pecans to cool down completely, then transfer them to jars or containers.
- Seal the containers tightly to be able to store them for 3 months.

## Crunchy Hazelnuts

|Intro|: These crunchy hazel nuts turn out fantastic! If harvest them or got a good deal on a big amount, the perfect way to preserve them is by dehydrating them. They come so crunchy and delicious, that you can add them to your homemade spreads, baked goods, and salads, or serve them as a healthy snack.

### Equipment:

Knife

Cutting Board

Dehydrator

Storing Jars

Bowl

### Nutrition Facts per 1/4 cup

| Calories | 211.01 kcal |
|----------|-------------|
| Carbs | 5.61g |
| Protein | 5.02g |
| Fats | 20.41g |

### Core Ingredients

- Raw Hazelnuts
- Salt (optional)
- Water

### Step 1 - Preparation

- Start by combining the hazelnuts with a big pinch of salt in a large bowl, and cover them with cold water. If you don't want them to be salted, you can omit the salt
- Allow them to soak for 8 to 12 hours. This will help the hazelnuts turn dry nicely and become crunchy.

### Step 2 – Dehydrating the hazelnuts in a dehydrator

- Prepare the dehydrator according to the manufacturer's instructions.
- Spread the hazelnuts evenly in a single layer on the dehydrating trays.
- Adjust the temperature to 105F, then dehydrate them for 16 to 24 hours until they become completely dry and crunchy.

### Step 3 – Storing the hazelnuts

- Allow the hazelnuts to cool down completely, then transfer them to jars or containers.
- Seal the containers tightly to be able to store them for 12 months in the fridge, and enjoy!

## Instant beans

|Intro|: Beans are known to take a long time to prepare, for you have to soak them and then cook them

until soft. Dehydrating them is the best way to preserve them for up to 12 months while reducing their prep time to 2 minutes and their cooking time to 0.

## Equipment:
Knife

Cutting Board

Dehydrator

Storing Jars

Bowl

**Nutrition Facts** per ¼ cup

| Calories | 165.32 kcal |
|----------|-------------|
| Carbs | 30.23g |
| Protein | 10.47g |
| Fats | 0.69g |

## Core Ingredients
- Homemade or store-bought back beans (or any other beans)

## Step 1 - Preparation
- Start by draining your beans and discard their liquid whether they are soaked or canned.

## Step 2 – Dehydrating the beans in a dehydrator
- Prepare the dehydrator according to the manufacturer's instructions.
- Spread the black beans in a single layer on the dehydrating trays.
- Adjust the temperature to 125F, then dehydrate for 8 to 12 hours until they become completely dry and crunchy.

## Step 3 – Storing the beans
- Allow the beans to cool down completely, then transfer them to jars or sealable bags.
- Seal the bags tightly to be able to store them for 12 months.

## Step 4 – Serving the beans
- When ready to serve use your black beans, place them in a large bowl, and cover them with water.
- Allow the beans to sit for 12 to 16 minutes until they soften.

- Drain them, then add and use them however you wish, and enjoy!

## Instant Chickpeas
|**Intro**|: Just like all beans, chickpeas also require planning and preparation beforehand to be able to use them. They make a great starchy and delicious addition to soups, stews, and salad. Instead of having to prep them for a whole day, you just have to actually soak them for 15 minutes only, then use them and enjoy!

## Equipment:
Knife

Cutting Board

Dehydrator

Storing Jars

Bowl

**Nutrition Facts** per 1/4 cup

| Calories | 188.92 kcal |
|----------|-------------|
| Carbs | 31.46g |
| Protein | 10.23g |
| Fats | 3.02g |

## Core Ingredients
- Chickpeas, homemade or canned

## Step 1 - Preparation
- Start by draining the chickpeas from the liquid whether they are soaked or canned.

## Step 2 – Dehydrating the chickpeas in a dehydrator
- Prepare the dehydrator according to the manufacturer's instructions.
- Spread the chickpeas evenly in a single layer on the dehydrating trays.
- Adjust the temperature to 125F, then dehydrate the apples for 6 to 12 hours until they become completely dry and crunchy.

## Step 3 – Storing the chickpeas
- Allow the chickpeas to cool down completely, then transfer them to jars or sealable bags.
- Seal the bags tightly to be able to store them for 12 months.

### Step 4 – Serving the chickpeas

- When ready to serve use your chickpeas, place them in a large bowl, and cover them with water.
- Allow the chickpeas to sit for 14 to 16 minutes until they soften.
- Drain them, then add and use them however you wish, and enjoy!

## Raw Cashews

|Intro|: Cashews have been getting more and more popular for their amazing taste and their versatility which makes them great to use for vegan sauces and cheeses. They taste so good, so it only makes sense to preserve them at home so you can have them on hand, ready to use whenever you need them.

### Equipment:

Knife

Cutting Board

Dehydrator

Storing Jars

Bowl

### Nutrition Facts per 1/4 serving

| Calories | 196.65 kcal |
|----------|-------------|
| Carbs    | 11.2g       |
| Protein  | 5.25g       |
| Fats     | 15.88g      |

### Core Ingredients

- Raw Cashews
- Water
- Himalayan salt

### Step 1 - Preparation

- Start by placing the cashews with salt and water in a large bowl then cover them with cheesecloth. The ratio for 1 cup of cashews is 2 cups of water and 1 teaspoon of salt.
- Allow them to soak for 3 to 4 hours. This will help the cashews turn out crunchy.
- Once the time is up, drain the cashews, wash them with fresh water, then drain them again and pat them dry or allow them to dry in the sun.

### Step 2 – Dehydrating the cashews in a dehydrator

- Prepare the dehydrator according to the manufacturer's instructions.
- Spread the cashews evenly on a single layer on the dehydrating trays.
- Adjust the temperature to 115F, then dehydrate them for 10 to 16 hours until they become completely dry and crunchy.

### Step 3 – Storing the cashews

- Allow the cashews to cool down completely, then transfer them to ziplock bags. Seal the bags tightly to be able to store them for 3 months in the fridge or 1 year in the freezer, and enjoy!

## Section 6: Dehydrated Herbs and Powders Recipes

### Homemade Chili Powder

|Intro|: Chili powder is a stable seasoning that's impossible not to find in every house. Even if you don't like spicy food, you're bound to still have it because some recipes just don't work without it. However, there is nothing like homemade chili powder, it's cheap, tasty, and will last you for up to 3 years.

### Equipment:

Knife

Dehydrator

Food processor

Storing Jars

Gloves

### Nutrition Facts per ½ pound

| Calories | 74.39 kcal |
|----------|------------|
| Carbs    | 17.59g     |
| Protein  | 3.72g      |
| Fats     | 0.37g      |

### Core Ingredients

- Fresh Chili peppers

### Step 1 - Preparation

- Start by washing the chili peppers, then pat them dry.
- Cut the peppers in half lengthwise, then discard the stems and seeds.
- You can leave the pepper halves as they are, or dice them to speed up the process.

### Step 2 – Dehydrating the chili peppers in a dehydrator

- Prepare the dehydrator according to the manufacturer's instructions.
- Spread chili pepper pieces on a single layer on the dehydrating trays.
- Adjust the temperature to 125F, then dehydrate them for 5 to 8 hours until they become completely dry and crispy.

### Step 3 – Turning the chili pepper into powder

- Allow the chili pepper pieces to cool down completely, then transfer them to a food processor.
- Process them several times until they turn into powder.

### Step 4 – Storing chili powder

- Transfer the chili powder into jars and seal them to be able to store them for up to 3 years, and enjoy!

## Homemade Turmeric Powder

|Intro|: Turmeric is a very special seasoning that adds so much flavor and beautiful color to all dishes, and the freshest it is, the better. Dehydrated turmeric preserves it, as it comes out cheaper, and tastier.

### Equipment:

Knife

Dehydrator

Food processor

Storing Jars

Gloves

### Nutrition Facts per ½ pound

| Calories | 972.72 kcal |
|----------|-------------|
| Carbs | 36.2g |
| Protein | 35.53g |
| Fats | 83.88g |

### Core Ingredients

- Fresh turmeric roots

### Step 1 - Preparation

- Start by washing the turmeric roots, and peeling them.
- Cut them into 2 inches thick cubes.

### Step 2 – Dehydrating the turmeric in a dehydrator

- Prepare the dehydrator according to the manufacturer's instructions.
- Spread turmeric root pieces on a single layer on the dehydrating trays.
- Adjust the temperature to 105F, then dehydrate them for 2 to 5 hours until they become completely dry and crispy.

### Step 3 – Turning the turmeric into powder

- Allow the turmeric pieces to cool down completely, then transfer them to a food processor.
- Process them several times until they turn into powder.

### Step 4 – Storing turmeric powder

- Transfer the turmeric powder into jars or zip lock bags and seal them to be able to store them for up to 1 year, and enjoy!

## Green Jalapeño Powder

|Intro|: Jalapeño provides a spicy and amazing taste that complements a lot of soups, stews, and meats, it comes in very handy to turn it into powder especially if you just harvested some jalapenos or got a good deal and a big amount but you don't know that to do with them. This method will enable you to preserve them as a powder for 12 months.

### Equipment:

Knife

Dehydrator

Food processor

Storing Jars

Gloves

### Nutrition Facts per ½ pound

| Calories | 53.93 kcal |
|---|---|
| Carbs | 12.09g |
| Protein | 1.69g |
| Fats | 0.69g |

## Core Ingredients

- Fresh Jalapeños

## Step 1 - Preparation

- Start by washing the Jalapeños peppers, then pat them dry.
- Cut the Jalapeños in half lengthwise, then discard the stems and seeds.
- You can leave the Jalapeños halves as they are, or dice them to speed up the process. If you would like your powder to be even spicier, you can leave it in the seeds.

## Step 2 – Dehydrating the Jalapeños peppers in a dehydrator

- Prepare the dehydrator according to the manufacturer's instructions.
- Spread Jalapeños pepper pieces on a single layer on the dehydrating trays.
- Adjust the temperature to 115F, then dehydrate them for 20 to 24 hours until they become completely dry and crispy.

## Step 3 – Turning the Jalapeños pepper into powder

- Allow the Jalapeños pieces to cool down completely, then transfer them to a food processor.
- Process them several times until they turn into powder.

## Step 4 – Storing Jalapeños powder

- Transfer the Jalapeños powder into jars and seal them to be able to store them for up to 1 year, and enjoy!

## Homemade Ginger Powder

|Intro|: Ginger is also yet another staple seasoning that is required in every kitchen. It adds its distinct amazing taste to a variety of dishes. Homemade ginger powder is cheaper, healthier, and will last you for up to 18 months.

## Equipment:

Knife

Dehydrator

Food processor

Storing Jars

Gloves

**Nutrition Facts** per 1 cup

| Calories | 145.15 kcal |
|---|---|
| Carbs | 32.24g |
| Protein | 3.3g |
| Fats | 1.36g |

## Core Ingredients

- Fresh ginger roots

## Step 1 - Preparation

- Start by washing the ginger roots, and peeling them.
- Cut them into 2 inches thick cubes.

## Step 2 – Dehydrating the ginger in a dehydrator

- Prepare the dehydrator according to the manufacturer's instructions.
- Spread ginger root pieces on a single layer on the dehydrating trays.
- Adjust the temperature to 105F, then dehydrate them for 2 to 5 hours until they become completely dry and crispy.

## Step 3 – Turning the ginger into powder

- Allow the ginger pieces to cool down completely, then transfer them to a food processor.
- Process them several times until they turn into powder.

## Step 4 – Storing ginger powder

- Transfer the ginger powder into jars or zip lock bags and seal them to be able to store them for up to 18 months, and enjoy!

## Homemade Sriracha Powder

**|Intro|:** You can never have enough spicy powders. Sriracha sauce is one of the most delicious sauces out there, which makes dehydrating it a perfect way to preserve it for up to 6 months.

## Equipment:

Knife

Dehydrator

Food processor

Storing Jars

Gloves

### Nutrition Facts per 1 cup

| Calories | 72.54 kcal |
|----------|------------|
| Carbs | 14.94g |
| Protein | 1.51g |
| Fats | 0.73g |

## Core Ingredients

- Sriracha sauce

## Step 1 - Preparation

- Start by lining the dehydrating tray with parchment paper.

## Step 2 – Dehydrating the sriracha sauce in a dehydrator

- Prepare the dehydrator according to the manufacturer's instructions.
- Spread the sriracha sauce on a single 1/8 inch thick layer on the dehydrating trays while making sure to keep the edges empty.
- Adjust the temperature to 135F, then dehydrate it for 8 to 12 hours until it becomes completely dry.

## Step 3 – Turning the sriracha sauce into powder

- Allow the sauce to cool down completely, then break it into chunks and transfer them to a food processor.
- Process them several times until they turn into powder.

## Step 4 – Storing sriracha powder

- Transfer the sriracha powder into jars or zip lock bags and seal them to be able to store them for up to 6 months, and enjoy!

## Dry Rosemary

**|Intro|:** Dry rosemary makes a great addition to a lot of dishes like soup, stews, and salad, and adds a very nice flavor as a topping for homemade bread. Dehydrating it is the perfect way to preserve it for up to 12 months.

## Equipment:

Knife

Dehydrator

Food processor

Storing Jars

### Nutrition Facts per 1 oz

| Calories | 375 kcal |
|----------|----------|
| Carbs | 73g |
| Protein | 6g |
| Fats | 17g |

## Core Ingredients

- Fresh Rosemary sprigs

## Step 1 - Preparation

- Start by washing the rosemary sprigs and pat them dry or allow them to dry for about 30 minutes under the sun.

## Step 2 – Dehydrating rosemary in a dehydrator

- Prepare the dehydrator according to the manufacturer's instructions.
- Spread rosemary sprigs evenly on a single layer on the dehydrating trays.
- Adjust the temperature to 95F, then dehydrate them for 2 to 5 hours until they become completely dry and crunchy.

## Step 3 – Turning the rosemary into powder

- Allow the rosemary sprigs to cool down completely, then pluck off the leaves and transfer them to a food processor.
- Process them several times until they turn into powder.

### Step 4 – Storing rosemary powder

- Transfer the rosemary powder into jars or Ziploc bags and seal them to be able to store them for up to 12 months, and enjoy!

## Basil Powder

**|Intro|:** Fresh or dry, basil has an amazing taste to everything that you decide to add it to. It's also a very easy herb to plant as you can plant it at home, if you happen to have a good bunch that you don't know what to do it, dehydrating it is the best option as it will allow you to enjoy it for up to 1 year

### Equipment:

Knife

Dehydrator

Food processor

Storing Jars

**Nutrition Facts** per 1 oz

| Calories | 66.06 kcal |
|----------|------------|
| Carbs | 13.54g |
| Protein | 6.51g |
| Fats | 1.15g |

### Core Ingredients

- Fresh basil leaves

### Step 1 - Preparation

- Start by washing with warm water the basil leaves, discard their stems and pat them dry or allow them to dry for about 15 minutes under the sun.

### Step 2 – Dehydrating basil leaves in a dehydrator

- Prepare the dehydrator according to the manufacturer's instructions.
- Spread basil leaves evenly on a single layer on the dehydrating trays.
- Adjust the temperature to 115 F or 120 F, then dehydrate them for 4 to 6 hours until they become completely dry and crunchy.

### Step 3 – Turning the basil leaves into powder

- Allow the basil leaves to cool down completely, then transfer them to a food processor.

- Process them several times until they turn into powder.

### Step 4 – Storing basil powder

- Transfer the basil powder into jars or Ziploc bags and seal them to be able to store them for up to 12 months, and enjoy!

## Dry Oregano

**|Intro|:** Oregano is yet another lovely aromatic herb to dehydrate and preserve for up to 1 year. You can plant it at home, dehydrate it, and save a lot of money.

### Equipment:

Knife

Dehydrator

Food processor

Storing Jars

**Nutrition Facts** per 1 cup

| Calories | 75.13 kcal |
|----------|------------|
| Carbs | 19.54g |
| Protein | 2.55g |
| Fats | 1.21g |

### Core Ingredients

- Fresh Oregano sprigs

### Step 1 - Preparation

- Start by washing the oregano sprigs and pat them dry or allow them to dry for about 20 minutes under the sun.

### Step 2 – Dehydrating oregano in a dehydrator

- Prepare the dehydrator according to the manufacturer's instructions.
- Spread oregano sprigs evenly on a single layer on the dehydrating trays.
- Adjust the temperature to 95F, then dehydrate them for 2 to 5 hours until they become completely dry and crunchy.

199

### Step 3 – Turning the oregano into powder

- Allow the oregano sprigs to cool down completely, then pluck off the leaves and transfer them to a food processor.
- Process them several times until they turn into powder or you can process them a few times only to preserve their shape and harsh texture.

### Step 4 – Storing oregano powder

- Transfer the oregano powder into jars or Ziploc bags and seal them to be able to store them for up to 12 months, and enjoy!

## Garlic Powder

|Intro|: Garlic powder has been very popular lately, for it is much easier to use than fresh garlic, and has a very nice taste. Dehydrating garlic at home and turning it into powder is very cheap, and healthy.

### Equipment:

Knife

Dehydrator

Food processor

Storing Jars

Gloves

### Nutrition Facts per 1 teaspoon

| Calories | 9 kcal |
|----------|--------|
| Carbs | 2g |
| Protein | 0.5g |
| Fats | 0g |

### Core Ingredients

- Fresh garlic cloves

### Step 1 - Preparation

- Start by washing the garlic cloves, then peel them, and cut them into very thin slices.

### Step 2 – Dehydrating the garlic in a dehydrator

- Prepare the dehydrator according to the manufacturer's instructions.
- Spread the garlic slices evenly on a single layer on the dehydrating trays.

- Adjust the temperature to 125F, then dehydrate them for 8 to 12 hours until they become completely dry and crispy.

### Step 3 – Turning the garlic into powder

- Allow the garlic slices to cool down completely, then transfer them to a food processor.
- Process them several times until they turn into powder.

### Step 4 – Storing garlic powder

- Transfer the garlic powder into jars and seal them to be able to store them for up to 3 years, and enjoy!

## Onion Powder

|Intro|: Onion powder is also another powder that has become super popular lately and a beloved seasoning. It doesn't replace fresh onion, but it does add a nice taste to all dishes if you don't wish to use fresh onion.

### Equipment:

Knife

Dehydrator

Food processor

Storing Jars

Gloves

### Nutrition Facts per 1 teaspoon

| Calories | 10 kcal |
|----------|---------|
| Carbs | 2g |
| Protein | 1g |
| Fats | 1g |

### Core Ingredients

- Fresh white onions (red, yellow...depending on what you prefer or have)

### Step 1 - Preparation

- Start by peeling and washing the onions.
- Cut them in half, then slice them into 1/8 inch thick slices.

### Step 2 – Dehydrating the onion in a dehydrator

- Prepare the dehydrator according to the manufacturer's instructions.

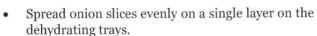

- Spread onion slices evenly on a single layer on the dehydrating trays.
- Adjust the temperature to 150F, then dehydrate them for 6 to 8 hours until they become completely dry and crunchy.

### Step 3 – Turning the onion into powder
- Allow the onion slices to cool down completely, then transfer them to a food processor.
- Process them several times until they turn into powder.

### Step 4 – Storing onion powder
- Transfer the onion powder into jars and seal them to be able to store them for up to 3 years, and enjoy!

## Section 7: Dehydrated Meat Recipes

### How to Dehydrate Beef

|Intro|: There is nothing like preserving beef meat by dehydrating it, which means making jerky. It's much cheaper than storebought Jerky and tastes much more delicious.

#### Equipment:
Knife

Cutting Board

Dehydrator

Plate

Oven

Baking sheet

Storing Jars/container

Large container

#### Nutrition Facts per 2.5 oz

| Calories | 151 kcal |
|----------|----------|
| Carbs | 5g |
| Protein | 21g |
| Fats | 4g |

#### Core Ingredients
- 3 pounds of beef eye of round

### Marinade Ingredients
- ¾ cup of soy sauce
- ¾ cup of Worcestershire sauce
- 1 ½ tablespoon of liquid smoke
- 1 ½ tablespoon of brown sugar
- ¾ tablespoon of red pepper flakes
- ¾ tablespoon of black pepper
- ¾ tablespoon of salt

### Step 1 - Preparation
- Start by washing the meat, and trimming off the fat.
- Transfer the meat to a large plate then freeze it for 70 minutes to 2 hours until it becomes partially frozen to be able to cut it easily.

### Step 2 – Marinating the meat
- Combine all the marinade ingredients in a large container then whisk them until they are well combined.
- Slice the meat into ¼-inch thick slices if you prefer easy to chew, and cut it with the grain if you prefer a more chewy texture.
- Add the meat slices to the marinade, then mix them well until the meat slices are coated with the marinade.
- Transfer the meat to the fridge, and allow it to sit for 2 nights so that it rests well and absorbs all the flavors.

### Step 3 – Dehydrating the jerky in a dehydrator
- Prepare the dehydrator according to the manufacturer's instructions.
- Place the meat slices evenly in a single layer on the dehydrating trays.
- Adjust the temperature to 165F, then dehydrate it for 3 hours.
- Once the time is up, lower the temperature to 145 F, then allow the meat to dehydrate until the jerky has a chewy and bending texture, do not over dehydrate it until it becomes crisp. The dehydrating process will take from 5 to 15 hours depending on your meat, and temperature....so make sure to check the jerky every hour to see if it's done.

### Step 4 – Dehydrating the jerky in the oven
- Preheat the oven to 175 F.
- Spread the meat slices evenly on foil lined-up baking sheets.

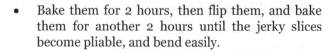

- Bake them for 2 hours, then flip them, and bake them for another 2 hours until the jerky slices become pliable, and bend easily.

## Step 5 – Storing the jerky

- Allow the jerky slices to cool down completely, then transfer them to air-tight containers/jars or zip lock bags and seal them tightly.
- If you store it in an airtight container, it could last for up to months in a dark cool place. If you store it in the fridge or a Ziploc bag, it can last for up to 2 weeks.

## How to Dehydrate Chicken

|Intro|: If you haven't tried dehydrating chicken before then you are missing a lot. With this recipe, you can easily dehydrate with your favorite marinade, and store it for months in the freezer. The outcome is lovely instant chicken that is packed with flavor.

### Equipment:

Knife

Cutting Board

Dehydrator

Meat thermometer

Oven

Baking sheet

Storing Jars

Container

Ziploc bags

### Nutrition Facts per 2.50 oz

| Calories | 150 kcal |
|----------|----------|
| Carbs | 7.5g |
| Protein | 27.5g |
| Fats | 0g |

### Core Ingredients

- Chicken breasts
- Marinade of your choice

## Step 1 - Preparation

- Start by washing the chicken, and trimming off the fat.

- Bring a large pot to a boil, then cook in it the chicken breasts until they reach an internet temperature of 165 F.
- Once the chicken is done, drain it and place it aside to cool down until becomes easy to handle.

## Step 2 – Marinating the chicken

- Pour the marinade that you wish to use into a large container.
- Cut the chicken breasts into bite-size pieces then add them to the marinade.
- Stir them well until the chicken pieces are well coated then leave the chicken in the container or transfer it to Ziploc bags.
- Transfer the chicken to the fridge and allow it to marinate for 2 hours to absorb the flavors.

## Step 3 – Dehydrating the chicken in a dehydrator

- Prepare the dehydrator according to the manufacturer's instructions.
- Drain the chicken pieces, pat them dry then spread them in a single layer on the dehydrating trays without allowing them to touch.
- Adjust the temperature to 145F, then dehydrate it for 6 to 8 hours while checking it every 2 hours until it becomes completely dry but not flaky or brittle.

## Step 4 – Dehydrating the chicken in the oven

- Preheat the oven to 275 F.
- Spread the chicken pieces evenly on foil lined-up baking sheets without them touching, and leave the door open 3 inches wide.
- Bake it for 1 to 2 hours until the chicken reaches an internal temperature of 160 F.

## Step 5 – Storing the chicken

- Allow the chicken pieces to cool down completely, then transfer them to air-tight containers/jars or zip lock bags and seal them tightly.
- If you store it in an airtight container, it could last for up two months in a dark cool place. If you store it in the fridge or a Ziploc bag, it can last for up to 2 weeks. You can store it for up to 6 months in the freezer.

## Step 6 – Serving the chicken

- When ready to serve your chicken, soak it in some hot water or broth until it becomes soft, then drain it, serve it and enjoy!

## How to Dehydrate Fish

|**Intro**|: Next time you are in the mood for fish, this recipe can come in handy! If you haven't tried dehydrating fish before then you are missing a lot. With this recipe, you can easily dehydrate it with your favorite marinade, and store it for months in the freezer.

### Equipment:

Knife

Cutting Board

Dehydrator

Oven

Baking sheet

Storing Jars

### Nutrition Facts per 1 oz

| Calories | 113 kcal |
|----------|----------|
| Carbs | 0g |
| Protein | 18g |
| Fats | 3.9g |

### Core Ingredients

- Fresh Salmon fillets (or any other fish of your choice)
- Marinade of your choice

### Step 1 - Preparation

- Start by discarding the innards and head of the fish.
- Cut the fish in half, then remove the bones, and skin of the fillets.
- Wash the fish fillets and pat them dry, then cut them into ¼-inch thick strips or cubes depending on what you prefer.

### Step 2 – Marinating the fish

- Pour the marinade that you wish to use into a large container.
- Add the fish pieces, and stir them well until they are well coated.
- Transfer the fish to the fridge and allow it to marinate for overnight to absorb the flavors.

### Step 3 – Dehydrating the fish in a dehydrator

- Prepare the dehydrator according to the manufacturer's instructions.
- Drain the fish pieces, pat them dry then spread them in a single layer on the dehydrating trays without allowing them to touch.
- Adjust the temperature to 145F, then dehydrate it for 10 to 12 hours while checking it every 5 hours until it becomes completely dry and slightly leathery.

### Step 4 – Storing the fish

- Allow the fish pieces to cool down completely, then transfer them to an air-tight container/jars or zip lock bags and seal them tightly.
- If you store it in an airtight container, it could last for up two months in a dark cool place. If you store it in the fridge or a Ziploc bag, it can last for up to 2 weeks. You can store it for up to 6 months in the freezer.

### Step 5 – Serving the fish

- When ready to serve your fish, soak it in some hot water or broth until it becomes soft, then drain it, serve it and enjoy!

# |Part 10| Freeze Drying Intro

## Section 1: What is freeze drying or Lyophilization

Lyophilization or in simple words freeze drying is the act of freezing a product that elongates its life to make it last for a long time without affecting it in any way.

During world war 2, freeze-drying was discovered by Jacques-Arsene d'Arsonval at the College-de-France in 1906, Paris. This invention had a great impact on the world because it was used back then to preserve penicillin, blood, and serums. It was super effective for medicine, so it quickly became a very popular preserving method for various products that includes food. It started with big companies who wanted to preserve certain foods so they could still provide them even when they were not in season, then technology evolved to a point where freeze drying became widespread and can also be done at home.

Many preserving methods help preserve foods for months and years but most of them require you to make alterations to your foods by adding to them other ingredients to be able to store them. Freeze drying, is the complete opposite, it enables you to freeze dry your foods in their original form, and the best thing about it is that instead of altering or taking away from the taste of your food, it preserves its flavor, and enhances it.

Freeze drying can be separated into 3 phases:

**Freezing:** This is the most important step of this process in which you have to freeze your food in a freezer, chilled bath...This action preserves the original form of the food and prepares it for the second phase.

**Primary drying:** Also known as freeze-drying is the act of lowering the pressure in the freezing chamber and introducing a certain amount of heat that sublimates the water from the food. In other words, it causes the water to change from a solid form to a gaseous state as in vapor instead of becoming a liquid first. This process is low and very delicate because to evaporate the water without melting it, a certain amount of heat needs to be maintained until 95% at least of the water is removed from the food.

**Secondary drying:** Also known as desorption drying require raising the temperature to become more than the one used in primary drying to remove any remaining water from the product and finally make it ready for storage.

The process might sound complicated but the machine will do all the work for you. This method is a brilliant way to store foods because unlike other methods that can last up to 2 to 5 years, freeze-dried foods can last for up to 25 years without needing you to do anything like rotating them, checking them...It's one of the greatest inventions to ever done.

Freeze drying can be done using 4 methods:
- Freeze-Dryer
- Freezer
- Dry Ice
- Vacuum Chamber

## Section 2: Preparing Food for Freeze-Drying

Freeze-drying is one if not the best way to preserve foods because unlike other preserving methods, freeze-drying actually preserves the shape, color, and nutrients of your food, enhances its flavor to make them taste even better, and sometimes it even increases its nutrients. The process is also very easy and doesn't require a lot of fuss.

If you wish to freeze-dry fresh foods like vegetables, fruits... you must **pick out the freshest ones**. If you are planning to buy them, and if you have a harvest that you wish to preserve then you should freeze-dry as soon as possible after the harvest to preserve its quality.

Next, comes cleaning. Makes sure to **wash and clean your foods really well** to make sure there is nothing left on them. After cleaning them, you should handle them with gloves, to keep them extra clean because once you freeze-dry them, if you leave any dirt behind, or if you freeze-dry your food without cleaning it first, the bacteria that you left behind is going to remain frozen with it until you decide to use it.

The final step is to cut your food into small pieces. Unlike big or whole pieces, the small pieces will help water evaporate quickly, and freeze-dry your food faster.

For cooked meals, you can just freeze-dry them as they are.

## Section 3: How to Freeze Dry Food in a Freeze-Dryer

Freeze-drying food using a freezer-dryer is a very easy process that requires very minimal effort. Freeze-dryers can be expensive indeed, but they are great to have at home because they will save you a lot of time since they have many trays that will enable you to freeze a big amount of food at the same time, and they are also fast.

The freezing process can be concluded through the following steps:

**Step 1:** Start by spreading the food that you wish to freeze on the freezing trays. If you are freezing fresh foods like meats, vegetables, or fruits...make sure to leave some space between them so they don't stick together.

**Step 2:** Put the trays in the dryer and close the door.

**Step 3:** Turn on your freeze-dryer by following the manufacturer's instructions, then adjust the temperature to the recommended setting for that food.

**Step 4:** Allow the process to be complete depending on the time required for the food that you are freeze-drying.

**Step 5:** Once the process is complete, transfer your food to mylar bags and seal them then store them. Mylar bags are the best bags to use for food storage because they protect against light, moisture, and insects.

## Section 4: How to Freeze Dry Food in a Freezer

If you are new to freeze-drying, or simply can't afford a freeze-dryer, then a freezer is the second best choice to use for freeze-drying food. The process is easy, and straightforward, its only downfall is that it takes a lot of time, and since the freezer is not as big, you will need to freeze your foods in batches.

**Step 1:** Spread your food on a tray that fits into your freezer without letting the food pieces touch.

**Step 2:** Adjust the temperature of your freezer to the lowest setting, then place the tray in the freezer.

**Step 3:** Freezing food in the freezer takes a long time, so depending on your food, the weight, and the moisture in your food, the freezing process could take from 2 to 4 weeks.

**Step 4:** Once the freezing process is complete, transfer your food into air-tight storage bags or mylar bags, then store your food in the freezer or a dark, and cold pantry.

## Section 5: How to Freeze-Dry Food With Dry Ice

Freeze-drying with dry ice is also a great way to freeze your foods without having to wait for weeks. The process takes around 24 hours typically, and it can be done in a few steps:

**Step 1:** Start by placing your food in freezer-safe bags, then transfer them to a cooler.

**Step 2:** You can get some dry ice from your market, pour it all over the food bags, then seal the cooler.

**Step 3:** Allow your food bags to sit in the cooler for 24 hours, then store your bags in the freezer or a cool and dry pantry.

## Section 6: How to Freeze Dry Food With a Vacuum Chamber

Freeze-drying food using a vacuum chamber is very efficient, fast, and the best freeze-drying method on this list, however, it can be expensive. If you get a lot of harvests, you might want to consider getting one, it's a great investment. Using a vacuum chamber is very easy, and the process consists of two parts:

### Part 1: Freezing the food

**Step 1:** Spread your food on a tray that fits into your freezer without letting the food pieces touch.

**Step 2:** Unlike the freezer method, in this case, leave the temperature as it is, and allow your food to sit in it for 6 to 12 hours until it becomes frozen.

## Part 2: Freeze-drying the food in the vacuum chamber

**Step 1:** Place the frozen food in the chamber then adjust the Torr and temperature according to the recipe you are following, or the manufacturer's recommendation for the food that you wish to freeze-dry.

**Step 2:** Allow your food to remain in the chamber for at least a week for optimal sublimation. This will ensure that most of the water evaporates, which increases the shelf life of your food, help enhance its taste, and make it even more nutritious.

**Step 3:** Once the process is complete, transfer your food into mylar bags or air-tight containers, then store them in the freezer or a pantry.

## Section 7: How to Reconstitute Freeze-Dried food

Reconstituting freeze-dried food is the easiest thing that you have to do in this whole process. Some of the most popular reconstitution methods that you can use are the following:

**Soak in Water** – If wish to rehydrate fruits, vegetables or meats, and firm foods, all you have to do is place your food in a container, big enough to hold the food and water. Then pour on top of them hot or warm water on. If you don't have the time to heat the water, cold water will also do.

Warm or hot water is best used when you wish to reconstitute your foods faster and don't have much time to do it. However, if you can allow them to sit overnight, then you can use cold water. It will enable reconstitution at a much slower pace, and retain the original shape.

**Spraying Water** – Some foods can't be soaked in water or they will be ruined like bread, for example, so the best way to preserve them is by spraying them with water. You can place the food on the kitchen counter next to you while going about your shores, and spritz them with water every once in a while until rehydration.

**Place Between Damp Paper Towels** – If you don't have the time to keep spritzing your food with water every once in a while, the second best option is to also cover it with damp paper towels, place it in a ZIP lock bag, then place them aside and let them soak the water until they become soft to your liking. For example, muffins, cake, bread...

**Adding it to Wet Ingredients** – If you are planning to add your freeze-dried food to already wet ingredients, like adding vegetables or fruit powder to soups, stews...then you don't have to rehydrate them at all because you will be adding them to water already, and heating them will also rehydrate them without you having to do it separately.

## Section 8: Freeze drying tips

Whether you are a beginner or expert at freeze drying, these tips will help you save a lot of time, money, and effort:

- Freeze drying takes a lot of time, so if you want to save time, you can freeze dry several foods at the same time just make sure they are of the same type. For example fruits with fruits, meats with meats...and if you are planning on freeze-drying onion or broccoli, it's best to freeze-dry them on their own because their smell will affect any food that you freeze dry with them.

- Yes, we all love cutting corners especially when freeze drying to save time, however, make sure to not freeze dry liquids and non-liquids in the same batch because they will affect each other's taste badly.

- If you plan to use a freeze dryer machine, you must place it in a chamber that is away from your bedrooms, preferably noise canceling because freeze drying takes more than 20 hours usually, and the machine might make loud sounds. You really don't want it anywhere near your sleeping chambers.

- The best way to freeze-dry all foods and save yourself a lot of time and effort is by cutting them into small pieces. Doing this will enable them to freeze dry quickly, and at the same time when you are ready to use them, you won't need to do anything but rehydrate them.

- If you wish to use your freeze-dried foods in a matter of months, you can feel free to store them in airtight jars. However, if you wish to save them for years, make sure to use mylar bags and oxygen absorbers. They will make your food last for up to 25 years.

# Section 9: Foods that don't freeze dry well

Freeze-drying is hands down of the best methods to preserve your foods and store them for a very long time. However, just like some foods can't be canned or pickled, they are also some foods that can't be freeze-dried. These foods are:

- Honey
- Butter
- Jam
- Jelly
- Peanut butter
- Chocolate syrup
- Mayonnaise

When freeze-dried, these foods don't turn out well become water is super important for their taste and texture. When you take it away from them, you will end up with very bad results.

# Section 10: Favorite Tools for Freeze Drying

Before you start freeze drying, you must prepare your tools first to make sure the process goes smoothly. The tools that you will be needing are:

- **Rolling cart:** Getting a rolling cart is super important if you are planning to use a freeze dryer because every time you freeze dry food, you have to have a bucket placed underneath it to collect all the water that will be removed from the food. Using a rolling cart will enable you to easily move it around, and access the backside of it.
- **Silicone Molds:** If you are planning on freeze-drying ice cream, yogurt...foods that you want to freeze dry in a certain shape, you will need silicone molds.
- **Mason jars or ZIP loc bags:** If you are planning on storing your food for weeks or months, storing them in mason jars is the best option.
- **Vacuum sealer:** If you want to store your food for a few years, a vacuum sealer is very handy. You can use it to vacuum seal both your food bags and jars.
- **Mylar bags and oxygen absorbers:** If you are planning on storing your foods for a long time, as in up to 25 years, then you really need mylar bags and oxygen absorbers. These kinds of bags absorb

oxygen when exposed to them, and ensure your food stays safe for years to come.

- **Storage Bins:** Using storage bins come in really handy when storing foods because thanks to them your pantry will remain always organized, and will also help you easily differentiate between the short-term and long-term stored foods. You can also mark them or attach notes to them so you can always know when you stored each food, and when is the best time to consume it.

# Section 11: FAQs

## 1) How long does it take to freeze dry food?

Freeze-drying foods actually depend on the method you are using and the food that you are dry freezing. If you are using a freeze dryer or vacuum chamber, the process will take less than 24 hours. However, if you are using the traditional method using dry ice or your freezer, then the process could take up to a month. Another factor that determines how long the freeze-drying process takes is the thickness of your foods. If you are freeze-drying powdered foods, or small foods such as corn, dry fruits, or thinly sliced foods...they will take a lot less time than freeze-drying whole fruits, veggies, and big chunks of meat.

## 2) How do you freeze-dry fruit at home without a machine?

Using a freeze dryer machine or a vacuum chamber are the best and fastest methods to freeze dry foods, however, if you don't have them or cannot afford them, you can easily freeze dry your food using your freezer or dry ice. For full instructions on how to do it, you can check the previous sections.

## 3) What is the shelf life of freeze-dried foods?

If you wish to store your food for a long time, meaning years, freeze-drying is the best option. However, the shelf life of your food will also be determined by the place and temperature where you are storing your food. If you want to maximize the shelf life of your foods, the best way to do it is to make sure to store your foods in a cool, and dry pantry. If you can control the temperature of it by lowering it to 40 to 60 F degrees, it's a huge bonus because a cold temperature will help your food stay fresh for a very long time, and preserve its nutrients.

## 4) Are any nutrients lost during the freeze-drying and dehydration processes?

Unlike other preserving methods like canning, and pickling that tend to take away from the stored foods' nutritional value, freeze drying does the exact opposite. It preserves all the vitamins and nutrients of the food and sometimes increases it with time. It also helps the food retain its shape, texture, and color, and enhances its flavor.

# |Part 11| Foods to Freeze Dry

## Section 1: Fruits to Freeze Dry

If you are planning on freeze-drying fruits, but you have no idea what fruit to start with or how to go about it, this simple list of the most suitable fruits for freeze-drying will help you kickstart your freeze-drying journey easily:

### Grapes

Grapes are one of the most versatile and easiest fruits to freeze dry. The best way to go about them is by slicing them in half, discarding the seeds then placing them with the open side facing down on the trays. After you freeze-dry them, you can serve them as a nice snack, or cake toppings.

### Apple Slices

Apples are an incredible fruit to freeze dry and store for you can use them for thousands of recipes varying from savory to sweet dishes. If you have some time, you should peel the apples because the skin tends to be tough and easier to use when you hydrate them. However, if you wish to store the with their peel, you can also do it. Cut your apples into bite-size cubes, and toss them with some fresh lemon juice to prevent them from oxidizing. Next, you can toss your apples with some caramel, or some sugar and cinnamon if you wish to use them mainly for sweets, or you can freeze dry them plain so you can feel free to add them to your casseroles, soups, pies.

### Pineapple

Pineapple is also a great fruit to start with for you can serve it as a snack, or easily add it to your savory and sweet dishes. You just have to peel it, cut it into slices or bite-size pieces depending on what you prefer, then freeze dry them.

### Blueberries

Freeze-dried blueberries are a very delicious treat, and go amazing with everything. However, they do take longer to freeze dry because they are juicy. The best way to freeze-dry them is by cutting them in half or poking them with a needle to make sure they are dried fully.

### Strawberries

There is nothing to say about strawberries because they are phenomenal in everything. To freeze dry them, you just have to wash them well, cut off the tops, then cut them in half, or slice them. Spread them evenly on the freezing tray and freeze-dry them.

### Mango

Mangos also make for a great addition to salads, smoothies, and cake toppings. You just have to peel it, cut it into bite-size pieces, then freeze-dry it.

### Mixed Fruit

Nothing beats mixed fruits in the summer for you can use them in smoothies and ice creams. So you just have to cut your favorite fruits into bite-size pieces, spread them on the freezing trays, and dry freeze them. When done, you can pack them into bags, then just pull out a bag whenever you are in the mood for ice cream or smoothie.

### Peaches & Apricots

Peaches and apricots are one of the most delicious and popular fruits to use in baked goods. So you just have to slice them in half, discard their pits, then freeze dry them as they are or slice them first. You can also add to them some sugar before freezing them to bring out their juice and make them taste even better when you hydrate them.

### Bananas

Bananas are yet another super versatile and easy-to-freeze dry fruit. You just have to peel the bananas, slice them and freeze-dry them. Some people like to freeze the bananas first in the freezer, then slice them to lower the time required for the dry freezing process, however, you should keep in mind that your bananas might come out slightly brown when frozen.

### Lemons & Limes

Lemons and limes are one of the most important fruits to have in hand because they add a very unique taste to all recipes, savory, sweets, ice creams, smoothies, and drinks as well, so it's always great to have around. You can choose to peel your fruit or not, slice it, discard the bones then freeze dry the slices.

## Watermelon

Freeze-dried watermelon is the perfect treat for summer, and tastes just like candy. Since it's a very juicy fruit though, dry freezing will take much more time than the other fruits. Also, taking out the seeds is essential.

## Raspberries & Blackberries

freezing raspberries and blackberries is a super easy and simple process. You just have to wash and spread them on freezing trays, then freeze dry them.

## Cherries

Cherries also make for a great snack, a yummy addition to cereals, and cake toppings...Pitting them does require a lot of time, but their taste is worth every minute of your time. You can freeze-dry them while they are fresh, or you can blanch them before pitting them for 2 minutes to reduce their chewiness.

## Avocado

Freeze-drying avocado is just like freeze-drying apples. To prevent it from browning, just toss it with some lemon juice, spread the pieces on freezing trays then freeze dry them and enjoy it with smoothies, guacamole, salads...

## Section 2: Vegetables to freeze dry

Here is yet another brief list of the best and easiest vegetables to start your freeze-drying journey with:

## Olives

Black and green lives are very underrated compared to other veggies, but they add a great taste to dishes, salads, and spreads which makes them perfect for freeze drying. If your olives are not pitted, make sure to pit them, spread them on freezing trays, then dry freeze them.

## Tomatoes

All types of tomatoes are perfect for freeze-drying. Once again, you can freeze-dry them whole, or slice them. If you are using cherry tomatoes, I highly recommend you slice in half them so that when you hydrate them you can add them right away to your salad and save prep time.

## Zucchini

Salads, soups, stews, casseroles, cakes, muffins..., zucchini is the perfect vegetable for all dishes so it makes sense to freeze dry it. You just need to cut it into the shape that you prefer first, slices, cubes, zoodles... then dry freeze it.

## Squash

Squash is also a great vegetable to freeze dry because you can use it in all seasons, and a lot of popular hearty dishes call for it. Cut it into the shape that you prefer and enjoy!

## Peas

If you have fresh peas, you just have to spread them on the freezing trays and freeze them. If you want to decrease the freeze drying time, even more, you can purchase frozen peas instead, and dry freeze them.

## Corn

If your family loves corn, then you will love dry freezing it because instead of worrying about chucking it every time and cutting it, you can get all the work out of the way in one day, and then have ready it on hand whenever you need it.

## Green Beans

If you wish to freeze dry green beans, it is best to blanch them first in water with a pinch of salt for a few minutes. The salt will give them a nice taste, and blanching them will make them ready to serve when hydrated.

## Carrots

Just like they are one of the easiest vegetables to plant, carrots are also very easy to dry freeze. They don't require any cooking, so you just have to cut them into pieces, or keep them whole, then freeze dry them.

## Onions

Onions come in very handy all the time, any time for they are essential to a lot of recipes. Once again, you just have to chop, slice, or dice them depending on what you like. Their only downfall is that they give a very strong odor that will remain in your house and whatever machine you used to freeze dry them with for a while.

## Broccoli

Broccoli might not look like it, but it does have a strong odor that sticks in your machine and house for days just like onions. The best way to freeze dry it and reduce the small is by cooking it first until tender but holds its shape, then freeze it in your freezer. Transfer the frozen broccoli pieces into freezing trays, then dry freeze them.

## Beans

There is nothing like storing beans and chickpeas for they come so handy in a lot of recipes, especially in the winter. You just have to cook them the way you prefer, strain them and air dries them, then freeze dry them and rest assured that if stored properly they will last for years to come.

## Potatoes

You might think because of their texture, freeze-drying potatoes is not a good idea, but it's actually the best idea to preserve them in their true form. Freeze-drying potatoes preserve their texture, so you can fry them, bake them, or add them to your casseroles, and soups...either way, they will taste just like fresh potatoes if not better. However, you need to blanch them first plain or with a pinch of salt, otherwise, they will become brown with time.

## Mushrooms

Mushrooms are yet another very versatile vegetable that you can use on their own, stew, soup, or sauce. You can slice them or dry freeze them whole, just make sure to remove the stems.

## Collard Greens

Freeze-drying greens is a super easy trick to be able to enjoy them all year without having to prepare them every time you need them. You just have to grab a bag and dump it in your dish. Make sure to wash your greens well, and discard their stems before freeze-drying them.

## Section 3: Meats & Eggs to freeze dry

If you are working or if you have a family, then you already have your hands full 24/7. This is why if you can freeze dry meats, you shouldn't hesitate. One or two days of prepping the meat and freeze-drying it will set you up for the rest of the year so you don't have to worry about it anymore. Cooked or raw, you can have both options. So here are some of the most popular meats to help you kickstart your dry freezing journey:

## Chicken

If you wish to freeze dry chicken, you can do it raw it by cutting into the pieces that suites you best, and know that you will be using a lot. Or, you can cook it the way you prefer or simply use rotisserie chicken. You can shred it, or cut it into pieces that can fit into your freezing trays, then freeze dry it.

## Ground Beef

Ground beef is another great meat to freeze dry for it is very versatile and can be used in various recipes. If you wish to freeze-dry it raw, make sure to use ground beef with the least amount of fat as possible because the fat in it will affect your meat's taste badly. If you wish to cook it instead, you can just cook your meat in a large pan while stirring often until it starts to become brown. When done, transfer it to a colander and let it sit for a few minutes to drain the fat from it. When done, pour over it some hot water to remove the remaining fat, pat it dry then freeze dry it. Cooking the meat first will save you a lot of time when you hydrate it.

## Ham

Ham can be used with salads, breakfast recipes, soups, and casseroles, so having freeze-dried cooked or raw ham is a lifesaver. Once again, make sure to get ham with the least amount of fat. Cook until it starts to become golden brown and drain it. Then freeze dry it and enjoy!

## Turkey

If you love turkey, then freeze-drying it will become your new hobby. Just like chicken, you can cook it or dry freeze it raw. You can also grind it, dice it, or cut it into pieces.

## Pork

Just like chicken and turkey, you can freeze dry pork raw or cooked, either way, make sure to cut off as much fat as possible from it.

## Beef and Lamb

There is nothing like dry freezing beef. You can freeze dry steaks, cubes, pieces, chops...whatever you want.

You can also cook them or freeze-dry them raw. Either way, freeze-drying really improves its taste and makes it last for a long time.

## Eggs

It's often that we all buy more eggs than we need, or if you have hens, then you must have a lot of eggs on your hands that you don't know what to do with, so why not freeze dry them? You just have to whisk the eggs and pour them into an eggs tray, then freeze dry them. You can transfer them to bags and seal them, or you can actually blend them in a food processor to turn them into a powder. Well-preserved freeze-dried eggs can last you for up to 20 years.

## Section 4: Dairy to freeze dry

Dairy products are super easy to dry and super easy to rehydrate and use again, so here are some of the best dairy products to start with.

## Yogurt

Next time you find a discounted big pack of yogurt or you made some homemade yogurt, you don't have to miss it anymore because you can freeze-dry it instead and enjoy it for years. You can freeze-dry it in the shape of small dots, or in silicone molds. One yogurt that this not recommended to dry freeze is Greek yogurt because it doesn't turn out well.

## Milk

Once you try freeze-dried milk you won't ever have to purchase milk powder anymore. You just have to pour the milk into the freezing trays, but be careful to leave at least ¼ inch of space on the top to prevent it from spilling, then freeze dry it. It turns out very flavorful.

## Cream Cheese

Once again, cream cheese is surely one of those ingredients that are super handy to have because they can be used in both savory and sweet dishes. The best way to freeze dry it is by allowing sit in the freezer for up to an hour until it becomes cold. Slice it into thick bars, then freeze-dry them.

## Sour Cream

Sour cream is super easy to freeze dry and rehydrate. You just have to spread it on a freezing tray, and dry freeze it. When you wish to use it, if you want to use it in a soup, stew, or something hot, then you just have to add it to the pot and cover it. If not, then just have to keep spritzing it with water until it becomes fresh again.

## Ice Cream

There is nothing like freeze-drying ice cream so you can have it ready whenever you need it. The most essential step is to make sure the machine that you will be using is cold so that when you put in the ice cream it doesn't melt. Next, you can cut it into chunks, or bite-size pieces. When ready to serve it, you just have to spritz it with milk until it regains its texture.

## Cheese

There is nothing like having shredded cheese bags ready to use. You can freeze-dry all cheeses by shredding them or cutting them into bite-size pieces.

## Eggnog

Christmas tends to be very hectic, so there is nothing like having dry frozen eggnog around that you can prep in a matter of minutes by adding to it milk.

## Section 5: Treats to freeze dry

Treats are an essential food to have on hand every day for a quick snack, for a hot summer day, or a simply delicious treat to enjoy when craving something sweet, so it only makes to freeze dry them and prolong their shelf life from days and months to years:

## Skittles

Freeze-drying skittle is a very simple task that yields very delicious candy. The process takes a lot of time, but it's worth every minute for freeze drying improves the taste of skittles and makes them taste even better.

## Jolly Ranchers

If you love Jolly ranchers, then you will love them when freeze-dried even more. They become crunchy and colorful, and they taste even much better than the original ones. You can freeze-dry them whole, or you can cut them in half with scissors.

## Other Candies

A lot of candies freeze dry really well and taste better than the original ones. There is no science behind which one is good and which one is not, so it's just a trial and error. Freeze dry small amounts of your favorite candies to see which ones you like most. It's important to stay away though from candies with chocolate because they won't freeze dry well.

## Marshmallows

Marshmallows taste great when freeze-dried, it turns out very crunchy, and flavorful. You can serve them whole with cereal, as a snack...or you can turn them into powder, and add them to your smoothies, milkshakes, and baked goods to boost their taste.

## Cheesecake

Freeze-dried cheesecake turns into an incredibly delicious crunchy snack. If you are using homemade cheesecake, make sure to freeze it first, if not you can just buy frozen cheesecake, then cut it into bite-size pieces. You can reconstitute it by spritzing it with milk or water, but it tastes much better when dry.

## Section 6: Other foods to freeze dry ideas

Some other foods that freeze dry really well and come in very handy especially when you are busy and don't have the time to spend hours in the kitchen are the following:

## Chicken and beef broth or stock

Preparing homemade broth or stock takes a lot of time, and you end up using it in a matter of days, then have to make another batch. Freeze drying is the best option since you can make a big batch or buy it, pour it into trays then freeze dry them. When ready to use it, you just have to mix it with some water.

## Meals

If you are a busy person or have a big family and don't like having to stand for hours in the kitchen cooking every day, being able to freeze dry your meals will save you so much time, and come in very handy when you don't feel like cooking anything. You just have to arrange your meals or spread them on freezing trays then freeze dry them. When ready to use, you just have to add to them some water and heat them.

## Soup

Freeze-drying soup is one of the best things to do because you will end up with a ready-to-eat homemade meal. You just have to pour your soup on freezing trays while making sure to leave at least ¼ inch of space on top to prevent it from spilling. After you freeze-dry it, you can break the soup into pieces and then store them in zip-lock bags or you can add them to a food processor and blend them smoothly. When ready to serve your soup, you just have to add some water and heat it.

# Measurement Conversion Chart
# & Cooking Chart

## Pan Size Equivalents

| | |
|---|---|
| 9-by-13-inches baking dish | 22-by-33-centimeter baking dish |
| 8-by-8-inches baking dish | 20-by-20-centimeter baking dish |
| 9-by-5-inches loaf pan | 23-by-12-centimeter loaf pan (=8 cups or 2 liters in capacity) |
| 10-inch tart or cake pan | 25-centimeter tart or cake pan |
| 9-inch cake pan | 22-centimeter cake pan |

## US to Metric Conversions

| | |
|---|---|
| 1/5 teaspoon | 1 ml (ml stands for milliliter, one thousandth of a liter) |
| 1 teaspoon | 5 ml |
| 1 tablespoon | 15 ml |
| 1 fluid oz. | 30 ml |
| 1/5 cup | 50 ml |
| 1 cup | 240 ml |
| 2 cups (1 pint) | 470 ml |
| 4 cups (1 quart) | .95 liter |
| 4 quarts (1 gal.) | 3.8 liters |
| 1 oz. | 28 grams |
| 1 pound | 454 grams |

## Metric to US Conversions

| | |
|---|---|
| 1 milliliter | 1/5 teaspoon |
| 5 ml | 1 teaspoon |
| 15 ml | 1 tablespoon |
| 30 ml | 1 fluid oz. |
| 100 ml | 3.4 fluid oz. |
| 240 ml | 1 cup |
| 1 liter | 34 fluid oz. |
| 1 liter | 4.2 cups |
| 1 liter | 2.1 pints |
| 1 liter | 1.06 quarts |
| 1 liter | .26 gallon |
| 1 gram | .035 ounce |
| 100 grams | 3.5 ounces |
| 500 grams | 1.10 pounds |
| 1 kilogram | 2.205 pounds |
| 1 kilogram | 35 oz. |

## Measurements Conversion Chart

### US Dry Volume Measurements

| MEASURE | EQUIVALENT |
|---|---|
| 1/16 teaspoon | dash |
| 1/8 teaspoon | a pinch |
| 3 teaspoons | 1 Tablespoon |
| 1/8 cup | 2 tablespoons (= 1 standard coffee scoop) |
| 1/4 cup | 4 Tablespoons |
| 1/3 cup | 5 Tablespoons plus 1 teaspoon |
| 1/2 cup | 8 Tablespoons |
| 3/4 cup | 12 Tablespoons |
| 1 cup | 16 Tablespoons |
| 1 Pound | 16 ounces |

### US liquid volume measurements

| | |
|---|---|
| 8 Fluid ounces | 1 Cup |
| 1 Pint | 2 Cups (= 16 fluid ounces) |
| 1 Quart | 2 Pints (= 4 cups) |
| 1 Gallon | 4 Quarts (= 16 cups) |

| Farenheit | Celsius | Gas Mark |
|---|---|---|
| 275° F | 140° C | gas mark 1-cool |
| 300° F | 150° C | gas mark 2 |
| 325° F | 165° C | gas mark 3-very moderate |
| 350° F | 180° C | gas mark 4-moderate |
| 375° F | 190° C | gas mark 5 |
| 400° F | 200° C | gas mark 6-moderately hot |
| 425° F | 220° C | gas mark 7- hot |
| 450° F | 230° C | gas mark 9 |
| 475° F | 240° C | gas mark 10- very hot |

Made in the USA
Las Vegas, NV
18 February 2024